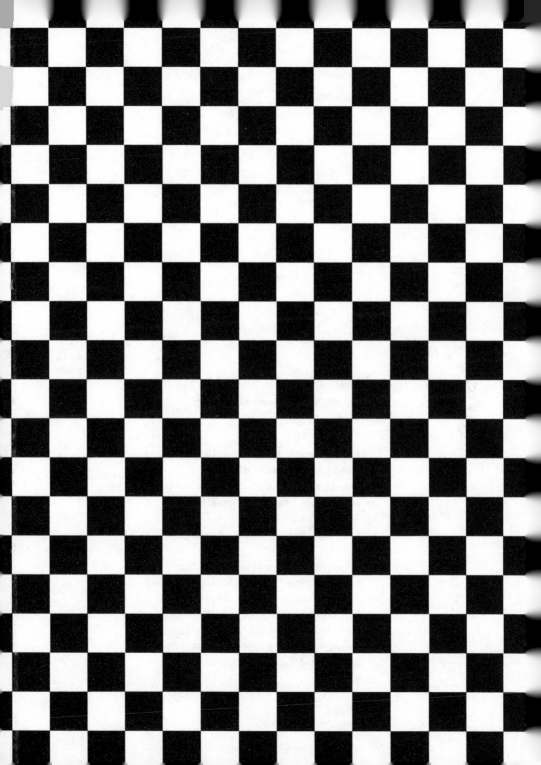

AMERICAN ★ MUSIC ★ HISTORY ★

Music shapes our world more powerfully than any other cultural product. To fully understand America, we must learn the complex, diverse history of American musical life. The books in this series tell the stories of the artists, forms, and innovations that define the musical legacy of the United States and fashion its ideals and practices.

THE RISE OF '90S
SKA AND SWING

Kenneth Partridge

THE PENNSYLVANIA STATE UNIVERSITY PRESS | UNIVERSITY PARK, PENNSYLVANIA

Library of Congress Cataloging-in-Publication Data

Names: Partridge, Kenneth, 1980– author.
Title: Hell of a hat : the rise of '90s ska and swing / Kenneth Partridge.
Other titles: American music history.
Description: University Park, Pennsylvania : The Pennsylvania State
    University Press, [2021] | Series: American music history | Includes
    bibliographical references and index.
Summary: "Examines the ska and swing music of the late 1990s as a pop-
    culture movement, telling the stories behind some of the era's most
    important bands"—Provided by publisher.
Identifiers: LCCN 2021012731 | ISBN 9780271090382 (hardback)
Subjects: LCSH: Ska (Music)—United States—History and criticism.
    | Swing (Music)—History and criticism. | Popular music—United
    States—1991–2000—History and criticism.
Classification: LCC ML3535.8 .P37 2021 | DDC 781.646—dc23
LC record available at https://lccn.loc.gov/2021012731

The Pennsylvania State University Press is a member of the Association of
University Presses.

It is the policy of The Pennsylvania State University Press to use acid-free
paper. Publications on uncoated stock satisfy the minimum requirements
of American National Standard for Information Sciences—Permanence of
Paper for Printed Library Material, ANSI z39.48–1992.

For Lindsey and Desmond

Contents

Acknowledgments

This is a book about the music I fell in love with when I was 14. It gave me an identity then and influenced pretty much everything I've done since. I'd like to start by thanking all the incredible artists and industry folk who spoke to me for this project. Every band profiled in these pages soundtracked some moment of my youth. I hope I did their stories justice.

I would also like to thank some of the bands I wasn't able to include for one reason or another: Spring Heeled Jack, Johnny Too Bad and the Strikeouts, the Smooths, Slow Gherkin, Filibuster, Thumper, Isaac Green and the Skalars, Pilfers, the Radiation Kings, Skavoovie and the Epitones, and the Allstonians. Your CDs are never far from reach.

Special thanks to my mom, Debra Partridge, for instilling in me a lasting love of music. And to my dad, Ken Partridge Sr., who drove me to many ska shows before I had my license. Shoutout to my dad's friend Larry Perosino for loaning me the Specials' *The Singles Collection* when he heard I was getting into this crazy music called ska. That CD changed everything.

A huge thanks to master wordsmith Vinnie Perrone for always encouraging my writing—even when I sucked. This book would not have happened without Eric Danton, who gave me my first freelance assignments back in 2003, and who has been a tremendous friend and sounding board ever since. Similarly, I'm eternally grateful to my dear friend Garland Walton for teaching me the grammar I should've learned in high school.

Speaking of high school, the music celebrated in this book will always make me think of my lifelong friends Geoff Bickford, Chris Taylor, and Logan Worsley. Geoff (who played in a terrific '90s ska-punk band called Jimmie Scooter) has accompanied me to more ska shows than either of us could tally. He also read my entire manuscript to make sure it wasn't crap. If you don't like this book, blame him.

Thanks to intrepid literary agent and fellow ska dad Eric Smith for helping me find this book a good home. Props to my friend Tracy O'Neill for reading my early proposal and helping me navigate the wild world of publishing. Thanks to the whole team at Penn State University Press, especially my smart and patient editor Ryan Peterson, who responded to all my frantic emails and guided me every step of the way. Thanks, too, to copyeditor Nicholas Taylor, whose comments in the final Word document were both informative and entertaining.

Thanks to Larry and Elizabeth Stanberry, Martin Stanberry, Rachel Maguire, Peter Drogin, Joe Lynch, Jason Heller, Jes Reiter, Brian Lee, Jennie Kwo, and my third-grade teacher, Ms. Lavey.

Last but not least, thanks to my son, Desmond, for inspiring me to do this, and to my amazing wife, Lindsey Stanberry, who did everything for this book except write it. Lindsey, you read drafts, tolerated my constant freak-outs, granted me time on weekends to write, and listened to more ska and swing music than any human should ever have to. Thank you a billion times.

Bring on the Horns

On June 28, 1997, about 14 months before he began hosting *TRL* and became Dick Clark for the dial-up generation, Carson Daly presided over the most glorious and bewildering programming block in MTV history. It was called *MTV Skaturday*, and for two hours, while enthusiastic extras skanked around the beach house, Daly introduced nothing but ska videos. He wore a black suit, black hat, and skinny tie, the standard uniform of the rude-boy subculture. This really did happen.

MTV Skaturday represented a surreal pinnacle for the "third wave" of ska, a movement that had been building since the '80s. In 1994, *Billboard* ran a story about ska being the next big thing. The *New York Times* followed suit in 1995, the same year Bay Area punks Rancid took their infectious "Time Bomb" to #8 on Billboard's Modern Rock Tracks chart. (The chart became known as Alternative Songs in 2009 and Alternative Airplay in 2020.) Goldfinger and No Doubt cracked the Top 10 of that tally with ska or ska-like songs in 1996. The summer of '97 belonged to Sublime's "Wrong Way," Reel Big Fish's "Sell Out," and the Mighty Mighty Bosstones' "The Impression That I Get," which hit #1 on Modern Rock Tracks.

Ska had arrived in America, and it sounded nothing like it did when it left Jamaica 30 years earlier. Born in the late '50s, just before Jamaica gained independence from Great Britain, ska was fast, brassy, optimistic music informed by American jazz and R&B and the island's own mento sound. Ska was built around the almighty "offbeat," with guitar, piano, and sometimes horns adding distinctive rhythmic chops in between the beats: one *and* two *and* three *and* four.

Trends come and go quickly in Jamaica, and by the mid-'60s, ska had mellowed into rocksteady, which in turn became reggae, the nation's most famous and lasting cultural export. Ska might've been forgotten had it not been for 2 Tone, a U.K. record label that spawned its own youth movement in the late '70s. Multiracial 2 Tone bands like the Specials, the Selecter, and the English Beat updated ska for their time and place. As Britain grappled with high unemployment and flaring racial tensions, the rolling buoyancy of Jamaica ska gave way to tense, anxious songs about racism, sexual politics, and Cold War paranoia.

While 2 Tone was never as big in the U.S. as it was in the U.K., where the label's first seven singles were Top 10 hits, many of the bands enjoyed a modicum of stateside success. Every third-wave American ska band took something from 2 Tone, though few focused on the politics at the heart of the movement.

There are some notable exceptions, but generally, American ska in the '90s was strikingly apolitical. This was in keeping with the overall trajectory of popular music in the '90s. At the beginning of the decade—a time marked by the Gulf War, the L.A. riots, and an economic recession—angsty grunge and nihilistic gangsta rap were all the rage. By the latter half of the '90s—with Bill Clinton in the White House and the economy kicking ass like Xena, warrior princess—sun-and-fun bands like Sugar Ray and Smash Mouth had begun crashing alternative radio playlists. Pearl Jam and Soundgarden were still huge, but so were Green Day and the Offspring, pop-punk bands with a sense of humor. Hip-hop, meanwhile, went from Glocks and chronic to the bombastic shiny-suit bling-rap of Puff Daddy. The shift culminated with the rise of teen pop in 1999, but not before ska and one other genre characterized by dudes with horns got some mainstream love.

Like third-wave ska, the swing revival had been growing organically for years. It began with the formation of Royal Crown Revue in Los Angeles in 1989 and spread to other cities, most notably San Francisco. The sound most often rehashed by neo-swing groups was not swing in the big band sense, but rather jump blues, a juiced-up '40s R&B precursor that often sounds a lot like rock 'n' roll. When third-wave ska finally broke in '97, it primed the world for retro-swing a year later.

However corny neo-swing wound up looking to outsiders, it started out pretty punk. "Our contemporaries were all into grunge," says Michael Moss, the San Francisco scenester who started *Swing Time* magazine in 1995. "They're walking around with their grungy clothes and their Nirvana wannabe lookalikes, and we were wearing zoot suits and crazy vintage fashions and looking sharp all the time. Suddenly, being sharp was punk."

The rise of ska can also be seen as a direct reaction to grunge. "That shit's great, but after a while it's kind of like, 'Gee, I'm depressed with this stuff,'" says Jon Pebsworth of Buck-O-Nine, who scored an alternative hit in 1997 with "My Town." "When you hear something like the Bosstones, all of a sudden you're like, 'Wow, this is fun. It's more musical, and it's easier on the ear.'"

Ska and swing overlapped in terms of fans and musicians, especially on the West Coast, where both scenes were the largest. When ska got hot in '97, followed by swing in '98, it was easy for the most casual, least informed alt-rock radio listeners to conflate the two. But there were crucial differences that went beyond musicology. Ska had been building longer, and the level of instrumental proficiency required to start a band was way lower. Consequently, the number of ska groups at all levels—MTV crossover down to local VFW shows—greatly exceeded the number of swing outfits.

Ska also lent itself better to hybridization. While the New Morty Show played kitschy covers of Metallica and Billy Idol songs, and Lee Press-On and the Nails invented "goth-swing," few retro-swing bands really got into the hyphen game. Third-wave ska, meanwhile, splintered off into ska-punk, ska-core, ska-jazz, ska-soul, and even metal-ska (check out underrated Boston-area greats Thumper). Mephiskapheles played satanic ska. Five Iron Frenzy and the O.C. Supertones were Christian. The Aquabats wore superhero costumes to perform their nerdy New Wave ska.

For as many bands as there were touring nationally, releasing albums, and landing songs on all-important compilation CDs, many released on the seminal NYC label Moon Ska, ska never really got *that* big. Of all the groups that made it onto MTV in some capacity—and there were plenty— only No Doubt, Sublime, Rancid, and the Mighty Mighty Bosstones have platinum albums. Of those, you might argue that only the Bosstones count as a ska band.

Thanks to the 1996 film *Swingers* and the Gap's 1998 "Khakis Swing" commercial, retro-swing was way more of a fad. That translated to a shorter shelf life but higher record sales. Cherry Poppin' Daddies sold 2 million copies of 1997's *Zoot Suit Riot*. Squirrel Nut Zippers, who notched a sur- prise hit with the fire-and-brimstone calypso curio "Hell" in 1997, moved a million copies of their 1996 sophomore album, *Hot*. Big Bad Voodoo Daddy went platinum with 1998's *Americana Deluxe*. Brian Setzer Orches- tra, who savvily released a version of Louis Prima's "Jump, Jive an' Wail" right after the Gap featured the original in its much-discussed TV spot, went double platinum with 1998's *The Dirty Boogie*.

Looking back through a twenty-first-century lens of political correct- ness, it's possible to view retro-swing as a little reactionary. Its sounds and aesthetics recalled an idyllic time when men wore hats, women favored lipstick and heels, and everything was right in the world. But these were ex-punks in San Francisco and L.A.—there was no MAGA element to the movement. "The swing scene was made up of incredibly intelligent peo- ple that were subversive and hip, before it got watered down," says Moss. "These were not misogynists. These were strong women that would kick your ass. Nobody was on that dance floor if it wasn't for the girls. They learned how and taught us and made us do it."

Compared to other genres, ska also presented safe spaces for females. "In hardcore punk, you'd go to the shows and it was, like, 80 percent dudes," says Dave Kirchgessner of Michigan ska-punks Mustard Plug. "Ska was great because it was a lot more open both in terms of there being girls at the shows, and it was theoretically way more open racially."

Simply put, ska and swing was music that allowed you to dress up (or not) and go dance. The lack of political content in much of the day's ska and nearly all of the swing reflected the times perfectly. For the mostly white teenagers and 20-somethings driving both scenes, this was precisely the right music for those final years before 9/11, when America was dreaming and didn't even know it. The period from 1991 to 2001 was the longest economic expansion in U.S. history to date, and from 1997 to 2000 GDP growth each year topped 4 percent, a number the nation hasn't seen since. During the Clinton years, America's only wars were in obscure places like Bosnia and Kosovo, and the handful of U.S. combat deaths wasn't going to be the thing that shaped your opinion of Slick Willy. Why not skank it up or jump, jive, and wail?

Neither ska nor swing was built to last as a mainstream phenomenon. By 1999, oversaturation and the industry's need for the next "next big thing" had killed both. There was also a substantial media backlash that's never gone away. In May 2016, when the music website Stereogum ran a story called "Let's All Remember the Late '90s Swing Revival," the first comment on the article read, "COUNTERPOINT: Dear God, please let's not."

For many, the mere mention of ska conjures images of goofy white guys in checkered pants running in place as inept high school band geeks yell "Pick it up!" and mangle the rhythms of the Skatalites. In 2005, when dance-rock was king, Brandon Flowers of the Killers dissed Sam Endicott of the Bravery for once playing in a ska band called Skabba the Hut. It was soon revealed that Killers drummer Ronnie Vannucci had been in a ska band called Attaboy Skip. *Spin* had a field day with the feud, publishing a full-page "Ska-letons in the Closet" chart exposing other rockers' secret ska pasts. When New York City mayor and presidential candidate Bill de Blasio professed his love of ska during a 2019 TV interview, Twitter mocked him for the rest of the day.

So why this book-length exploration, defense, and celebration of frequently maligned sounds that temporarily captured imaginations in the '90s? In addition to being vibrant music perfectly suited for those peaceful, prosperous years before 9/11, ska and swing encouraged and rewarded curiosity. If you were passionate about these sounds, there was a universe of great music waiting for you to discover it. Third-wave ska led back to 2 Tone and the Skatalites, plus all the incredible music that's come out of Jamaica since. Kids who flipped for swing might have gone back to Louis Prima and Cab Calloway and all the other men and women who moved the masses before rock 'n' roll.

Swing and ska encouraged young people to actively engage with music, not just sit on the sidelines. You didn't have to become a mod or a rude boy or fill your house with swanky mid-century furniture. Learning to tie a tie and wearing it while dancing yourself dehydrated at a ska show was enough. Even having the open-mindedness to let a little trombone into your life was something.

Regardless of whether '90s ska and swing fans stuck with these genres into the '00s, they learned from the Bosstones and Royal Crown Revue what it means to interact with pop culture on a deeper level. "Straight-up rock with a capital R doesn't ask anything of you," says Steve Perry of Cherry Poppin' Daddies. "But swing and ska do. They're kind of elitist in a way, because you can't just roll out of your bed and be into swing and ska. You have to figure it out."

CHAPTER I

Noise Brigade

The summer of 1997 was the Summer of Ska, and the Mighty Mighty Bosstones provided its soundtrack with "The Impression That I Get," the most commercially successful single of the American third wave. As "Impression" exploded on the radio, reaching #19 on Billboard's pop-centric Mainstream Top 40, #17 on the pop-for-parents Adult Top 40, and #1 on the theoretically anti-pop Modern Rock Tracks chart, there was no escaping the track's choppy guitar intro and big-hearted horns. Best of all was the chorus, where Bosstones front man Dicky Barrett stops trying to sing all nice and growls like only he can: "*Iiiiiiiiiii've* never had to knock on wood . . ."

If you were listening casually in your car or even reading the lyrics without paying too close attention, it was easy to think Barrett was singing about how he'd never needed to rap his knuckles on a piece of wood, a superstitious act that's supposed to keep bad things from happening. But that doesn't make any sense. He's really saying he never had to face any of the hardship he mentions in the verses: "Have you ever been close to tragedy / Or been close to folks who have?" The "knock on wood" bit is a parenthetical. Barrett tells us he's never suffered rough times, then realizes he doesn't want to jinx himself. It's a subtle point that's key to understanding the song.

And yet there's something poetic about fans in 1997 being too busy singing along or simply living their lives as teenagers to contemplate the deeper meaning. In part, Barrett wrote the lyrics to "The Impression That I Get" about what a relatively easy time everyone was having in the '90s. It's a commentary on the very cultural climate that allowed ska songs like "The Impression That I Get" to reach the mainstream in the first place.

"The second verse is about the challenges of the generation," Barrett says. "'Have you ever had the odds stacked up so high you need a strength most don't possess? / Or has it ever come down to do or die? / You've got to rise above the rest.' At that time, we were a ska-punk band, and the biggest problem is trying to put together a record. Or, 'Ugh, touring is so hard.' Then you think, 'Well I doubt if it was as hard as Vietnam.' I think of other generations that came before us. We were right in that sweet spot, that window of 'This is pretty good.'"

The song started out as something more personal. Barrett came up with the idea at the funeral of a close friend's brother. As he witnessed the pain of grieving family members, Barrett realized he'd never been through anything so trying. He jotted down some of the lyrics on the bereaved family's front porch.

So there's a lot in "The Impression That I Get": social commentary, self-reflection, and warm acknowledgment of people and places that came before. These elements have always been present in the music of the Mighty Mighty Bosstones, a band that ignored trends, wore its heart on its gaudy plaid sleeves, snuck saxophones into Alternative Nation, spoke out against racism, and took the long way to the top. The Bosstones Americanized ska in a brawny, guitar-heavy manner that made sense to their audience, and when it counted, they carried the music into the mainstream without abandoning its core elements.

The quintessential '90s ska band formed in Boston in 1984, after several members had their lives changed by 2 Tone. Barrett saw the English Beat with the Pretenders at the Orpheum Theater in 1980 when he was 16. "The next day I was buying everything on the 2 Tone label I could get my hands on and became Boston's first 'rude boy,'" Barrett told the *Chicago*

Tribune in July 1997. Barrett even took a Greyhound from Boston to New York City to see Madness perform on *Saturday Night Live* in 1984. After the broadcast, he and a friend spent the night carousing with their heroes. It was a life-altering experience Barrett would write about in the liner notes for the 1997 compilation *Total Madness*.

Joe Gittleman, bassist and musical architect for the Bosstones, found 2 Tone a few years later. In April 1983, when he was 15, he saw the English Beat at Walter Brown Arena on the Boston University campus. (Opening act: R.E.M.) Hailing from just over the Charles River in Cambridge, Gittleman had been to a few punk shows. But the Beat were something altogether different. "That was the most amazing thing that I witnessed to date," Gittleman says. "That show had lasting repercussions on me and all my friends."

Those friends included guitarist Nate Albert, a classmate at the hippy-dippy Fayerweather Street School, where the curriculum featured "a lot of music and puppetry and shit like that," Gittleman says. Coming of age in super-liberal Cambridge in the '70s, Gittleman and Albert were sensitive to the racial issues at the heart of 2 Tone. That, plus the energy of the music, made ska irresistible. Before long, Gittleman and Albert were decorating their lockers and skateboards with black-and-white checkered 2 Tone designs.

Barrett was a known quantity on the Boston punk scene when Gittleman and Albert approached him with the idea of starting a band. He'd lent his angry-bulldog vocals to the hardcore group Impact Unit and the ska band the Cheapskates, neither of which played more than a handful of shows. Even though he was a few years older, Barrett decided to join up with the young bucks from Cambridge. "That he agreed to play music with us at all was in and of itself like a victory," says Gittleman. "The Cheapskates had broken up, and I was working in a restaurant," Barrett says, downplaying the notion he was slumming. "I certainly had free time."

The band grew to include Josh Dalsimer on drums, Tim Bridwell on trumpet, and Tim "Johnny Vegas" Burton on saxophone. At one early gig,

Bosstones roadie buddy Ben Carr was denied entry to the venue on account of being underage. Barrett told the club owner that Carr was part of the band, and then to sell the lie, Carr jumped onstage and skanked around while the guys played. So it transpired that Carr became a full-time dancer. He's credited as the "Bosstone" on every album.

This first incarnation of the Bosstones only lasted until 1987 and played for tiny local crowds consisting mainly of friends. That lineup did, however, stumble on the mix of Jamaican rhythms, hardcore, punk, and occasionally metal that would make them one of the biggest and most influential ska bands of all time. The concept was there from the start—putting it into practice was another story.

The Bosstones realized just how much work they needed when they opened for Fishbone at Jonathan Swift's, a sandwich shop in Harvard Square where Barrett worked. This was the biggest gig the Bosstones played in their first go-round, and it was a humbling experience to say the least. On some level, the Bosstones were excited to play with another group that had roughly the same idea of mixing ska and punk and other styles of music. "But they were actually executing it," says Gittleman. In those days, the Bosstones used to end one of their songs by playing the theme from the Bill Cosby cartoon *Fat Albert*. Unbeknownst to them, Fishbone also covered the tune as part of their set, and the difference between the two versions was night and day.

"They just do this fucking dirty, soulful, funky—like four-part vocal harmony—incredible version of that," Gittleman remembers. "Honestly, it was almost depressing on some level. On one hand it was like, 'Wow, people are taking this to the next level.' But at the same time, 'We can't do that.'"

Nobody thought there'd be more to come when the group split up in 1987. Over the next couple of years, Gittleman toured overseas with the Boston hardcore band Gang Green and Albert finished up high school. They all kept in touch as much as possible in those pre-Internet days, and after Gittleman got booted from Gang Green, they decided to get the band back together.

Now it was 1989, and everything was different. Gittleman had been around the world and learned the business. Albert was out of high school. The band modified its name with the "Mighty Mighty" prefix after learning there'd been a Beantown doo-wop group called the Bosstones in the '60s. Resplendent in the plaid suits they'd make their trademark for the next six years, the Bosstones were ready to take things seriously—though not everyone believed them. When they signed with the local indie label Taang! Records, their contract stipulated they had to play at least 20 shows per year to promote their music. In hindsight, it's a laughable addendum, as the band would spend much of the next decade on the road.

The Bosstones went screaming into the next era with the release of their 1990 debut album, *Devil's Night Out*. It opens with the title track, a heavy metal chugger that abruptly shifts into cheery ska, complete with ripping saxophone. As the lyrics tell us, the Devil himself is watching the band and very much digging the beastly metalliska.

"The metalness of that was almost a joke on some level," Gittleman says. There's undoubtedly a light side to *Devil's Night Out*. There are also early indications that Barrett was a lyricist with more on his mind than drinking and partying. Take "Howwhywuz, Howwhyam," a springy ska tune that finds Barrett, then in his mid-20s, taking stock of his life: "Am I getting older? / Are things getting harder? / I used to never cry when I would think about my father." Barrett says he was only trying to keep up with his bandmates and contribute lyrics that matched the inventiveness of the music. "I took everything I learned from teachers I had growing up, people who realized that I could write poetry and said, 'Write about what you know,'" Barrett says. "All of those clichés."

Devil's Night Out includes "The Cave" and "Drunks and Children," songs the early incarnation of the Bosstones had recorded for the '80s ska compilations *Mash It Up* and *Mashin' Up the Nation*, both released via Razorbeat Records, the label run by Boston ska stalwarts Bim Skala Bim. Bim's trombonist, Vinny Nobile, guests on *Devil's Night Out*, as does Jimmy G of New York City hardcore heroes Murphy's Law. When Murphy's Law took the Bosstones on their first national tour soon after the album dropped, Gittleman started to realize they were on to something. "I remember playing little basement dive bars in Milwaukee, but it was packed," says Gittleman.

Around this time, the Bosstones recruited saxophonist Kevin Lenear, who brought with him trombonist Dennis Brockenborough, his roommate at Boston's revered Berklee College of Music. Lenear and Brockenborough were jazz guys unschooled in ska and punk, but their musicianship added a lot to the band. That both were Black was a welcome fact but not the product of calculated hiring. "It wasn't lost on me," says Gittleman. "I knew what the Specials looked like. I understood that they were a mixed-race band, and I thought that was a part of what made them cool. But I'll be honest, when we first called Kevin, I don't know if we knew that he was African American. It wasn't intentional, but it was meaningful to me."

Energized by the newly stacked horn section and the addition of drummer Joe Sirios, the Bosstones eased back on the metal and hardcore for their next album, 1991's *More Noise and Other Disturbances*. The LP is loaded with breakneck, horn-forward ska songs like "Cowboy Coffee" and "He's Back," plus the less frantic "Where'd You Go," a radio-ready head-nodder the Bosstones would lip-sync in the 1995 generational touchstone film *Clueless*. *More Noise* would be the group's final album for Taang! They were beginning to build a following in New England, and around this time, they even appeared in a nationally televised commercial for Converse sneakers. The major labels naturally came calling.

After early interest from Atlantic, the Bosstones signed with Mercury Records, where former Gang Green manager and Boston hardcore promoter Alec Peters was working as an A&R rep. The year was 1993, and nobody was thinking ska was about to blow up. Certainly not Mercury

FIG.1 The Bosstones unleash their ska-core fury in Providence, Rhode Island, June 18, 1990. Photo: Jonathan Knight.

Records vice president of A&R Bob Skoro, who signed the band for reasons he didn't even understand. Gittleman remembers what Skoro told the Bosstones after catching one of their sold-out gigs: "I don't get it, but there are people lined up around the block dressed like you."

"It was really on the strength of this unique scene that was going on and the connections with our fans," says Gittleman. "It was more about the proof that he was seeing than any kind of belief in our songwriting ability or visions or ska becoming a thing. He signed Ugly Kid Joe next, if that's any indication."

The Bosstones had always been fiercely independent, and that wasn't about to change just because they were on Mercury. Their major-label debut, 1993's *Ska-Core, the Devil, and More*, is an eclectic seven-song EP highlighting the extremes of what the Bosstones could do. On the one hand, there's a bright and sunny cover of "Simmer Down," the 1963 debut single by Bob Marley's group the Wailers, featuring instrumental backing by the Skatalites. The Bosstones version is pretty faithful, with no distorted guitar breaks killing the groove. But the EP also features covers of not one, not two, but *three* brutal hardcore classics. It was an unspoken message from the Bosstones to their new bosses: "We're going to do whatever we want."

FIG.2 Dicky Barrett (*left*) grins as Bosstones dancer Ben Carr (*right*) skanks it up. Photo: Jonathan Knight.

The Bosstones continued to bring the heavy on 1993's *Don't Know How to Party*, their third studio album and first for Mercury. The band worked with producer Tony Platt, whose resume included AC/DC and Bob Marley. The Bosstones saw themselves as bastard children of those two artists, and that's the sound they went for. On songs like the title track and "Last Dead Mouse," the band fuses buoyant reggae with crushing hard rock. "Holy Smoke," all about religious hypocrisy, and "What Was Was Over," which pinpoints the moment heartbreak becomes resignation, are the best bets for ska-heads hoping to get a little skanking in.

Far and away the most palatable track is the lead single, "Someday I Suppose," a punky reggae cut that first appeared on *Ska-Core, the Devil, and More*. "Someday I Suppose" earned steady MTV rotation and peaked at #19 on Billboard's Modern Rock Tracks chart. The Top 20 placement looks impressive on paper, but as Gittleman points out, there weren't a ton of alternative radio stations in America in 1993. "To call it #19 on the chart, you're only getting played in 20 or 30 markets in the whole country," says Gittleman. "So it really wasn't that big a thing, but it made the label happy. We started to maybe become a little bit more of a priority, because it outpaced their expectations." Skoro from Mercury was pleased enough with the album's performance to make a bold prediction that would ultimately come to pass. In a 1994 *Billboard* story titled "Hunt for 'Next Big Thing' Unearths Ska Underground," Skoro says his long-term goal for the Bosstones is platinum sales.

In the wake of *Don't Know How to Party*, the Bosstones found themselves selling out larger venues across the country. The touring schedule became so hectic that the group went into their fourth album with nothing written. To get the ball rolling, Mercury sent the Bosstones to Philadelphia to record with red-hot producers Phil and Joe Nicolo, aka the Butcher Brothers. A few years earlier, Joe Nicolo had co-founded Ruffhouse Records, the label behind hip-hop mega-sellers Kriss Kross, Fugees, and Cypress Hill. Mercury must've thought some of that magic would rub off on the Bosstones.

The Philly sessions yielded three songs that don't sound like anything else in the Bosstones catalog. "Kinder Words" opens with heavy bass throbs and almost hip-hop–style drums. Then Nate Albert crashes in with some heavy rock riffage, but that's also a diversion, because at 0:53, it turns into a full-on ska-punk song, with horns and organ doubling the offbeat guitars. "Toxic Toast" starts even more strangely, with stately, sentimental piano that seems like another fake-out. But the keys hang around for the verses, providing a bittersweet backdrop for Barrett's nostalgic lyrics about a booze-soaked crash pad he once shared with friends. The third Butcher Brothers cut, "365 Days," is metal-with-horns mayhem that must've left even Brillo-throated Barrett wanting a lozenge.

All three songs made it onto 1994's *Question the Answers*, an album Gittleman and Barrett hear as disjointed and incohesive. After the Butcher Brothers sessions, the Bosstones linked back up with producer Paul Q. Kolderie, who'd worked on their first two albums. The band recorded in four studios before all was said and done, and the sonic textures vary greatly from track to track. That said, for material written on the fly, the songs are remarkably strong. "A Sad Silence" is a gutter-reggae elegy for a kid struck down in the streets. "Jump Through the Hoops" is a frustrated smile of a ska song about the soul-sucking daily grind and unpleasantness of holidays. "Hell of a Hat" starts punk, then morphs into a jazzy reggae tune about a dapper dude who's freaking everyone out with the pistol on his waist. "Hell of a Hat" flopped as a single, as did "Pictures to Prove It," a solid alt-rock tune with reggae verses and a lovelorn lyric from Barrett. The album outperformed *Don't Know How to Party* on the Billboard 200, reaching #138 in October 1994, but nobody would've called it a hit.

The Bosstones spent the next summer on the road with Lollapalooza, the traveling festival that had become synonymous with the '90s alt-rock revolution. Headliners included Sonic Youth, Hole, Cypress Hill, and Pavement. For the first time, the festival played amphitheaters instead of open fields, and that left lower-tier acts like the Bosstones to perform early in the day for rows of empty seats. According to Gittleman, it was a miserable experience made all the worse by the band's excessive partying. Autumn couldn't come soon enough.

Back in the real world, the Bosstones faced an uncertain future with Mercury. "The sense of us overachieving at the label was long gone by that point," Gittleman says. "We didn't have that song that did the same thing 'Someday I Suppose' had done. People at labels start to get a little fidgety and nervous." Gittleman remembers conversations where the label suggested they lose the horn section for the next album. While that was obviously a nonstarter, the band did think long and hard about its next move. During this period of contemplation, a funny thing happened: ska got popular.

Late 1995 saw the release of No Doubt's *Tragic Kingdom* and another album that made a much bigger impression on the Bosstones, Rancid's ... *And Out Come the Wolves*. Gittleman heard early mixes and was awed by ska tracks like "Time Bomb." When *Wolves* came out, Gittleman bought a copy at a Massachusetts mall and played it all the way through in the parking lot. "Every song was good, and 'Time Bomb' was getting played on the radio," says Gittleman. "People were ready for a more upbeat, sunnier mood. There was a lot of change in the air."

Sensing the opportunity before them, the Bosstones took their time writing their next batch of songs. They recorded demos upon demos, crafting songs that were more focused than any they'd written before. Previously, Barrett had been interested in making "anti-records," songs that went against the grain as a matter of principle. He began to change his approach after a conversation with Danny Goldberg, the former Nirvana manager who'd become Mercury's president in 1996.

"[Goldberg] was basically telling me that he knew what I was doing," says Barrett. "He said, 'What you're doing is fine, and that can go on for as long as you want, and I don't disrespect it, and I don't not like it. But there's another way to go about it. It doesn't have to be "fuck everything."

You can actually make songs that appeal to a lot of people without compromising who you are and what you are.'" Then Goldberg told Barrett something that really stuck with him: "You're afraid to write a hit song."

Goldberg's challenge and ska's ascension created the perfect environment for the Bosstones to record their masterpiece. Instead of shuffling between studios and producers, as they'd done the last time out, the band set up shop on familiar ground, Boston's Fort Apache Studios, where they'd made their first two albums. Produced by Fort Apache co-founders Kolderie and Sean Slade, *Let's Face It* is softer and sweeter than *Don't Know How to Party* and more streamlined than *Question the Answers*. It was the band's most ska-centric album since *More Noise and Other Disturbances*, but the songs didn't feel like breathless sprints. As the cover photo shows, the band swapped its plaid suits for sharper black and gray.

Let's Face It opener "Noise Brigade" gets the dance party going with clean skanking guitars and a brisk tempo that continues into track two, "The Rascal King," all about infamous '40s-era Boston politician James Michael Curley. The Democratic boss served four terms as mayor—one of them while behind bars for mail fraud. "If you grew up Irish Catholic, like I did, in Boston, there was always three pictures hanging up in your father's den: the pope, JFK, and James Michael Curley," Barrett told MTV in August 1997.

As the album's second single, "The Rascal King" reached a respectable #7 on the Modern Rock Tracks chart. It was icing on the cake after the success of "The Impression That I Get," a song that almost didn't make the album. It originally appeared on the 1996 compilation *Safe and Sound: A Benefit in Response to the Brookline Clinic Violence*. Released on the Bosstones' own Mercury imprint Big Rig Records, *Safe and Sound* was a fundraiser organized by Boston musicians after the December 1994 killings of two women at reproductive health facilities in Brookline, Massachusetts. When the version of "Impression" on the comp began getting radio airplay, the band decided it should be on the album.

Barrett remembers "The Impression That I Get" being a tricky song to write. He felt strongly about the chorus he'd penned on the porch that day at his buddy's brother's funeral, and he didn't want to change a thing. Gittleman, who came up with the music, thought the chorus packed in too many words before getting to the song's title phrase. In the end, Barrett refused to budge. "It wasn't like, 'I know that this will work, and I know that people will love it, and it's going to buy everybody a house,'" he says. "But I couldn't let it go."

Elsewhere on *Let's Face It*, The Bosstones tackle drug addiction ("Royal Oil," "Nevermind Me"), alcoholism ("Another Drinking Song"), and the numbing effects of mass media ("Desensitized"). On the title track, the Bosstones nod to their 2 Tone roots by declaring open season on closed-mindedness: "Be racist, be sexist / Be bigots, be sure / We won't stand for your hate." The message reached a lot of kids. *Let's Face It* peaked at #27 on the Billboard 200 and went platinum in September 1997.

Goldberg was right: The Bosstones were capable of writing radio-friendly songs that actually said something. The band's reward for making the best album of its career was touring the world for the better part of the next two years—a not-so-grand prize that took its toll on everyone. Even by their own road-dog standards, the Bosstones ran themselves ragged. It all came to a head in Cologne, Germany, in the summer of 1998. Midway through a show, Lenear kicked over Albert's amplifier and smashed his saxophone to bits. He quit the band soon after.

At some point during the grueling tour, Albert applied to Brown University. He'd dropped out of Hampshire College in 1992 to be a full-time Bosstone, and after six years of spreading the ska-core gospel, he was ready to finish his education. Albert was also caring for his cancer-stricken mother, and as the band began work on its next album, he told Gittleman he was leaving.

Albert stuck around long enough to finish 2000's *Pay Attention*, the band's longest (16 tracks) and most experimental album to date. Noticeably lacking in the ska department, it's anything but a sequel to their commercial blockbuster. Only "Let Me Be," "All Things Considered," and "Where You Come From" might've made sense on *Let's Face It*. "So Sad to Say," the lead single, is pop-punk with minimal horns. "She Just Happened" is a calypso-like lover's lament with steel-drum accents. "High School Dance" is a funk-reggae-pop ballad sung from the perspective of a Columbine-style high school gunman. "Riot on Broad Street" is another Boston history lesson, à la "The Rascal King," done in the style of Celtic-punkers Big Bad Bollocks, who guest on the track.

It might've looked like the Bosstones were ditching ska because it wasn't cool anymore, but that wasn't the case. Barrett says *Pay Attention* was about continuing the songwriting journey that had begun on the previous album. Despite some industry shakeups that resulted in Mercury being absorbed by Island Def Jam, the Bosstones were given license to make whatever kind of record they wanted. They worked at scenic Long View Farm Studio in North Brookfield, Massachusetts, with a hefty budget and no self-imposed rules.

"Nothing we've ever done has been pure ska anyway," says Barrett. "We've always reserved the right to make whatever kind of song we wanted to make. I love that album. Lyrically, I never felt stronger. I wasn't drinking at the time. I was writing very clear-headed and just super into being on that farm. I felt like it had to be *Let's Face It* on steroids."

"So Sad to Say" made it to #11 on the Modern Rock Tracks chart, and *Pay Attention* managed #74 on the Billboard 200. Without the major radio airplay they'd enjoyed with *Let's Face It*, the Bosstones saw their popularity level course correct. "It settled back into what it had always been on some level, where it was more about us and our fans," says Gittleman. Albert wasn't the only member to leave after *Pay Attention*. Brockenborough also jumped ship, leaving a trombone vacancy filled by Chris Rhodes of the Bosstones-approved Connecticut ska band Spring Heeled Jack. Rhodes fit comfortably alongside Burton and Roman Fleysher, who'd taken Lenear's place prior to the *Pay Attention* sessions. A lengthy search to find Albert's replacement ended when the band hired Lawrence Katz, an Atlanta guitarist who'd been doing session work in L.A. That's the lineup that would keep things moving after the Bosstones parted company with Island Def Jam in 2001.

The Bosstones signed with the L.A. indie label SideOneDummy for 2002's *A Jackknife to a Swan*, another eclectic album with offbeat guitars on five of the 13 songs. The collection ends with "7 Ways to Sunday," a blues-gospel number about the quest for salvation. It was a philosophical note on which to end the second phase of the Bosstones' career.

The band went on hiatus from 2003 to 2007, during which time everyone found interesting ways to keep busy. Gittleman produced records for other bands and founded the punky rock 'n' roll combo Avoid One Thing. Sirois banged the skins for numerous bands, including Beantown punks Street Dogs. Rhodes joined up with the Toasters until the travel became too much. Fleysher flew private jets. Burton worked in the film industry. Barrett got into radio broadcasting, moved to L.A., and became the announcer on the ABC late night show *Jimmy Kimmel Live!* Everyone seemed happy and productive, but once a Bosstone, always a Bosstone.

In 2007, the group recorded three new songs for *Medium Rare*, a collection of B-sides and rarities, and reunited to revive the Hometown Throwdown, a yearly run of intimate Boston shows the band initiated in 1994. After the 2007 Throwdown sold out its entire run, the Bosstones stayed permanently reactivated, albeit on a part-time basis.

As of 2020, they've toured every year since 2007, kept the Throwdown going, launched a summertime New England ska-punk festival called Cranking & Skanking, and released three additional albums: *Pin Points & Gin Joints* (2009), *The Magic of Youth* (2011), and *While We're at It* (2018). Produced by Ted Hutt, the trilogy of latter-day Bosstones albums is marked by up-tempo ska songs made by eight middle-aged guys clearly enjoying themselves.

"I really like the way we have it now," says Gittleman, who spends his non-Bosstones time molding young minds at Northern Vermont University, where he's an associate professor of music and performing arts. "There are nights when I feel like we're playing our best shows we've ever played. It allows us to put a lot of thought and energy into the things we do and the way that we approach our music. And to approach it with the right spirit and energy and attitude and excitement that's required.

"It's perfect to be able to still do it on that level, but also have these other things going on that give your life new challenges and hopefully some additional meaning."

CHAPTER 2

Trapped in a Box

The two '90s ska bands that sold the most albums and made the biggest impact on pop culture formed 30 miles apart in Southern California in the latter half of the '80s. Both had charismatic blond lead singers and weathered enough tragedy to earn episodes of VH1's *Behind the Music*. Neither was really a '90s ska band.

"We were a ska band in the '80s, getting into the early '90s a little bit," says No Doubt drummer Adrian Young, who joined the Anaheim outfit in 1989, three years into their run and a good six before they finally broke through to the mainstream. "After that, we kind of became a clusterfuck of a lot of different things."

"We used to laugh when people said we were ska because Brad never thought that was our scene," said Miguel Happoldt, original manager and producer of Sublime, in a 2012 interview with *OC Weekly*. Brad, of course, is Sublime lead singer, guitarist, and songwriter Brad Nowell, who died of a heroin overdose in May 1996 at age 28. "That was just one part of cool music that he liked. He liked rap, reggae, and punk rock just as much and he always said, 'Ska? Whatever, we're just a band.'"

Young and Happoldt make valid points. No Doubt started out as a real-deal suits-and-checkers ska band in 1986 but stopped being one long before 1995's largely ska-free *Tragic Kingdom* began selling in the millions, making front woman Gwen Stefani the biggest female rock star of her generation.

Sublime's default sound was punky stoner reggae, though plenty of ska tracks pepper the three albums they recorded before Nowell's death.

So no, these weren't '90s ska bands, but it's impossible to imagine the ska boom echoing as loudly as it did without either of them. No Doubt and Sublime put the word "ska" in the mouths of journalists and American teenagers and made MTV and alt-rock radio safe for every horn-toting band that followed. Asked why ska exploded in 1997, Aaron Barrett of SoCal's Reel Big Fish gives props to his local heroes. "It was 100 percent about No Doubt and Sublime," he says. "Because they were so successful and they had so many huge hits."

In many ways, No Doubt and Sublime were very different. Hailing from idyllic Orange County and co-founded by siblings Eric and Gwen Stefani—two nice kids from a good Catholic family—No Doubt were paragons of professionalism from the beginning. "They were always rehearsed, all the songs arranged, they looked good, you know what I mean?" said Happoldt. Sublime came from the edgier port city of Long Beach and ran with a different crowd.

"Sublime showed up in the van half-drunk and played whatever they wanted to," said Happoldt. "Sublime loved that about No Doubt and No Doubt loved that about Sublime. No Doubt was like Richie Cunningham and Sublime was like Fonzie. Brad admired the professionalism. He said, 'One day we're going to have to be like that.'"

The odd-couple relationship made for some great double bills and collaborative recordings. Gwen sings her butt off on "Saw Red," a furious ska-punk reworking of reggae great Barrington Levy's "She's Mine" on Sublime's 1994 sophomore album *Robbin' the Hood*. Nowell sings and toasts on "Total Hate '95," an equally rambunctious track off No Doubt's 1995 set *The Beacon Street Collection*.

Nowell's untimely passing meant the two bands experienced stardom in different ways. No Doubt kept the hits coming on two follow-up albums before Gwen went solo in the '00s and became a TV star and *Us*

Weekly fixture in the '10s. Sublime maintained their visibility via post-humous releases and offshoot bands like Long Beach Dub Allstars and Sublime with Rome. In 2019, even as conversations about the sexism and cultural appropriation in Sublime's music sparked thoughtful criticism on websites like Pitchfork, postmodern pop star Lana Del Rey released a critically acclaimed cover of their hit "Doin' Time." She tapped into the seedy SoCal vibes common to her and Sublime's music and gave the band about the greatest endorsement it could've asked for.

■ ■ ■

Gwen Stefani had her life saved by ska. Before discovering the Specials, the Selecter, and most importantly Madness via her older brother Eric, she was a suburban wallflower without much direction. At Loara High, where she graduated in 1987, the future fashionista A-lister was an average student obsessed with *The Sound of Music*. "I was a fat little nerdy kid who desperately wanted to be cool," Stefani told the *Sunday Telegraph* in 2007. Her parents were strict Catholics, and she dreamed of getting married and starting a family.

Eric Stefani was more ambitious. He was also obsessed with ska, just like his Loara High classmate John Spence, a Black scenester who wore Fred Perry shirts and drove a P200 Lambretta scooter. Spence worked at Dairy Queen with Eric and Gwen, and that's where the idea was born to form a band. Speaking with *Interview* magazine in 2012, Stefani credited Spence with starting everything. "He's the one who got the band going," Stefani said, "because he said, 'I want to be in a band,' and he forced my brother to go get a keyboard." Spence's favorite expression—"Yeah, no doubt!"—gave the band its name.

Eric taught himself piano by playing along with records like the mischievous 1980 Madness single "Baggy Trousers." It figured Eric was a quick study; he was also a gifted illustrator who won awards at school and sometimes got detention for doodling on desktops. "Eric was the really talented and overly hyper older brother who was always pounding on the piano, and I was the lazy girl watching *The Brady Bunch*," Stefani said. "I wasn't doing anything, and he would say, 'Come in here and sing with me!' I owe everything to him, and I learned how to write songs and how to be in a band because of him."

Stefani soon became a self-proclaimed "ska chick" who crushed on Madness singer Suggs and took her fashion cues from the rude-girl cartoon character on the back cover of the English Beat's 1980 debut album, *I Just Can't Stop It*. Before joining No Doubt as Spence's co-lead vocalist, Stefani took the plunge into the world of ska performance by singing the Selecter classic "On My Radio" at a school talent show, lyric sheet in hand.

Eric put together a lineup that included guitarist Jerry McMahon, drummer Chris Webb, bassist Chris Leal (soon replaced by Kirk Hofstetter), trombonist Paul Caseley, and brothers Alan and Tony Meade on trumpet and saxophone, respectively. The band made its debut with a backyard show in 1986. The set list included "On My Radio" and the Specials' "Gangsters," plus at least one Eric Stefani original, "Stick It in the Hole," a song that was about a pencil sharpener but—wink, wink, nudge, nudge—also wasn't.

No Doubt's first proper gig took place on March 12, 1987, at the Fender Ballroom in Long Beach. The seedy venue would become a favorite spot for the band, and it was there that Tony Kanal—a U.K.-born child of Indian immigrants who moved to Anaheim at age 11—would first lay eyes on Gwen (and the rest of the group) later that year. No Doubt soon found themselves in the market for a new bassist, and as luck would have it, Kanal was a Prince-obsessed funk slapper with work ethic and drive to match his musical chops. Not long after Kanal joined, he and Gwen began dating. Their relationship would be enormously beneficial for No Doubt, insofar as its demise would inspire their multiplatinum *Tragic Kingdom*. But at the time, it was a secret to be kept from their bandmates.

By the time No Doubt got rolling, the roots of third-wave ska had already been firmly planted in Southern California. No Doubt were heavily influenced by the Untouchables and Fishbone, both of whom they befriended. One night in 1987, when No Doubt were supporting Fishbone at Fender's, a 2 Tone–loving Long Beach teen named Adrian Young was in the audience. Young saw No Doubt about 10 times before he joined in 1989. "They just had this thing, an energy and a sound," he says. "There were a lot of bands at that time that were also very good, like the Skeletones and Donkey Show. But I have to say No Doubt did stand out to me on those multi-bill lineups. It would be 10 bands or something, and you would dance for eight hours and somehow not get tired."

No Doubt in 1987 were a fairly textbook post–2 Tone ska band. Blurry camcorder footage of their performance at Mod Expo III at Fender's shows nine young musicians skanking and bopping nearly as zealously as the audience. Spence appears totally in his element, working the crowd and sometimes leaping into its waiting arms. But all that outward confidence was masking deeper issues.

On December 21, 1987, days before No Doubt were to play an industry showcase with the Untouchables at the Roxy in L.A., Spence committed suicide. It took his bandmates completely by surprise, and even nine years later, when *Spin* asked Stefani why Spence took his own life, she couldn't really say. "Obviously he was in a lot of pain," she said. "It's really hard to understand why anyone would commit suicide. Mostly I have happy memories about him. He was a very important part of the band." No Doubt thought about giving up but decided Spence would've wanted them to continue.

In 1988, as No Doubt moved with uncertainty into their next phase, a new band was making noise over in Long Beach. After two years at the University of California, Santa Cruz, Brad Nowell transferred to California State University, Long Beach. The move home meant he could play regularly with bassist Eric Wilson and drummer Floyd "Bud" Gaugh, local ne'er-do-wells who grew up across an alley from each other. Wilson's dad was a professional drummer and music professor who taught Gaugh to hit the skins. He taught Eric, too, but the younger Wilson gravitated to guitar and bass. Wilson and Gaugh teamed up for a series of go-nowhere punk bands, including the Juice Bros., which they'd later revive briefly following Nowell's death.

In a 2019 interview with *High Times*, Wilson recalled being "kind of a loser kid" before Sublime. Nowell, it seems, was quite the opposite. Although he was a child of divorce who took Ritalin to treat his ADHD, he did well in school and developed a deep love for music. When he was 11, his father took him on a sailing trip to the Caribbean, where he found reggae, the music he'd convince his reluctant punk friends to play in the years ahead.

Nowell and Wilson were members of a pre-Sublime teenage ska band called Sloppy Seconds. Nowell played guitar, a guy named Eric Ward sang lead, and Ruth Goodman, sister of eventual Sublime coconspirator and sometime drummer Marshall "Ras MG" Goodman, was on saxophone. "We covered a lot of ska songs," says Wilson. "That's how they got written into our own sound."

Nowell and Wilson were big fans of 2 Tone, though Wilson knew little about the music's roots. "For the longest time, I thought ska was from England, until I found out differently," he says. A flier from one of Sloppy Seconds' few house-party gigs shows a cartoon skeleton in a porkpie hat, suit, and checkered socks high-kicking while playing guitar. Modeled after a photo of Clyde Grimes, rhythm guitarist for the Untouchables, the drawing suggests that Sloppy Seconds embraced the whole rude-boy look. But that wasn't the case. "I always thought that'd be cool," Wilson says. "But I've never gotten any band I've been in to wear any type of uniform."

Sublime began booking gigs on the Cal State Long Beach campus and met Miguel Happoldt, a sound-engineering student with access to free studio time. The ensuing sessions yielded 1991's *Jah Won't Pay the Bills*, a 10-song demo released on Skunk Records, founded by Happoldt and Nowell for the purpose of putting out Sublime material. Considering everyone's lack of experience, *Jah Won't Pay the Bills* is a surprisingly strong document of Sublime's blossoming beach-bum reggae-rock fusion. The gorgeous "Badfish" and harder-edged "New Song" present Nowell as a self-aware waster who wants to straighten up but knows he's weak. His voice is sweet and sad and heavy from experience. He sounds older than 23.

There are also two tracks with ska elements: "Ball and Chain," Nowell's treatise on the obsolescence of marriage in modern society, and "Date Rape," the controversial morality play that would give Sublime their breakthrough hit a few years later. Stronger versions of both appear on 1992's wonderfully messy *40oz. to Freedom*, Sublime's first proper album and definitive statement as a band. Happoldt was again at the controls, with Marshall Goodman behind the drums, subbing for Gaugh while he was away at drug rehab. On *40oz.*, Brad and the boys guzzle down and belch back up every musical influence they can think of. There's plenty of reggae, obviously, plus punk rock (a cover of Bad Religion's "We're Only Gonna Die for Our Own Arrogance"), a folk tribute to hip-hop icon KRS-One, a Grateful Dead cover, and healthy doses of ska. There are even horns on "What Happened," Nowell's hung-over attempt at piecing together the previous night's escapades, and the new version of "Date Rape."

"Date Rape" is the cringiest song in Sublime's often-problematic catalog. Nowell was inspired by some guy at a party who actually said the now-infamous phrase, "If it wasn't for date rape, I'd never get laid." Nowell's lyrics tell of a man who picks up a woman at a bar, commits sexual assault, and lands in jail, where a fellow inmate gives him a taste of his own medicine. On an *extremely* superficial level, it's an anti-rape song where justice arguably prevails. On the other hand, it makes light of a supremely unfunny topic. Plus, as critic Evan Rytlewski points out in his scathing 2018 Pitchfork review of *40oz. to Freedom*, there's some degree of homophobia in the suggestion the rapist "now takes it in the behind."

In his review, Rytlewski also charges Nowell with cultural appropriation, citing his "broad" reggae voice and recycling of misogynistic hip-hop tropes, like the word "ho" on "Right Back." "There's a fine line between homage and caricature," Rytlewski writes. "Sublime's appeal rested on never asking fans to consider it." In his lifetime, Nowell knew he was treading on dangerous ground. "I have a lot of self-criticism when I sound like a Black person or when I accidentally find myself singing like a damn Jamaican," he told *Slam Magazine* in 1995.

In his defense, Nowell rarely sang in anything but his own soulful world-weary surfer-dude croon. Like the Clash before them, Sublime adapted reggae for their environment, switching out the standard one-drop drums for a more propulsive rock style and abandoning political-spiritual messages for songs about what screwups they and their friends were. Nowell isn't someone who awakens your political consciousness, like Bob Marley or Joe Strummer. He's a flawed hero—someone you root for even when you know how the story ends.

Wilson doesn't care what the critics say. He describes Sublime's hybridization of reggae as a natural evolution of styles. "We're just glad to be one of the first bands doing it, at least in this country," he says. "The whole thing about writing music and being a band is taking influences you grew up listening to and making it yours."

Back in Orange County, No Doubt also released their debut album in 1992. It was a long road to get there. Their debut studio release had come four years earlier, on the 1988 Moon Records compilation *Skaface*. The song was "Everything's Wrong," an eerie minor-key number that starts creepy-crawly, then sprints into the chorus. Gwen is squeaky-voiced and hesitant, while Eric gets his Jerry Dammers mojo working on the keyboard. A decade later, when No Doubt were filling arenas, Moon contacted the band in hopes of reissuing *Skaface*. "I got a really nice call from Tony Kanal, who was like, 'We're really flattered, but we don't want to do it,'" says Moon's then director of marketing and communications, Steve Shafer. "The track that's on there, it's not a great song. He was very gracious about it."

Spence's suicide didn't immediately make Gwen the lead singer. Throughout 1988 and into '89, she shared the spotlight with Alan Meade, who was promoted from trumpeter to co-vocalist. Less than a year after joining, Meade left to marry his pregnant girlfriend. Around the time he quit, No Doubt added two other members who would hasten the group's transition away from ska.

One was Tom Dumont, a metal guitarist whose band Rising used the same rehearsal space as No Doubt. Dumont was growing disillusioned with the metal scene, and when No Doubt posted a flier seeking someone to replace Jerry McMahon, he took a chance, even though he knew little about ska. "Their scene seemed so much healthier to me," Dumont told *BAM* in November 1995. "People would come to shows, dance, and just have fun." The other key addition was Young, a drumming novice who'd only owned a kit for about 12 months. He told his future bandmates he'd been at it for years, then learned every song on their demo before the audition. Young clearly wanted the job, and not because he thought he was joining a ska band.

"When I joined, the current song list had already had influences of funk and some more punk-leaning rock at times," Young says. "The experimenting had already begun, and I wasn't trying to influence them to remain a ska band. I was onboard for stepping out of the box and really finding out what the sound of this band would eventually become." That was a problem for purists, because there were "ska rules" that were not to be broken.

"We weren't going to follow any rules," Young says. "We were going to play whatever the fuck we wanted to. We did get some early day backlash when we really started to branch out stylistically. We had to just deal with it. We would hear, 'They're not a fucking ska band.' And in a sense, eventually, we weren't. Even when *Tragic Kingdom* became a successful record—it's not really a ska record, but we would still be labeled a ska band. I thought that was a little bit unfair to the ska bands who stayed true to just being 2 Tone ska."

Live footage and demos from 1989 and '90 bear this out: No Doubt were becoming a punky, funky pop-rock band with ska tendencies. In his role as lead songwriter, Eric Stefani brought a cartoonist's sensibility to the music. He was responsible for novelties like "Ache," all about a trip to the dentist, and "Paulina," a one-handed salute, ahem, to model Paulina Porizkova. No Doubt were highly capable and certainly unique, especially as grunge came to the fore. The band just lacked a cohesive vision and songwriting voice.

Nevertheless, Interscope Records A&R exec Tony Ferguson saw the potential and signed No Doubt in 1991. He did so with the blessing of label boss Jimmy Iovine, who also had the foresight to sign Dr. Dre and Trent Reznor around the same time. "Jimmy took me aside and said, 'Gwen, you are going to be a huge star in six years,'" Stefani recalled in a 2008 interview with *Vogue*. "I was like, 'First of all, who the hell are you?' And second of all, 'I'm not going to be *in* this band six years from now. I'm going to be having fourteen children and be married.'"

No Doubt went into the studio with producer Dito Goodwin and emerged with a spotty self-titled album that couldn't have been more ill-suited for the times. Released in March 1992, *No Doubt* is all bright horns and bass pops, with guitars that skank and wah-wah more than they crunch. The lead single, "Trapped in a Box," is a pseudo-ska bouncer based on a poem Dumont wrote about the evils of television. Eric Stefani composed the music, so naturally there are zany jazz breaks and a heavy bridge that comes out of nowhere. MTV was too busy playing Guns N' Roses and Pearl Jam to pay attention, and the single failed to chart.

For as much as No Doubt weren't a ska band anymore, they still kind of were. "Ache," the one about the dentist, is quite skankable, as are "A Little Something Refreshing" and "Paulina," Eric Stefani's odes to binge eating and wanking, respectively. "Get on the Ball," a quick tutorial from Gwen on how to keep a girlfriend, is another bone thrown to the ska crowd. With its reggae verses and punky chorus, "Move On" is the most important song on the album. It functions as a quickie band history ("one was a female, four were mad men") and a justification of their evolution beyond ska. "We moved on, moved on, moved on / To our house in the middle of the street," Gwen sings, quoting from the 1983 single "Our House" by their heroes Madness, who also went increasingly pop throughout their career.

Needless to say, No Doubt had no clue in '92 that there was a ska revival just around the bend. "We were plugging away in our garage, just continuing to try and make music," says Young. "At that time, you've got to remember, at least after our self-titled record, grunge was dominating KROQ and alternative music. Our goal was to get on KROQ, no question. But we didn't really see a clear path to us being played on major radio like that. It just didn't seem viable or likely."

As the alt-rock winds began shifting, Sublime and No Doubt took strange detours on their next albums. After deftly mixing and mashing genres on *40oz. to Freedom*, Sublime smashed them into sonic mush on 1994's periodically brilliant, largely frustrating *Robbin' the Hood*. The album is filled with half-baked song ideas, sloppy dub experiments, trippy sound collages, and the bizarre rants of a schizophrenic man named Raleigh Theodore Sakers. There's only a handful of legit songs, three of which have ska elements. One is the Gwen Stefani team-up "Saw Red," a playful duet that's a lasting testament to her and Nowell's unlikely friendship. The far darker "STP," which stands for "secret tweaker pad," finds Nowell and his buddies holed up in their drug hangout, too paranoid to venture into the light of day. It's probably not a total work of fiction.

In a 1997 interview with *Rolling Stone*, Nowell's widow, Troy Dendekker, said *Robbin' the Hood* was made at the height of Brad's heroin addiction. She pointed to "Pool Shark," which appears on the album twice, in punk and acoustic form, as a snapshot of Nowell's lifestyle at the time. "'Now I've got the needle / I can shake but I can't breathe," Nowell sings. "Take it away and I want more, more / One day I'm gonna lose the war." According to legend, *Robbin' the Hood* was recorded in a crack house. Wilson says that's not true—though you did literally have to jump over a crack in the ground to get into the place. That's because the house had been damaged in an earthquake, and some buddies of Brad's were squatting there. "A crack house, to my understanding, is a condemned house for a bunch of crack heads," Wilson says. "I couldn't see any music going on [there]. But it's a good story, though."

Sublime also recorded some of the album at Bad Religion's studios, as that band's guitarist Brett Gurewitz was interested in signing them to Epitaph, which he owned. "Their engineer was used to tracking with the bass buried, like on Bad Religion songs, and he refused to turn the bass up," Wilson recalls. "He took off for a little bit to eat lunch or something, and we cranked up the bass, made a mix, and left before he got back. So it was appropriate to call the album *Robbin' the Hood*. Everything we recorded didn't cost us any money."

Following the lackluster sales of their debut album, No Doubt entered into a limbo period with Interscope that would last for several years. "We were getting hung out to dry, going back to college and working jobs and trying to finish this record," says Young. "But Interscope kept telling us we didn't have the record yet. We didn't have the record yet. We didn't have the record yet." All the while, No Doubt stockpiled songs, recording demos at the studio they built in the two-car garage of their shared house. They knew many of these songs wouldn't make their next studio album, so they bundled them together on *The Beacon Street Collection*, an outtakes record they initially released on their own, despite being under contract to Interscope.

Beacon Street includes "By the Way," a Latin-flavored pop-rock tune written by Gwen and Dumont, and two songs penned by Gwen and Kanal, her soon-to-be ex. The Tony-Gwen jams, "Greener Pastures" and "Snakes," are hooky rock tunes with sludgy guitars and no traces of ska. It's worth noting that Eric Stefani didn't contribute to writing any of these songs. Of the three he composed entirely by himself, two, "Squeal" and "Doghouse," have horns and offbeat guitars. One might surmise Eric was clinging to No Doubt's ska roots, while Tom and Tony were pushing toward a more mainstream rock sound.

"That's a perception that's very general and not entirely accurate," Young says. "I don't think that Eric wanted to keep it strictly a 2 Tone band. In the early days, he was writing a lot of the music—not all of it, but a good portion of it—and he was writing songs that were not ska songs, too. As far as Tom and Tony and myself, we were all onboard with experimenting and trying different things, especially as we were improving as musicians."

Arguably the best song on *Beacon Street* is "Total Hate '95," a retooled version of a song No Doubt had been kicking around for years. The song is credited to John Spence and two other '80s-era members, bassist Chris Leal and trumpeter Gabe Gonzalez. Brad Nowell steals the show with his toasting section, ending with the line, "Long beat, Long Beach, and it feels so fine / Rock this shit straight back to Anaheim."

By the time No Doubt had released *The Beacon Street Collection* in 1995, Nowell's star was on the rise. In 1994, Sublime signed with the MCA subsidiary Gasoline Alley, and in early 1995, the two-year-old "Date Rape" went into heavy rotation on KROQ. This was all thanks to Tazy Phyllipz, co-founder of the long-running and influential radio show *The Ska Parade* on KUCI at the University of California, Irvine. While working in KROQ's promotions department, Phyllipz gave a copy of *Step on It: The Best of the Ska Parade Radio Show* to the assistant music director. It featured a live recording of "Date Rape," and within a month, the studio version was on the air, lighting up request lines. Other stations around the country quickly began adding the song, despite reservations about the subject matter.

In October 1995, No Doubt finally released their proper sophomore effort, *Tragic Kingdom*. After false starts with numerous producers, they'd found momentum with Matthew Wilder, the one-hit wonder behind the

1983 synth-reggae pick-me-up "Break My Stride." *Tragic Kingdom* happened despite *and* because of two major shake-ups that nearly sank the band: Eric Stefani quit, and Tony dumped Gwen. This left poor Gwen to soldier on without her brother and *with* her ex-boyfriend. Her only recourse was to write about it.

Eric had been pulling away for a long time before officially giving his notice in late 1994. Of the 14 tracks on *Tragic Kingdom*, he wrote just two and co-wrote five others. That left half the album to Gwen, Tony, and Tom, who were finding their voices as songwriters. Some speculate Eric was uneasy about relinquishing creative control, and that's why he left to focus on being an animator on *The Simpsons*. Speaking with the *Los Angeles Times* in October 1996, by which time *Tragic Kingdom* had gone double platinum, Eric put things in cloudier terms. "That whole passage of my life is unclear," he said. "I was messed up inside. I was troubled. I didn't know what direction to go." He said the rise of other songwriters in the band gave him the opportunity to step aside. "It was like being the father of a kid, and it was time to let go," he said. "For the long run it worked out for the best for everyone, including myself."

The most improved player on *Tragic Kingdom* was Gwen, who went from tagalong kid sis to self-assured 20-something with something to say. That was evident from the album's lead single, "Just a Girl," a jagged little New Wave rocker about feeling underestimated and overprotected on the basis of gender. (Perhaps coincidentally, the phrase "Don't ask me—I'm just a girl" was uttered by Lisa Simpson's Barbie-esque doll Malibu Stacy in a 1994 episode of *The Simpsons*.) "Just a Girl" instantly transformed No Doubt from a female-fronted band to a band with a female point of view. "I wrote that because my dad got mad at me for going to Tony's house and driving home late at night," Stefani told *BAM*. "I mean, c'mon, I'm, like, going on 30 here! I wouldn't trade [being female], but I really don't think guys understand what a burden it can be sometimes." "Just a Girl" reached #23 on the Billboard Hot 100 and #10 on the Modern Rock Tracks chart. The video—featuring a red-lipped, platinum-coiffed Gwen in a midriff-baring tank top with a bindi on her forehead—was tailor-made for MTV. With grunge in the rearview, the station was finally ready to give this bubbly Anaheim crew some shine.

No Doubt struck right back two months later with a second excellent single, "Spiderwebs." Written by Stefani and Kanal, it's another blast of New Wave rock with flashes of brassy reggae bookending the song in the intro and outro. Stefani wrote the lyrics about a doofy would-be suitor who used to call her up and sing awful poetry with an acoustic guitar. As per Billboard rules, "Spiderwebs" wasn't eligible for the Hot 100, since it wasn't released as a commercial single, but it made #5 on the Modern Rock Tracks chart and #18 on Hot 100 Airplay, a good indicator it was reaching teens everywhere. (Hot 100 Airplay, a component chart of the Billboard Hot 100, was renamed Radio Songs in 2014.)

The album's third single, "Don't Speak," truly made No Doubt a household name. The plaintive ballad originated with Eric Stefani and was rewritten by Gwen to reflect her split with Kanal. The song's music video is notable for two reasons. The magazine photo-shoot scene, where the boys are cropped out and Gwen is given a close-up, reflects the growing tension in the band as Stefani emerged as the star. Second, Young sports a Madness T-shirt in the scene where the band is playing in the garage. Madness later told Young they appreciated the nod.

"Don't Speak" reached #2 on Modern Rock Tracks and spent 16 weeks at #1 on the Hot 100 Airplay chart. (Like "Spiderwebs," it wasn't eligible for the Hot 100.) As the song seeped into the brains of millions, reaching teens who shopped at Hot Topic and the moms who drove them there, so too did the story of Gwen and Tony. The drama made No Doubt the Fleetwood Mac of ska-pop, and that gave the group another useful marketing hook. Suddenly, a band that nobody outside of Southern California had cared about for nine years was under the microscope, sharing its most intimate inner workings with the world.

Though not as successful as the other singles, the follow-up reggae rocker "Sunday Morning" is perhaps the album's strongest bridge between old and new No Doubt. Lyrically, it's another post-breakup anthem signaling Gwen's transformation from "sappy" and "pathetic" to empowered. The clip features a cameo from Specials front man Terry Hall, who'd get No Doubt to appear in his video for "Ballad of a Landlord" a few years later.

Tragic Kingdom reached #1 on the Billboard 200 in December 1996. By then, it had already shipped 5 million copies, and in 1999, it was certified 10x platinum, same as Nirvana's *Nevermind* and Green Day's *Dookie*. Taking those Fleetwood Mac comparisons to their logical conclusion, *Tragic Kingdom* is like the alternative generation's *Rumours*, a breakup album every white suburbanite of a certain age owned. Sturdy deep cuts like "Different People" and "Sixteen" just about elevate *Tragic Kingdom* to classic album level. It's certainly more than three hits and a bunch of padding.

Nowell lived long enough to see his buds in No Doubt achieve the level of fame he might've enjoyed had things turned out different. In a 2012 interview with *OC Weekly*, manager Miguel Happoldt recalled a 1995 show in San Diego where No Doubt actually opened for Sublime. After the show, Kanal gave Sublime a cassette with "Just a Girl." They played it on the drive home and knew instantly it was a hit. "It was like, 'Jesus Christ, we're going to be opening for them for the rest of our lives,'" said Happoldt. "Within two weeks, every time we'd go to 7-Eleven to buy beer, we'd hear that damn song. It was like, 'Hoo-ly shit, they're blowing up.'"

For all his self-destructiveness, Nowell took the MCA deal seriously. He checked himself into rehab and stayed sober for six months while Dendekker was pregnant with the couple's first and only child, Jakob James Nowell, born June 25, 1995. But by February of 1996, when Sublime decamped to Austin to record their third album, Nowell had relapsed hard. "There were times where someone had to go into the bathroom to see if Brad was still alive," producer Paul Leary of Butthole Surfers told *Rolling Stone*. It got so ugly that Leary sent Nowell back to Long Beach before the album was finished.

There was a lot working against Sublime. Fortunately, they had some good people in their corner. John Phillips, the Gasoline Alley A&R rep who landed them their deal, secured a $150,000 recording budget and brought on producers Leary and David Kahne—the latter with experience recording iconoclastic ska-fusion bands. Kahne's résumé includes Fishbone's mega-influential self-titled 1985 debut EP as well as the two albums that followed, 1986's *In Your Face* and 1988's masterful *Truth and Soul*.

Leary and Kahne proved the right men for the job, though they didn't do it alone. Happoldt was also integral to the sessions. In the 1998 documentary *Sublime: Stories, Tales, Lies & Exaggerations*, Leary describes Happoldt as "the glue that holds it together." Happoldt played wrangler for the hard-partying band, co-produced "Paddle Out," deployed "space echo" on two other tracks, sang harmony vocals, and even laid down the acoustic guitar solo on "What I Got," the album's lead single. Happoldt is credited in the liner notes as "production coordinator," a title usually reserved for film sets.

A week after returning home from Texas, Nowell cleaned up again and seemed to be turning a corner. "For once, Brad really seemed to be serious about living drug free," Sublime road manager Jason Westfall told *Guitar World* in 1997. "And there was a gleam in his eyes that no one could recall ever having been there before." On May 18, 1996, he and Dendekker got married in Las Vegas. Seven days later, following a show in Petaluma, California, Nowell overdosed on heroin in a San Francisco motel room.

When *Sublime* was released two months later, plenty of new fans didn't realize Nowell was dead. Millions of kids discovered the band through "What I Got," the obvious—and most heartbreaking—pick for lead single. As with many tracks on *Sublime*, it borrows heavily from Nowell's favorite music, in this case dancehall star Half Pint's 1986 jam "Loving." Nowell nicks Half Pint's chorus wholesale but delivers a new lyric in which he counts his blessings and tries to remind himself that happiness is within reach if he'll just embrace it. Whatever was going through Nowell's mind when he wrote it, "What I Got" is upbeat pop music with rolling acoustic guitars, crisp hip-hop drums, and turntable scratching. The single reached #1 on Billboard's Modern Rock Tracks chart, #11 on Mainstream Rock, and #29 on Hot 100 Airplay. Sublime were a hit.

Equally infectious was the follow-up single, "Santeria," another song about Nowell's search for elusive inner peace. It's ostensibly a love song, with strolling reggae-rocking accompaniment and one of the sweetest melodies Nowell ever wrote. But the final line, "My soul will have to wait," played like another possible epitaph for the late singer, following the more hopeful "Lovin' is what I got." "Santeria" became Sublime's second straight Top 5 Modern Rock Tracks single, reaching #3 in March 1997. *Sublime* had already gone platinum, and by August it would move another million units.

The disc's third single, "Wrong Way," dropped in May 1997, just in time for the Summer of Ska. Like "Date Rape," it's a jovial song about an abused woman—or rather girl, as Nowell's lyrics center on a 12-year-old forced into prostitution by her father. Nowell plays her would-be rescuer, a Prince Not-So-Valiant who can't help himself when the opportunity comes to take advantage of her. It's a complex story for a song that clocks in at 2:16, trombone solo included. The single peaked at #3 on Modern Rock Tracks and #47 on Hot 100 Airplay, eliciting little or no controversy along the way.

"Wrong Way" isn't the most troublesome track on *Sublime*. That would be "April 29, 1992 (Miami)," Nowell's play-by-play of what he was supposedly doing during the L.A. riots. If the lyrics are to be believed, he was looting alcohol, home furnishings, and the very guitar heard on the song. Nowell assures us the unrest "wasn't about Rodney King," the Black motorist whose videotaped March 1991 beating at the hands of four white LAPD officers dominated national headlines for months. When the officers were acquitted of using excessive force, years of pent-up anger and frustration spilled into the streets. In Nowell's version of history, the riots were about everyone—Blacks, Mexicans, and yes, whites—rising up against out-of-control cops. Nowell might've thought he was preaching solidarity against a common enemy, but "April 29, 1992" plays like a white dude taking advantage of a situation in order to score some free stuff. Sublime haters looking to brand the band as tone-deaf appropriators need only play this song to make their case.

The key thing to remember is that Nowell wasn't a prophet or moral exemplar. He was, however, a gifted musician and storyteller whose superpower was musical synthesis. As with *40oz. to Freedom*, many of the best songs on Sublime recycle bits from Nowell's record collection. "Jailhouse" starts out like a cover of the 1966 Wailers tune "Jail House," but as Nowell gets into the verses, he borrows the melody from Jamaican singjay Tenor Saw's 1985 tune "Roll Call." Nowell does something similar on "Pawn Shop," a reworked version of the Wailing Souls' 1984 reggae jam "War Deh Round a John Shop."

The greatest example of this is the album's fourth and final single, "Doin' Time," which flips a sample of jazz great Herbie Mann's 1961 version of George Gershwin's "Summertime." Credit goes to Marshall "Ras MG" Goodman for finding the sample and building the track—that's why Nowell shouts him out in the chorus. "Doin' Time" is hazy and vaguely sinister, with Nowell fixating on a cheating girlfriend he daydreams of murdering. Nowell and Goodman share writing credit not just with Gershwin, but also Beastie Boys and their producer Rick Rubin, as the track lifts a snippet from "Slow and Low," off the Beasties' 1986 smash *License to Ill*. In terms of problematic behavior, there are parallels to be drawn between Sublime and the Beasties, though the latter ultimately atoned for their loutish early material by decrying sexism in later years.

On the ska-punk tip, *Sublime* delivers four skankable songs, each with pretty gnarly lyrics. Nowell beds a tween prostitute and offers to kill her dad on the aforementioned "Wrong Way." On "Seed," he deflowers, impregnates, and/or morally corrupts a girl he's not planning on sticking with. "Burritos" finds him too depressed to smoke weed or look at porn.

"Same in the End" is a cryptic barrage of low-life imagery evoking drugs, sex, and absentee fathers.

Sublime was certified platinum in February 1997, weeks after No Doubt headlined Enough Already, a benefit show at the Hollywood Palladium raising money for the Musicians' Assistance Program and a scholarship fund for Nowell's son. The lineup featured Cali ska champs Voodoo Glow Skulls and Filibuster and the debut appearance of Long Beach Dub All-stars, a new project formed by Nowell's surviving bandmates. Wilson and Gaugh hadn't jammed for nearly a year after Nowell's death. They found it therapeutic to play together again.

In the months following Enough Already, ska reached the peak of its popularity on MTV and alternative radio. This left No Doubt in a strange position: just as they outgrew the music that fueled their early creativity, America was ready to skank it up. "I really didn't know what to think about it," says Young. "I think it's probably a good thing, but by that time, we had really solidified the band that we were becoming, which was more or less a rock band / pop band. So we already felt kind of removed from it." On the tour bus in the *Tragic Kingdom* days, Young says, No Doubt listened to Radiohead and 311. There wasn't much third-wave ska on the stereo.

All remaining traces of ska would disappear on No Doubt's next album, 2000's *Return of Saturn*. The band fired Matthew Wilder after lightning didn't strike twice and hired hitmaker Glen Ballard, then swimming in money and accolades after co-writing and producing Alanis Morissette's 1995 juggernaut *Jagged Little Pill*. Benefiting from a rhythm section that now included Kanal, Young, and the ticktock of Stefani's biological clock, No Doubt toned down the cartoon splashiness of *Tragic Kingdom* and delivered an album of gloomy New Wave songs inspired by Gwen Stefani's budding relationship with Bush front man Gavin Rossdale. The rainy-day reggae-pop of "Magic's in the Makeup" and "Marry Me" maintained a through line of Jamaican music that would become more pronounced on 2001's *Rock Steady*.

Contrary to what the title suggests, *Rock Steady* doesn't revive the harmony-rich post-ska, pre-reggae sounds of the Paragons and the Melodians. The sound du jour was dancehall, as heard on the hit single "Hey Baby" and vacation-ready album cut "Start the Fire," produced by Sly & Robbie and Steely & Clevie, respectively. Dance-pop cuts like "Hella Good" anticipate Gwen's solo career, another ska-free adventure that would nevertheless result in two worthwhile '00s pop albums.

Meanwhile, Long Beach Dub Allstars evolved into a proper band and released two highly Sublime-y albums before dissolving in 2002. Wilson and Gaugh kept busy with various side projects and formed a new group—called Sublime with Rome—with Nowell superfan Rome Ramirez in 2009. Gaugh left a couple years later, expressing regret they'd resurrected the Sublime name in the first place. Wilson continued on with a new drummer, and Sublime with Rome released their third album, *Blessings*, in 2019.

In his Pitchfork review of *40oz. to Freedom*, critic Evan Rytlewski predicts that "Sublime's well of young fans may dry up," and that the band might ultimately fade from public consciousness, as changing cultural mores have left Nowell and the boys looking like relics from a more permissive, less progressive era. That may be true, but as of 2020, the continued viability of Sublime with Rome, tribute acts like Badfish, and inferior clones like Slightly Stoopid indicates there's still a healthy appetite for the music and lifestyle represented by Nowell.

No Doubt are more of a question mark. In June 2018, *Gwen Stefani—Just a Girl* opened in Las Vegas. Stefani's set list for the concert residency was built on solo and No Doubt hits, though it wasn't quite career-spanning. There was nothing from *No Doubt*, *The Beacon Street Collection*, or No Doubt's mostly slept-on 2012 comeback album *Push & Shove*. Stefani expressed her disappointment with *Push and Shove* in a 2017 *Rolling Stone* interview that didn't exactly bode well for a follow-up. "When Tony and I are connected creatively, it's magic," she said. "But I think we've grown apart as far as what kind of music we want to make."

As of the summer of 2019, Young had "no idea" whether there might be another No Doubt album, or whether it might continue the band's love affair with Jamaican sounds. "I would like that to be the case if we made another record," Young says. "But with our band, there's a lot of cooks in the kitchen, so it's hard for me to really predict it."

The Contender and the Kings of Swing

The issue of *Life* magazine dated August 8, 1938, features an article titled "Swing: The Hottest and Best Kind of Jazz Reaches Its Golden Age." It talks about how haters claim that swing is dying, even though it's still really popular and impossible to define in the first place. Here's the hot take: "The public wants swing, even though it isn't sure what swing is."

Amazingly, all of this would've passed for astute pop-culture criticism six decades later, in 1998. That was the year Cherry Poppin' Daddies cracked Billboard's Mainstream Top 40 with "Zoot Suit Riot," forcing Casey Kasem to say the words "Cherry Poppin' Daddies" on his national radio show. That same year brought the ubiquitous "Khakis Swing" Gap ad and the Brian Setzer Orchestra's timely cover of the very same song. If swing wasn't king, it was definitely a thing.

As neo-swing rocketed toward the height of its unlikely popularity, Royal Crown Revue and Big Bad Voodoo Daddy, the two California bands most responsible for putting the music on the map, were largely absent from MTV and pop radio. Although they never quite earned the distinction of becoming one-hit wonders, both came away from the swing revival with plenty to show for their efforts.

Royal Crown Revue, the band that started the whole thing, released two fantastic major-label albums, cameoed in a comic book movie, opened for Kiss and Neil Diamond in the same week, and backed Bette Midler on tour. They had the chops to play the Playboy Jazz Festival and the ferocity to start mosh pits on the Vans Warped Tour. Big Bad Voodoo Daddy scored a platinum album, appeared in an era-defining comedy, performed at the Super Bowl, and built a career that's continued well past retro-swing's sell-by date.

■ ■ ■

Like many trailblazers, Royal Crown Revue suffered the curse of being first. They were ahead of their game in neo-swing's infancy, when only a handful of scenesters were paying attention, and they were behind the curve a few years later, when there was real money to be made. They were victims of bad breaks, bad timing, and a stubborn musical integrity that made them the baddest neo-swing band of all.

Royal Crown Revue formed in Los Angeles in 1989. Nirvana, leaders of the movement neo-swing would be seen as a reaction against, were still a little-known indie outfit Dave Grohl had yet to join. RCR weren't consciously reacting against anything. The band was just a nifty way for a bunch of aging L.A. punks to try something new. Or, rather, something really old.

One of these punks was Eddie Nichols, the jive-talking, street-smart charmer who would give Royal Crown Revue its voice and character. Nichols was born in New York City to a Vegas lounge singer father and ballet dancer mother. After his folks split up, his mom remarried a man Nichols has called his "evil stepfather," a strict disciplinarian with a habit of using his fists. To his credit, he taught young Eddie about doo-wop and a cappella music—sounds Eddie would come to love as much Elvis Presley, Frank Sinatra, and British punk.

Nichols moved with his family to San Diego in 1984 and left for L.A. at 17. He got into hardcore, roadied for the band Rigor Mortis, and took odd jobs, like cleaning the bathrooms at the grimy punk club Cathay de Grande. Nichols also spent time living on the streets and developed a heroin addiction that would plague him for years.

Nichols could sing and play guitar, and along the way, he formed a rockabilly band called the Rockomatics. He also linked up with a second guitarist and an upright bassist to start another group, a roots combo that would morph into Royal Crown Revue. "It was kind of like discovering American music because we didn't know the music first," Nichols told the *Lake Tahoe Action* in 2008. "We were a bunch of punk rock kids. We were learning our instruments. Nobody taught us how to play 1-6-2-5, which is a common jazz chord progression. When we figured that out, I'd write a song to it."

Nichols caught a lucky break when he got a job working in a Hollywood tattoo shop frequented by Mando Dorame Sr., a Mexican American custom-car expert from Watts who played tenor sax. His son, Mando Jr., also blew a mean tenor and inherited his old man's love for old-school R&B, jump blues, jazz, and doo-wop. When Mando Jr. was a kid, his pop would take him around L.A. and convince bar owners to let the youngster hop onstage. Thanks to his dad's persistence, Mando Jr. got to play with local heroes like Joe Houston and Big Jay McNeely, the "King of the Honking Sax."

Nichols and the younger Dorame formed an instant and intense connection. They did a couple gigs as the Rockomatics, but it wasn't really working, so they found new players for the group that would change their lives—and the course of '90s music. "There was a punk scene, there was a rockabilly scene, and there was a ska scene," Dorame says. "I'm sure there was R&B somewhere. Being the only saxophone in the band at the time, I brought more of the jump R&B influence."

The initial Royal Crown Revue lineup featured guitarist James Achor and siblings Andy and Mark Stern, founding bassist and drummer of the seminal SoCal hardcore band Youth Brigade. Their brother Jamie Stern joined on alto sax, fulfilling a Stern family swing dream that dated back to the late '70s. In the 2009 documentary *Let Them Know: The Story of Youth Brigade and BYO Records*, the fourth Stern brother, Youth Brigade singer and guitarist Shawn, talks about how he and his siblings nearly tried punk 'n' jive all the way back in 1980.

"It was right at the time of the whole 2 Tone thing, the ska bands coming out of England," Shawn says. "I thought, *These guys are doing ska music—we should do swing music. Like punk-rock swing music.* Originally, we were going to be a swing band called the Swing Skins Brigade." There was just one problem. "All the people he knew who were horn players were music school geeks who only read charts," Jamie says in the doc. "And then you had all the punk rockers who didn't read any music at all." Plus, the band geeks didn't want to shave their heads, so the whole thing tanked after a few rehearsals, and the Sterns formed Youth Brigade instead. Fast-forward to 1989, when the SoCal punk scene had started to fizzle out, and the timing was finally right. "Punks were tired of getting beat up by the cops because of how they looked," Dorame says. "They started wearing suits and going out and getting into jazz and ska and rocksteady."

The RCR crew began hanging out at King King, a former Chinese restaurant on 6th and La Brea that Dorame credits with birthing the entire '90s L.A. retro scene. "You'd go see a show, and there'd be cats dressed up in '40s and '50s suits," Dorame says. "You'd see punks there. You'd see skinheads there. You'd see cats dressed up in skinny ska suits. Everybody was all mixed in. No one thought to call it 'retro' yet."

If you threw on your finest suit and went to the King King on a Wednesday night between '89 and the club's closure in '93, you saw Jump With Joey, a seven-piece band that defined the club's aesthetic as well as any. Led by upright bassist, composer, and all-around retro aficionado Joey Altruda, Jump With Joey started out covering everyone from jump blues legend Louis Jordan to ska originators the Skatalites. As they began writing their own material, Jump With Joey gravitated toward the Jamaican stuff, playing ska and rocksteady with a jazzy Latin vibe. Jump With Joey's masterful 1991 debut, *Ska-Ba*, anticipates both the ska and swing revivals right around the corner.

There'd already been a long history in L.A. of punk rock comingling with American roots music. The greatest of the city's first-wave punk bands, X, featured bona fide rockabilly guitarist Billy Zoom, a pompadoured virtuoso who'd played with Gene Vincent and Etta James. The first two X albums arrived on Slash Records, a punk label with a serious Americana bent. Slash was home to Los Lobos, a group of Chicano kids from East L.A. who blended their parents' traditional Mexican folk music with rockabilly, Tex-Mex, R&B, soul, zydeco, and more. The Slash roster also included the Blasters, a punk-adjacent band from Downey, California, whose sound was best summed up by the title of their 1980 debut, *American Music*.

Blasters guitarist Dave Alvin would team up with X, minus Billy Zoom, for a country side project called the Knitters in 1985. By this time, bands like Gun Club and Lone Justice had found ways to repurpose country and blues for the post-punk era. On his 1986 solo debut, *Un "Sung Stories,"* Blasters singer Phil Alvin tapped the Dirty Dozen Brass Band and Sun Ra's Arkestra to back him on a collection of songs that included three Cab Calloway tunes.

Another antecedent to neo-swing was English singer-songwriter Joe Jackson's 1981 album *Joe Jackson's Jumpin' Jive*. Jackson arrived on the scene in 1979 a kind of Elvis Costello clone, another "angry young man" with reggae-tinged New Wave songs and geek-chic style. Over time, Jackson proved exceedingly Costello-like in his musical ambition and curiosity. *Jumpin' Jive* finds him paying tribute to the music of Louis Jordan, Cab Calloway, and others. Jackson didn't just foretell the swing revival years before it happened—he also produced early recordings by third-wave ska pioneers the Toasters.

Dorame has described *Joe Jackson's Jumpin' Jive* as "kinda milquetoast," and he never listened to much punk rock—not even Youth Brigade. He was strictly an old-school cat. In the early days of their friendship, he and

Eddie would spend hours listening to records they'd buy for a quarter apiece at local thrift shops.

Nichols was also into pulp novels, gangster flicks, film noir, and classic cars. He peppered his vocabulary with terms he learned from a book of '30s street slang. The songs he wrote for Royal Crown Revue existed in a mythical mid-century America populated by hoodlums, doomed prizefighters, and Hollywood lowlifes. Because the cartoon drama reflected the darkness in his own life—and because his lyrics were so sharp and funny—he managed to avoid sounding corny. In concert, Nichols would glide across the stage while shadowboxing to the beat and land magnificent jump-splits with the greatest of ease.

Like his singing, his gracefulness was hereditary. In his youth, Nichols had followed in his mother's footsteps and studied ballet. According to Dorame, young Eddie was good enough to be hand-picked for Mikhail Baryshnikov's New York City Ballet. "When you see him jump in the air and do 11 pirouettes, that's ballet training," Dorame says. "He never really told anyone about his ballet. I was fascinated by it and encouraged him. But people used to make fun of him when he was a kid and call him 'ballerina' and shit. He'd get into fights over it. I think that really messed with him and changed his mentality."

By January 1991, Royal Crown Revue had enough material to enter the studio with Thom Wilson, who'd produced records for Cali punk heavyweights like the Vandals, Dead Kennedys, and T.S.O.L. Royal Crown Revue called the album *Kings of Gangster Bop*, a fitting title given their sound at that point. They weren't quite playing swing or rockabilly, but rather a jumpin' hybrid of those and other vintage American sounds, with plenty of punk rawness to boot.

Kings of Gangster Bop features all original tunes except for "Swingin' All Day" and "Stormy Weather," a '30s standard that gives Nichols the chance to go full Rat Pack crooner. The strongest cuts are the tom-tom bonanza "Hey Pachuco" and the winking mobster fantasia "Zip Gun Bop,"

FIG.3 Mando Dorame and Eddie Nichols of Royal Crown
Revue mug for the camera. Photo: Mark Jordan.

both of which would play important roles later in the group's career. The hopped-up "Jumpin' in G" features cool back-and-forth banter between Eddie and the boys. The dual saxes are lighter than air on "Inner City Swing," a toe-tapper with a hint of desperation.

"There was a lot of passion in what we were doing, but we were also learning how to play the music," Dorame says. "It's a reckless record. But we were just going for it. We were happy to have something we felt was different."

Royal Crown Revue may have been completely out of step with the music industry in the early '90s, but there were a couple places they felt at home. In L.A. they had the King King, and in San Francisco they received a warm welcome at Club Deluxe, a newly refurbished '40s-era bar on the corner of Haight and Ashbury. Neo-swing's fervent early adopters bought into a retro lifestyle that, for some, went beyond clothing and music. "The swing movement is about cultural rebellion in its most subversive form: one that uses the symbols of the status quo for its own intents and purposes," V. Vale writes in his 1998 book *Swing! The New Retro Renaissance*. "This is achieved through the simple means of rejecting corporately dictated consumption and embracing forgotten and/or ignored aspects of the American experience (e.g., music, dance, manners, clothing, etc.)."

This retro rebellion was happening unbeknownst to Scotty Morris, an aspiring singer, songwriter, guitarist, and bandleader from Ventura, California. Like Nichols, Morris had served time as a teenager punker, playing bass for False Confession, a key band in the "Nardcore" scene based in the town of Oxnard, California. Morris loved the energy of punk, but it wasn't his destiny to scream over distorted guitars. His fate had been sealed at age five or six, when he picked up his older brother's trumpet and taught himself to play along with a Louis Armstrong record.

As a teenager, Morris switched from trumpet to guitar and began writing and recording his own songs. He also devoured all types of music—not just punk. His taste for vintage and contemporary sounds led him to the

Slash roster. "You'd go to the punk clubs, and you'd hear Fear or Bad Religion . . . and they would have grinding power and aggression," Morris says. "Then a band like the Blasters would come on, and they'd have the exact same intensity as those bands. Only they were playing tunes that just *transcended*. The groove these guys had was so thick and deep. As a musician, I'd lock into it and be like, *This is the shit I'm into.*"

After False Confession ran their course in the late '80s, Morris studied at the Musicians Institute in Los Angeles, then took gigs as a hired-gun musician. The experience of touring behind established artists and being treated like garbage gave Morris a distaste for the L.A. music industry. Once he'd saved enough money to walk away, he went back to Ventura and opened a surf shop with his brother. The job gave him plenty of time to play guitar and write songs. He soon met drummer Kurt Sodergren through a mutual friend.

By now it was 1991 and grunge was ascendant. It made *zero* sense to start a swing band, and yet that's the music Morris heard in his head. It was more than he and Sodergren could make by themselves, so they did the best they could. "In hindsight, we were doing almost exactly what the Black Keys were doing," Morris says, referencing the Ohio garage-rock duo that would form a decade later. Morris would need a lot more musicians to bring his vision to life, starting with a bass player. He found a guy by placing an irresistible newspaper ad: "Imagine Tom Waits, Duke Ellington, and Jimi Hendrix smoking pot in a hot tub."

"Our thing was to play more like jazz and jump swing," says Morris. "But it was all original tunes. They would be really loud and have a lot of aggression. It was almost like a punk-rock swing band."

In early 1993, Morris replaced the original bassist with Dirk Shumaker and added baritone sax player Andy Rowley. It was all coming together. Even the origin of the band's name suggests the gods wanted Morris to make it. A few years before forming the group, Morris caught a blistering performance by Texas blues guitar god Albert Collins. After the show,

Morris ripped a poster off the wall and asked Collins for an autograph. Collins signed it, "To Scotty, the Big Bad Voodoo Daddy."

In light of everything Big Bad Voodoo Daddy would accomplish, it's tempting to think Morris picked up some business savvy from his time in the L.A. music scene. In the band's early touring days, Morris would collect data on how much alcohol clubs sold whenever Big Bad Voodoo Daddy played. He'd use those figures to score more bookings and further grow the fan base. And yet Morris says there was nothing calculated about what he was doing.

"When I was putting my own thing together, I didn't pick guys I thought were great musicians," Morris says. "I picked guys I wanted to hang out with. I wasn't starting a swing band in '92 or '93, at the height of Nirvana, to make money. If I wanted to play any kind of music, that's the kind of music I wanted to play." Morris definitely had the touch when it came to picking bandmates. As of 2020, Sodergren, Shumaker, and Rowley were still in the band.

By early 1993, Morris had some songs, a horn section, and a clear direction in mind. Now he needed an audience. Whereas Royal Crown Revue created a sound for an existing scene, Big Bad Voodoo Daddy had the challenging task of convincing regular people, not big-city retro-philes, to come out and dig the music. "We were 60 miles away from L.A., but we could've been 150,000 miles away," Morris says.

At this point, Big Bad Voodoo Daddy weren't attracting proper swing dancers. But they were beginning to draw larger crowds, and that meant they needed a demo. Local engineer Russ Castillo, whose résumé included Pink Floyd's *The Wall*, heard the band and told Morris he'd love to help them make a record. Castillo guessed they could do it for $2,000—precisely the amount up for grabs at a Ventura battle of the bands. It was another lucky break Big Bad Voodoo Daddy had the talent and wherewithal to capitalize on. They won the prize and recorded their self-titled debut album, released on their own Big Bad Records.

Big Bad Voodoo Daddy isn't quite "punk-rock swing," but it does radiate energy. Even at this early stage, the group had found a way to present pre-rock sounds with rock-band vigor. Morris wrote great hooks and sang them with a modern inflection that made the band sound fresh. His lyrics were lighter and friendlier than Royal Crown Revue's: the disc's two strongest cuts, "Jumpin' Jack" and "King of Swing," are basically about how awesome swing is. But there is some edge on the record. "Machine Gun" tells of a guy who breaks out of jail, goes on a killing spree, and gets sentenced to death. His final words before they switch on the electric chair: "I don't care."

Still smarting from his L.A. experience, Morris had no desire to venture south from Ventura and deal with industry politics. Instead, he turned his attention north, establishing a routine whereby Big Bad Voodoo Daddy would travel to San Francisco and back, stopping midway to play extra gigs on both ends of the trip. They consigned copies of their CD in stores up and down the coast and sold them out every other week. For all Morris knew, Big Bad Voodoo Daddy were cruising in their own lane. But after a show in San Francisco, someone came up to Morris and told him they should play with this band called Royal Crown Revue. Morris had never heard of them, but he wrote down the name of the club they played every Wednesday night: the Derby.

Located at 4500 Los Feliz Boulevard in L.A., the Derby would become neo-swing's most famous venue. It's where the Royal Crown Revue and Big Bad Voodoo Daddy stories intersect, then briefly follow similar arcs before jutting off in opposite directions.

By the time Tony and Tammi Gower opened the Derby in 1993, the dome-roofed building had been through a few revivals of its own. Built in 1929, it originally housed a drive-in restaurant called Willard's Chicken Inn. Then in 1940, cinema legend Cecil B. DeMille rebranded the place as the fourth restaurant in L.A.'s famous Brown Derby chain. The spot became an Italian eatery called Michael's Los Feliz in the '60s and fell into disrepair by the early '90s. That's when the Gowers moved in and gave the place a snazzy Art Deco makeover, complete with velvet curtained booths and the oval bar from the 1945 film *Mildred Pierce*.

Royal Crown Revue began a two-year Derby residency in 1993. When Morris and Rowley drove down from Ventura to check them out, the band was red hot. "I remember standing there for their first song, and I was like, 'Oh shit, we'd better do some practicing,'" Morris says.

As Royal Crown Revue became the "it" band around L.A., director Chuck Russell tapped them to appear in his big-screen adaptation of the Dark Horse comic book *The Mask*. The 1994 film starred a then-unknown Cameron Diaz and a rapidly rising Jim Carrey, who'd mugged his way to mega-stardom with *Ace Ventura: Pet Detective*. *The Mask* was an apt showcase for Royal Crown Revue. The offbeat superhero comedy had a cool retro look and eye-popping special effects inspired by golden-age Warner Bros. animator Tex Avery. Royal Crown Revue appear in a scene where Carrey's character—decked out in a yellow zoot suit and fortified by superpowers he gets by wearing a magical mask—seeks to impress Diaz's lounge-singer character by doing a number with her band. At first, the musicians are dressed in staid white tuxes. Then Carrey spins them around like tornadoes, transforming them into gangster hepcats. "Let's rock this joint!" Carrey says, and right on cue, the band launches into "Hey Pachuco," a sufficiently lively soundtrack for some Looney Tunes rug-cutting.

The movie hauled in $119 million at the box office and became the second-highest-grossing superhero movie up to that point, behind 1989's *Batman*. It was a big win for Royal Crown Revue and the first indication that neo-swing might catch on outside of California. The only downside was the choice of song. "Hey Pachuco" was the closest Royal Crown Revue had come to making a political statement. The lyrics touch on the heinous racial violence of the 1943 Zoot Suit Riots, wherein American servicemen on shore leave in L.A. took to the streets to beat and humiliate zoot suit–clad

Mexican American youth known as *pachucos*. Dorame wrote the song with Nichols and felt a deep personal connection with the subject matter.

"When I was first in the band, I was the only guy that wore a zoot suit around the scene," Dorame says. "The reason I wore a zoot suit is I'm half Mexican. My grandfather was a zoot suiter. I started collecting *Lowrider* magazines from the '70s, and cats were dressing in zoot suits at all the car shows and disco dances. I went and bought a zoot suit because no one else did. That was my own little punk-rock thing. Never did I think there would be some guy wearing a yellow zoot suit in some blockbuster movie. We were happy to be in the movie, but it kind of made a circus of everything."

On the heels of *The Mask* and the increasingly buzzworthy Derby residency, Royal Crown Revue could feel something starting to happen. Unfortunately, things were also happening again for Youth Brigade, who'd reunited in 1992. With Mark and Adam Stern suddenly dividing their time between two bands, Royal Crown Revue needed a substitute rhythm section if they were going to continue playing the Derby every Wednesday. After one Youth Brigade tour, the Stern brothers came back to find they'd been permanently replaced. In the *Let Them Know* documentary, the Sterns suggest they were fired over a disagreement about whether to leave Youth Brigade's own BYO Records and sign with Warner Bros. Dorame says that had nothing to do with it.

"The truth was we were on this mission, and we felt like we were really gaining a lot of momentum," Dorame says. "We started playing the Derby and getting these big crowds. Out of nowhere, [Mark and Adam Stern] said they were going to Europe to do some Youth Brigade stuff. We had no idea what that even meant. We couldn't understand why they would leave the band to do another band. This was our brotherhood."

The Sterns were replaced by bassist Veikko Lepisto, who'd studied jazz at the University of Minnesota, and drummer Daniel Glass, a Honolulu native who'd earned a bachelor's at Brandeis University and honed his skills at the prestigious Dick Grove School of Music in Los Angeles. A finesse player with the raw power to take punk-swing to the next level, Glass had known the Royal Crown guys since 1992 or '93, when he began playing with them in the side project Jazz Jury. "We were all on this scene in L.A., this mesh of swing bands, rockabilly bands, ska bands, blues bands," Glass says. "Things were very open. Nothing got separated as it did later in the decade."

The great Royal Crown reorg of 1994 also saw the addition of trumpeter Scott Steen and baritone sax player Bill Ungerman. This new seven-man lineup had the skill and versatility to keep the band from falling back on tired clichés. "We were not an oldies band," Glass says. "We were looking at all the styles of music we'd grown up with—rock 'n' roll, punk, ska, rockabilly, which were all rebel styles. We were looking to find that energy in the old swinging stuff. We could see the parallels."

Glass describes the '90s-era Royal Crown Revue as a "street gang," with all the loyalty that suggests. When he and Lepisto first joined up, Nichols insisted on making both of them full partners, not just sidemen for hire. That meant they had to look the part. "Eddie took me to get my first haircut," Glass says. "I had long hair when I joined the band. So did Veikko. Scott gave me my first suit. They gave me some vintage ties. They really welcomed me in."

The new and improved Royal Crown Revue continued packing the Derby, drawing celebrities like Bruce Springsteen, Quincy Jones, and the cast of *Friends*. Also, Ted Templeman, the Warner Bros. A&R man who'd produced the first six Van Halen albums, as well as records by Van Morrison, Little Feat, and the Doobie Brothers. "We very consciously tried to walk that line between being a rock band and a swing band or whatever," says Glass. "[Templeman] grew up listening to jazz. He understood all these references."

Having found an industry guy they could trust, Royal Crown Revue signed with Warners, becoming the first neo-swing group to land a major-label deal. That led to more and more bookings outside of L.A., which made it tougher and tougher to play the Derby every Wednesday. The group knew they weren't going to be around in April 1995, so they asked Big Bad Voodoo Daddy if they wanted to sub for one evening.

"It was exciting—there was a scene," Morris says. "It was their scene. I was like, 'No, I don't want to do it.' Tammi, the owner, called me and said, 'Listen, I need you to come in. You'd be doing me a huge favor.' I was like, 'I don't even know you.' She was like, 'We'll make it worth it with the money.'"

Morris was nervous. This was an important gig, and he didn't think trumpeter Ralph Votrian was up to snuff. (Morris played a lot of the wilder trumpet parts on *Big Bad Voodoo Daddy* himself.) Big Bad Voodoo Daddy subbed at the Derby twice with Votrian before replacing him with classically trained Glen "the Kid" Marhevka, another guy still in the band in 2020.

With Royal Crown's schedule refusing to let up, it eventually transpired that Big Bad Voodoo Daddy took over the Wednesday night residency altogether, which wound up being one of the luckiest breaks in the band's career. At the time, it was a nice bit of validation for Morris and his crew. Big Bad Voodoo Daddy had formed out in Ventura, where there was no retro culture to speak of, and here they were taking over the hottest club in L.A. "[Royal Crown Revue] just wanted us to fill in—I don't think they liked that we took that Wednesday night over, and it just exploded," says Morris. "But that is what happened. It wasn't by design. There was nobody who was a bigger fan than I of that band."

By this time, the Derby's clientele had come to include a fledgling actor and screenwriter named Jon Favreau. The New York City native had recently moved to Los Angeles from Chicago after breaking up with his girlfriend, and he was feeling pretty lousy. Like some of his actor buddies, Favreau was frustrated by how hard it was to find work, so he wrote a screenplay based on their boozy adventures in the city's retro-lounge scene. He called it *Swingers*, and in 1995 he and director Doug Liman scraped together enough dough to shoot the thing.

Favreau played the lead role, and because money was tight, his friends Vince Vaughn, Ron Livingston, and Alex Désert, who also sang in the L.A. trad ska band Hepcat, played supporting roles. While writing *Swingers*, Favreau listened to a lot of Frank Sinatra and Royal Crown Revue, whom he'd seen at the Derby. Favreau originally wanted to get Royal Crown Revue for the film's climactic Derby dance scene, but the bosses at Warner Bros. didn't think the band should waste its time on some low-budget movie starring a bunch of nobodies. The label demanded a fee that would've broke the bank for Favreau and his team. "Warner was like, 'If you want to use three tracks, that's gonna be 30 grand,'" Glass says. "We were screaming and yelling and saying, 'You don't understand. This is gonna be a big deal.'"

Morris questions whether Warner Bros. actually killed the deal. "I think Royal Crown Revue didn't want to do it because they'd already done *The Mask*," he says. "[*Swingers*] was a little indie thing. I'm speculating, but I think they turned it down and blamed it on Warner Bros. because it was such a small thing." Either way, Favreau wound up going with Big Bad Voodoo Daddy. "We were the backup plan," says Morris, who'd befriended Favreau prior to being offered the movie. "But when push comes to shove, I think it was just fate they turned it down, and we were able to do it."

Big Bad Voodoo Daddy may not have been Favreau's first choice, but they were perfect for *Swingers*. In their big scene, they play the lighthearted boozer anthem "You & Me & the Bottle Makes 3 Tonight" as our heroes enter the Derby, then the equally gleeful "Go Daddy-O" as Favreau forgets his ex while spinning Heather Graham around on the dancefloor. It's a feel-good scene where the band is meant to fuel the dancing without distracting from the action. It's hard to imagine Favreau and Graham sharing the same moment with Royal Crown Revue tearing through "Hey Pachuco" or "Zip Gun Bop." Royal Crown Revue looked and sounded harder. They had personality for days, moxie out the wazoo. The chemistry would've been all wrong.

Released in October 1996, *Swingers* flopped at the box office but found a second life on home video. By the end of the '90s, young men everywhere were calling women "beautiful babies" and telling each other "You're so money." Annoying catchphrases notwithstanding, *Swingers* is a smart, likable sign-of-the-times comedy that brought retro culture to Blockbuster outlets around the country. Morris has only seen the movie once, on the night of its premiere. "It's such a good movie that I remember it really clearly," says Morris. "My kids really want to watch it with me. I'm like, 'Give me a little more distance, and I'll be OK.'"

Around the time *Swingers* was happening for Big Bad Voodoo Daddy, Royal Crown Revue had other things to worry about. In Vale's *Swing! The New Retro Renaissance*, Eddie Nichols speaks candidly about how his heroin addiction returned with a vengeance in 1995. Nichols told Vale it was Dorame who saved him from self-destruction. "Mando is Mexican American," Nichols said. "He grew up in Watts and has a strong sense of loyalty—has a sense of family. That's just what you do, and you don't even question it. It's the luckiest thing that ever happened to me."

With Nichols back from the brink, Royal Crown Revue were able to hit the studio with Ted Templeman and record their Warner Bros. debut, *Mugzy's Move*. The album arrived in June 1996 with cover artwork inspired by vintage pulp novels. The illustration shows a guy in a suit and fedora hiding in a shadowy alley while bad men with machine guns creep around the corner. Instead of a blaster, our hero clutches a saxophone. The tagline reads, "Mysteries, Thrills, and Hard-Boiled Swing."

Mugzy's Move opens with the one-two punch of "Hey Pachuco" and "Zip Gun Bop," the only two numbers recycled from *Kings of Gangster Bop*. Both benefit enormously from the new rhythm section, which makes the old one sound like recruits from a high school jazz band. The title track is even better. As Glass lays down an anxiety-attack rhythm, Nichols moves beyond pulpy playacting to seemingly relay some real-life experiences: "My blood is burning / My veins on fire / No one cares / Just a fiend / Just a liar." After the spoken-word intro, the band goes off on a jazzy joyride, horns bleating a punchy riff that distracts from what Nichols is singing about.

Elsewhere, Royal Crown Revue get bluesy on the Willie Dixon cover "I Love the Life I Live" and deliver a supercharged version of the Jesse Powell Orchestra's 1952 jump gem "Walkin' Blues." Nichols indulges his Bobby Darin fantasies on "Beyond the Sea," featuring a string arrangement by Artie Baker, who played piano on Darin's 1959 version. With its belching bari sax and a hard-swinging beat, "Trouble in Tinsel Town" plays like a '40s version of X's 1977 punk classic "Los Angeles." "Me and Eddie did not feel limited anymore," says Dorame. "When you listen to *Mugzy's Move*, there's all kinds of jazz on there."

The trouble was, Warner Bros. wasn't sure how to handle a swing band in the years immediately following grunge. Right around the time the band inked its deal, Danny Goldberg replaced Mo Ostin as head of the label. Glass recalls Goldberg visiting the studio while Royal Crown Revue were recording *Mugzy's Move* and standing with his arms crossed for five whole songs. "We could make *anybody* move," Glass says. "And then he said, 'That's not really going to do very well on the radio, is it?'" Warner didn't push a *Mugzy's* single on radio or commission any music videos. When it came to touring, the label left Royal Crown Revue to figure things out for themselves. Beginning in 1996, the seven musicians would cram themselves, their instruments, their extensive wardrobe of gabardine suits, and their two-man crew into an RV meant for five people. They'd sometimes play two dozen one-nighters in a row and drive all night after gigs to save money on hotels.

In 1997, Warner agreed to let Royal Crown Revue release the live album *Caught in the Act* on their manager Dave Kaplan's Surf Dog Records label. (Kaplan also managed Brian Setzer, whose second wedding Royal Crown Revue played in 1994.) It wasn't any kind of cash-grab: Royal Crown Revue wanted a cheapo CD they could offer fans that summer on the Vans Warped

Tour. The "punk-rock summer camp" was only in its third year, and the lineup reflected ska's growing influence in the punk world. The Mighty Mighty Bosstones, Reel Big Fish, Less Than Jake, and Hepcat all joined the circus, horn sections in tow. As the lone swing reps on the bill, Royal Crown Revue did their scene proud.

Warped Tour creator Kevin Lyman's business model involved playing parking lots and giant fields. These big open spaces could get pretty hot in July and August, but Royal Crown Revue made a point of sticking with (and probably sticking *to*) their retro threads. They also played hard and fast enough to win over anyone who questioned their punk cred. "We went out and beat the shit out of those audiences," Glass says. "Within five minutes, we had total respect amongst all the bands. Because we could actually play our instruments. We were playing upright bass and horns, and Eddie was more punk rock than any of those motherfuckers. What, are you gonna go up and tease Eddie Nichols? Not gonna happen."

At one Warped stop, Royal Crown shot a grainy black-and-white video for "Barflies at the Beach," their riotous reimagining of Louis Prima's 1936 swing staple "Sing, Sing, Sing (With a Swing)." "Barflies" was originally released on *MOM II: Music for Our Mother Ocean*, a charity album featuring tracks by the Mighty Mighty Bosstones, Sublime, and Brian Setzer Orchestra, as well as Jimmy Buffett, Counting Crows, and Moby. Since *MOM II* was out on Surfdog, a subsidiary of Interscope, Warner wouldn't promote "Barflies," Glass says, and neither would Interscope.

In the end, Warner reissued *Mugzy's Move* with "Barflies" included, but the whole thing was a missed opportunity. With a proper push, the song might've been a hit—something that was made apparent in the fall of 1997, when "Barflies" enjoyed a triumphant run on MTV's 12 *Angry Viewers*, a short-lived show that gave a panel of music fans the power to pick which videos went into rotation.

Big Bad Voodoo Daddy were presumably having an easier time with Coolsville, the subsidiary of Capitol Records they signed with after

Swingers. Coolsville was founded by Brad Benedict, the veteran Capitol producer who'd spearheaded the *Ultra-Lounge* series, a point of entry for newcomers discovering the exotica and "space-age bachelor-pad" music of Martin Denny, Les Baxter, Esquivel, and others. Big Bad Voodoo Daddy's first project with Benedict was rerecording "Jumpin' Jack" for a swing compilation. They got to use Morris's dream studio, Capitol's Studio B, where Frank Sinatra, Bob Dylan, and the Beach Boys made some of their most indelible recordings. For the session, Capitol hired an extra sax player, trombonist, and lead trumpeter to flesh out the horn section. Morris loved the robust sound so much that he's used the session trombonist and trumpeter on all subsequent recordings.

Big Bad Voodoo Daddy finally released their big-league debut, *Americana Deluxe*, in February 1998. (The title doesn't appear on the cover, so a lot of people mistake the record as being self-titled.) By this time, the band had grown to include piano player and arranger Joshua Levy, whose sparkling keyboard work complements the double-stacked horns. *Americana Deluxe* included three songs from the group's self-titled record, plus the *Swingers* favorites "You & Me & the Bottle Makes 3" and "Go Daddy-O." Morris practically dares you not to enjoy yourself with the standout "Mr. Pinstripe Suit." There's also the Cab Calloway cover "Minnie the Moocher" and "Mambo Swing," which predicts the Latin boom of the following year. The bongos and bluesy guitar of "Please Baby" anticipate "Smooth," the hit 1999 collaboration between Carlos Santana and Rob Thomas.

By no means as edgy or challenging as *Mugzy's Move*, *Americana Deluxe* is an immensely likable and well-crafted album. And yet lead single "You & Me & the Bottle Makes 3" stalled at #31 on the Modern Rock Tracks chart and never crossed over to pop radio. Its limited radio success was partially a result of the label's marketing plan. The Capitol division E-Prop focused on promoting *Americana Deluxe* via in-store displays in markets where they knew swing sold. Radio was a secondary concern. Even without a smash single, *Americana Deluxe* went platinum in March 1999. Morris believes it could have sold 2 or 3 million, but in April 1998, two months after the album dropped, E-Prop folded, leaving Big Bad Voodoo Daddy without promo support for months before they signed with Interscope.

Big Bad Voodoo Daddy plugged the record by appearing on *Late Night with Conan O'Brien* and *The Roseanne Show*, where they were upstaged by everyone's favorite septuagenarian sex therapist, Dr. Ruth Westheimer. The band had stipulated that it didn't want any swing dancers accompanying the performance—they looked really cheesy on these shows—but as they launched into "Mr. Pinstripe Suit," Dr. Ruth got up and started boogying with a dancer who'd been brought to the set. "They immediately take away from what I feel is the best song on the record," Morris says. Roseanne's producers were elated. "They were like, 'We didn't have it lit right. Let's do it again,'" Morris says. "'And this time, we'll film Dr. Ruth dancing.'"

By the spring of 1998, neo-swing had come a long way. The movement launched in underground L.A. and San Francisco clubs had vaulted a handful of bands to national attention and spawned two genuine hits, Squirrel Nut Zippers' "Hell" and Cherry Poppin' Daddies' "Zoot Suit Riot." Ska was still hanging around. Even mainstream rock was trending toward beachy bands Sugar Ray and Smash Mouth. Everything was building toward some kind of reverse "Smells Like Teen Spirit" moment, an expression of late-'90s exuberance that later generations would look back on with wonder.

The Gap's "Khakis Swing" was not that moment. It was a commercial for pants—albeit a very effective one. Set to Louis Prima's 1956 classic "Jump, Jive' an Wail," the ad quickly got people talking (and dancing) when it premiered in April 1998. It was a boon for the Gap and even better for the Brian Setzer Orchestra, who released a cover of Prima's song two months later on their third album, *The Dirty Boogie*. Setzer's version of "Jump, Jive an' Wail" peaked at #14 on Billboard's Adult Top 40 chart. The swing revival had its third and final radio smash.

As with *Swingers* and "Barflies at the Beach," the Gap commercial may have been a near miss for Royal Crown Revue. "We were doing 'Jump,

Jive an' Wail' when I first joined the band," says Glass. "We quit doing it because it wasn't cool enough, because everyone else was doing it. The Gap came to Royal Crown Revue and said, 'We hear you have a version of 'Jump, Jive an' Wail.' I think they thought it was going to be too expensive to license the Louis Prima version. We said, 'No, we don't, but we could record one tomorrow.'"

The next day, Glass says, the Gap folks called back and said they could afford Prima's original after all. Because Royal Crown Revue were between albums, it didn't make sense for them to cut a version and capitalize on the Gap spot. Setzer, on the other hand, was just finishing *The Dirty Boogie*. He had enough time to record "Jump, Jive an' Wail" (with Nichols on background vocals) and consequently score his first big band hit. (Dave Kaplan says he has no knowledge of the Gap ever contacting Royal Crown Revue.)

Morris had his own reasons to be disappointed. "That's when I knew we were in trouble, because Setzer did not write that song," he told the *Dig Me Out* podcast. Morris believed the scene needed original music to thrive, and he knew encroachment from Madison Avenue meant swing's days were numbered. He advised his bandmates to save their money, saying bluntly, "We're Chubby Checker right now, and this is 'The Twist.'"

The bubble hadn't yet burst when Royal Crown Revue released their third studio album, *The Contender*, in August 1998. With Templeman again producing, the group made a conscious effort to write more radio-friendly material while pushing into new territory. Gnarly surf-garage guitars underpin the title track—essentially a retelling of the great 1949 boxing noir *The Set-Up*, if not the Bruce Willis segment from *Pulp Fiction*, if not Royal Crown Revue's very own underdog story. Nichols's spoken-word verses on "Friday the 13th," about a lowly hood searching for his stolen car, are straight out of a Raymond Chandler novel. The tropical-flavored "Port-Au-Prince" tells the story of how pinup queen Bettie Page lived in Haiti for four months and supposedly witnessed a voodoo ritual.

"By the time we got to *The Contender*, we felt like, 'This is who we are. This is how we want to be represented,'" says Dorame. "I still to this day don't know what to call it. I guess retro music or alternative music. I don't know what you call it. That's always been our problem."

The album's lead single was "Zip Gun Bop—Reloaded," yet another version of a song Royal Crown Revue had first recorded seven years earlier. This time, though, it had a chance. The band shot a tongue-in-cheek prison-break-themed music video featuring cameos by Mike Ness of Social Distortion and the guys from Hepcat. Glass says MTV censors were nervous about the guns carried by the prison wardens, so few people ever saw it. The single went nowhere and the album topped out at #172 on the Billboard 200. "I think we were too late," says Glass. "Two or three songs from the genre peaked, and after that . . ."

Royal Crown Revue earned some unwanted publicity on October 24, 1998, when Nichols and the group's guitar technician got into a fistfight with off-duty police officers following a show in Toledo, Ohio. Nichols claimed the men—who he didn't know were cops—provoked him by shooting spitballs. He spent the weekend in jail and faced numerous charges, including assaulting a police officer, disorderly conduct, and resisting arrest. A month later, the prosecutor lowered the charge to disorderly conduct; Nichols pleaded no contest and was given credit for time served. The Lucas County Police Internal Affairs Department said it would investigate the arrest, since the spitball shooters had reportedly been drinking, but according to MTV the department concluded that no investigation was necessary.

The incident forced the band to cancel shows and contributed to Nichols's bad-boy reputation. "He had a hardened exterior, although he was a very sweet guy once you got to know him, and a very giving guy," Glass says. "He had a lot of issues related to his upbringing. It's part of what made the band great, and it's what made the band authentic. Eddie was the heart and soul of that band in terms of what it was all about."

As 1998 wound to a close, Big Bad Voodoo Daddy booked the gig that would represent neo-swing's peak pop-cultural achievement: Super Bowl XXXIII. They were asked to open the show with "Go Daddy-O," then join co-headliner Stevie Wonder for his 1976 Duke Ellington tribute "Sir Duke." Morris knew the song well. When he was 12, he complained to his junior high jazz band teacher that all the music they played sucked. The teacher told him if he didn't like it, he should write something better. So Morris busted out the staff paper and whipped up a jazz band score for "Sir Duke." When Morris shared that story with Wonder, the Motown legend offered to sign the score. (The blind music legend's autograph is a thumbprint.)

"At the Super Bowl, it felt like, 'Boom, here it goes. Now where?'" Morris says. "This thing had been snowballing so perfectly for so many years. At the time, I didn't realize that was the pinnacle." But after you've performed for a global audience of 83.7 million people, there's nowhere to go but down. It didn't help that Big Bad Voodoo Daddy were playing five or six nights a week and burning themselves out. When they finally came off the road, the label told Scotty it needed a new album in six weeks. "I had to make up something," Morris says. "I had to make up anything."

What he came up with was *This Beautiful Life*, released in October 1999. Only three of the 13 songs weren't brand new: "I Wanna Be Like You," originally recorded by Louis Prima for the 1967 Disney film *The Jungle Book*; "2000 Volts," a reworking of "Machine Gun"; and a cover of Frank Sinatra's swinging '60s version of "Ol' MacDonald." New originals like "Big and Bad" and "What's Next" are tight, catchy, and right for dancing, '90s swing 101. About the worst you can say about *This Beautiful Life* is that it's more of the same, *Americana Deluxe II*. Critics weren't impressed. "I assumed the record was getting bad reviews because [it] wasn't good," Morris says. "But the backlash was in full effect. We had to deal with terrible reviews. Terrible turnouts at venues we'd been playing for years."

One reason for the backlash was that radio simply stopped playing swing. Someone once told Morris they overheard KROQ programming director Kevin Weatherly say, "I'm going to kill fucking swing music." Morris puts some of the blame on the bands themselves. "There wasn't a lot of variety in what was happening," he says. "Either it sounded like us, it sounded like Royal Crown, or it sounded like Brian Setzer. I don't think anything came out unique enough to break further. That's just the nature of the beast. This music is really hard to create original authentic music. The footsteps are huge."

Since 2000, Morris has managed to keep Big Bad Voodoo Daddy together and playing to fans across the country. That longevity is once again due to savvy decision-making. Morris shifted from clubs to performing arts centers and took on sensible recording projects. With the world not exactly jonesing for more original '90s-style swing songs, Morris and his band have turned in a series of conceptual tribute albums. They honor New Orleans jazz on 2003's *Save My Soul*, Cab Calloway on 2009's *How Big Can You Get?: The Music of Cab Calloway*, and messieurs Armstrong, Jordan, and Prima on 2017's *Louis, Louis, Louis*.

After the poor performance of *The Contender*, Royal Crown Revue asked Warner Bros. to release them from their contract. They promptly signed with the L.A. indie label SideOneDummy and recorded their fourth album, 1999's *Walk on Fire*, with Squirrel Nut Zippers producer Mark Napolitano. They got some help from Warped Tour founder Kevin Lyman, who was teaching a music business course at Citrus College an hour from L.A. The school had a state-of-the-art recording facility, and as long as a couple of Citrus students worked as engineers, Royal Crown got free studio time.

Just because Royal Crown Revue had access to a cutting-edge studio, they weren't about to make a modern-sounding album. They recorded the old-fashioned way, using all vintage equipment and even positioning the entire horn section around a single microphone. Stylistically, *Walk on Fire* goes further afield than *The Contender*, defying anyone to use the "swing" label. Resplendent with timpani drums and mariachi horns, opener "She Walks on Fire" plops a fez on your head and ushers you into an exotic soiree in some sand-swept faraway land. The rollicking jump-blues sin-galong "Watts Local" buses you back to familiar territory, but it's a wild ride from there to "Mr. Meschugge," which ends the disc with some das-tardly '20s jazz experimentation. "We lost a lot of people with that record," Glass says. "I think it's one of our best efforts. Eddie's songwriting is just amazing. He really dug into his characters."

Walk on Fire came out in July 1999, just as Royal Crown Revue embarked on their second Warped Tour. By this time, the band had begun to feel the pinch Big Bad Voodoo Daddy were experiencing. The backlash was on, and nobody—not even the punk-as-fuck band that started everything and maintained its integrity all the way through—was safe. "They threw out the baby with the bathwater," Glass says. "Nobody acknowledged we did it differently. We had been around longer. We did it first. It didn't matter at that point."

In Dorame's estimation, it was 9/11 that finally lowered the curtain on neo-swing. "I remember we played the Flamingo in Vegas the day after," Dorame says. "There was no one on the strip. It was the eeriest shit. No one was at the gig. The whole world changed. From that point on, it was pretty much dead. We were doing corporate gigs and going overseas. We were still keeping our head above water in Australia, or we'd got to Europe. But we couldn't do shit in the States anymore."

In 2001 Royal Crown Revue released *Passport: Live in Australia*, and in 2004 the band's horn section backed Bette Midler on her Kiss My Brass Tour. By this time the group had begun to shed original members, and by the end of the decade only Glass, Dorame, and Nichols remained. They hired replacement horn players and continued touring periodically, most notably in Australia. In 2009, to celebrate their twentieth anniversary, Royal Crown Revue added Mando's girlfriend, retro-fabulous singer Jenni-fer Keith, and debuted a new stage show, complete with burlesque dancers.

Royal Crown Revue played a mere three shows in 2013 and went on indefinite hiatus. Glass moved to New York City, where teaching gigs and session work enabled him to settle down with his wife and enjoy life off the road. Dorame got engaged to Keith, with whom he formed the Jennifer Keith Quintet in 2007. In October 2019, Royal Crown Revue surprised fans by announcing plans to headline the Viva Las Vegas Rockabilly Weekend in April 2020. Unfortunately, the festival was cancelled due to the COVID-19 pandemic.

Looking back, Morris thinks the rise of neo-swing—like the ska boom that preceded it—had a lot to do with grunge. "When the uplifting part of ska and swing presented itself, it was new," Morris says. "When you'd go see a grunge band, the guys and girls aren't hanging out together. The guys are usually rocking, or they're in the pit. But then swing comes along, and it's this more romantic music. Girls are dressing up and guys are dressing up, and they're dancing together and drinking cocktails together. It was this real revolt against what had been going on for a while."

Dorame sees the '90s as "the last decade of bands." Ever since, it's been all about the DJ. That's why kids on their way into the trendy Marquee nightclub in Las Vegas used to stop and gawk at the Jennifer Keith Quintet when the band played an adjoining lounge during a mid-'10s residency. "These kids would stop and listen to this music because there was a band," Dorame says. "They've never seen instruments before. Do you realize I've met kids who don't know who Elvis Presley is? Don't know who Frank Sinatra is? That's American history. How do you not know who that is?"

CHAPTER 4

Skanking Behind the Orange Curtain

In the '90s, perhaps no place in America was better equipped to produce and export jubilant third-wave ska bands than Orange County, California. On top of all the good stuff happening for the nation on a macro level (high GDP growth, low unemployment, plummeting crime rates, minimal conflict with other nations), this was the fabled O.C., an oasis of sunshine and wealth that had always been considered a nice place to live. As soon as you cross over the county line heading south from Los Angeles, Californians say you've gone behind "the Orange Curtain," an invisible barrier separating well-to-do WASPs from the rest of the region.

"We had enough money to buy nice instruments and learn an instrument in school, and we didn't really have a lot of issues," says Monique Powell, lead singer of Save Ferris, one of the two O.C. ska bands not called No Doubt that scored national radio hits in the '90s. "We weren't political. We didn't really deal with any of that. Everybody just wanted to party."

As it happened, Powell didn't have the happiest of home lives, but in Orange County, that was OK. "The kids with the problems just blended in with the majority, and the majority were kids who didn't have a lot [of drama] going on," she says. "Big families. Didn't really struggle with money. It was pre-9/11, and the country, we felt like we were impenetrable."

That's Powell's theory on why Orange County became the ska capital of the world for a little while in the '90s. Her hypothesis squares nicely with the shiny-happy skanking of Save Ferris, who exploded onto the radio with a cover of Dexys Midnight Runners' 1983 New Wave fave "Come On Eileen," and the wiseass party music of Reel Big Fish, who swam even further into the mainstream with "Sell Out," a song that defined '90s ska for a lot of people, for better and for worse.

"We're like the guilty-pleasure band," says Reel Big Fish lead singer and guitarist Aaron Barrett. "We're like the band that you use as the example if you hate ska and you want to make fun of it. But we're also the band that people talk about when they love ska. Like, 'Oh yeah, bands like Reel Big Fish will carry the torch.'"

Save Ferris and Reel Big Fish were easy points of entry for American teenagers with zero knowledge of ska. Historical perspective wasn't a prerequisite for understanding or enjoying what they were doing. Barrett sported a pompadour, sideburns, and Hawaiian shirts. His look was more Ace Ventura than Walt Jabsco, 2 Tone's cartoon rude-boy mascot. Powell was a ska-pop pinup with dyed red hair and vintage style. They stood as good a chance as anyone of getting this music on MTV.

Before Powell and Barrett emerged as mini ska celebs—both Save Ferris and Reel Big Fish appeared in feature films before the '90s were out—they were classmates at Los Alamitos High School. Powell was there thanks to Orange County School of the Arts (OCSA), an auditions-based program for promising young talents. She was studying to become an opera singer, a dream born after she slayed her sixth-grade talent show.

For a Jewish girl from a working-class family who didn't quite fit the O.C. stereotype, OCSA was a chance to attend a fancy school where people believed in her talent. "I went from being a very shy girl who never cut or dyed her hair or wore makeup to starting to find my voice," Powell says.

While at Los Alamitos, Powell met the guys in Reel Big Fish, already an active band that included Barrett, bassist (and fellow OCSA student) Matt Wong, and singer Ben Guzman. Barrett started playing guitar at 15, soon after his family got MTV. Like many an impressionable lad, he was into hair metal and classic rock, and that's what Reel Big Fish played from its inception in 1991 until Barrett graduated from high school the following year. "We didn't understand that there was any kind of local music scene or anything," says Barrett. "We thought some man with a contract was going to come knocking on the garage door: 'Hey guys, you sound great!'"

Barrett credits Guzman with hipping him to ska, music he actually already dug. "One of my favorite bands was the English Beat," says Barrett. "And Madness and all the old 2 Tone stuff. But I didn't realize it had a name until later. We kind of fell into the ska scene backwards. I was like, 'Oh, I love this music. Let's do this!'"

Powell also discovered 2 Tone as a youngster, thanks to her KROQ-loving older sister. "'Ghost Town' and 'Too Much Too Young' [by the Specials] were on the radio all the time, and I was really into it," says Powell. "But I was studying opera, so my exposure to pop and modern music was a little bit limited."

■ ■ ■

Around 1993, Reel Big Fish made the switch from Poison and Jimi Hendrix covers to ska. By this time, Barrett had started going to see local bands like No Doubt and Sublime. "It was the tail end of the super-purist 2 Tone [era], where you had to wear a skinny tie and a porkpie hat. If you didn't, they'd fight you," Barrett says. "There was tension between the purists and the kids that just wanted to go to shows and have fun. But then as we started playing more shows, it became more about, 'Everyone's welcome. You can dress however you want to. You can play whatever style of music you want to.'"

Reel Big Fish's metamorphosis into a ska band came with some lineup changes. Guzman, guitarist Lisa Smith, and keyboardist Zach Gillitrap were out. Barrett jumped on lead vocals and convened a two-piece horn section. By 1995, when Reel Big Fish self-released their debut album, *Everything Sucks*, the lineup included Barrett, Wong, drummer Andrew Gonzalez, saxophonist Adam Polakoff, trumpeter Tavis Werts, and trombonists Dan Regan and Robert Quimby. Around this time, KROQ was spinning Sublime's "Date Rape" on the regular, and Barrett could sense a ska moment on the horizon.

In sound and subject matter, *Everything Sucks* presents a rougher, dirtier version of the Reel Big Fish the world would love (or hate) in a couple of years. Stuffed with bright, rubbery horn lines and guitars that toggle between chipper upstrokes and heavy power chords, the album features 10 songs the band would rerecord for its big-league debut, 1996's *Turn the Radio Off*. These include "Join the Club," "Trendy," and "I'll Never Be," all of which contribute to an overall conceptual thread about starting a band, worrying your band will suck, wrestling with the desire to fit in, and fearing you'll never get on MTV. Although Barrett's constant longing for fame is couched in jokes that make the whole thing seem ironic, *Everything Sucks* is actually pretty sincere.

"Once I decided that I wanted to be in a band, that was all I thought about," says Barrett. "I just wrote about what I was thinking about all the time. I was obsessed with making it and being a rock star."

Everything Sucks sold well locally and attracted fans that didn't mind the album's amateur vibe. "David Lee Roth says, 'If you can't do it right, do it anyway,'" Barrett says. "In Orange County, it wasn't about great musicianship and trying to show each other up with our hot licks or anything. It was just, 'Can you make a noise? Yeah? Get up onstage! Can you hold a horn above your head and at least wave it around? All right, you're in the band.'"

In October 1995, Reel Big Fish played a "Skalloween" show with the Skeletones at the Barn in Riverside. As the opening act they were only supposed to have 20 minutes, and of course they went over. When the soundman tried to shut them down, Barrett freaked out, declaring "Fuck

you! I'm going to play anything I want to!" His tantrum impressed a guy in the audience named John Feldmann, lead singer of a fledgling ska-punk group called Goldfinger. Feldmann needed a horn section to play on Goldfinger's debut album, soon to be released on a new label called Mojo Records, and he tapped Reel Big Fish to join him in the studio.

Mojo was a joint partnership with Universal Music founded by Jay Rifkin, the music and film producer who'd recently worked on *The Lion*

King. The label took an interest in Reel Big Fish and wanted to sign them for a split 7-inch with Goldfinger. Reel Big Fish's manager pushed Mojo to let the band make a full album, and since the label hadn't yet signed many acts, they agreed. Reel Big Fish were at the right place at the right time to get on Mojo, and Mojo lucked into having two bands that would be at the forefront of the "next big thing."

■ ■ ■

As Reel Big Fish readied for their close-up, Powell was also taking steps toward her ska destiny. After graduating from Los Alamitos in 1993, she enrolled at Cal State Fullerton, where her love for ska really took hold. It seemed like all of her friends were in ska bands, and when she saw the Skeletones on campus, that cemented it. One of the bands in her orbit was Suburban Rhythm, an O.C. ska outfit immortalized in the Reel Big Fish song "S.R.," which opens with the line "What ever happened to Suburban Rhythm? / Why did Ed and Scott quit?" As it turns out, bassist Ed Kampwirth quit to join a new band called Larry, featuring Monique Powell as one of the vocalists. They were not a ska band—Powell has described the Zappa-influenced funk-rock troupe as "music major music"—but thanks to their connection with Suburban Rhythm, they played on lots of ska bills. Either slightly before or during Larry, Powell also fronted a short-lived all-girl ska band called the Shanties. "They were rad," Powell says. "They were a bunch of tough girls. I loved hanging out with them. That opened up the space for me to say, 'Well, I wanna be in a ska band.'"

Powell got her chance when another local ska band, Los Pantalones, went finito. Following the split, several ex-members—including singer-guitarist-songwriter Brian Mashburn, bassist Bill Uechi, and saxophonist Eric Zamora—decided to carry on with a new singer. When the first guy they found didn't work out, they thought of Powell. Los Pantalones had opened shows for Larry, so they knew she had pipes. What they didn't know was her phone number. Luckily, one of their girlfriends had access to the old OCSA phone roster, and they tracked down Powell's parents' home phone. Since Powell had never been the lone front woman in Larry or the Shanties, the offer to take the helm of this new group was too good to pass up. "I thought the songs were cute, and that I could do a lot with them," Powell says.

She could also see Save Ferris as a kind of exit ramp from the career path she'd been following since the start of her opera training. "I remember being the youngest and weirdest person in the [Cal State] opera department by a number of years, and just feeling like I didn't fit in at all," Powell says. "Going to [ska] shows was my calling, because I felt comfortable."

Powell claims she laid down some ground rules before taking the job. "I was like, 'Listen I really want to do this full-time,'" Powell says. "'I want to quit Fullerton. I don't want to go back, because I want to do music full-time, and I want to stick with this until it happens. So who doesn't have the time, or who isn't serious about it?'"

The original trombone player wasn't ready for that level of commitment, so Powell brought in her friend T-Bone Willy, formerly of the O.C. ska band the Nuckle Brothers. T-Bone had a house with a star-shaped pool where he'd throw parties and host local bands. That's how Save Ferris got the name for Starpool Records, the indie label they used to release their debut EP, *Introducing . . . Save Ferris*, in 1996. (The name Save Ferris, of course, comes from the 1986 teen comedy *Ferris Bueller's Day Off*.) Powell's sister fronted the band money for studio time, and the group knocked out the seven songs in 24 hours. "Some of us would sleep while the others were playing," Powell recalls.

Released a month after the group formed, *Introducing . . . Save Ferris* is appropriately billed as "Ska/Pop/Swing" on the bright-red retro-style cover artwork. The music is tight and catchy and completely devoid of the sarcastic edge favored by Reel Big Fish. Save Ferris don't waste any time fretting about trendiness or whether they'll get on MTV. The swinging "Super Spy" puts a flirty spin on the secret-agent song, a popular trope in third-wave ska. "Under 21" is a battle cry for teens without fake IDs.

"Spam" celebrates Hormel's iconic brand of canned pork. The other four tracks are straightforward love songs carried by Powell's mighty vocals and the energy of the performances.

Another one of Powell's stipulations before joining was that she wanted to serve as manager. Thanks to her time with Larry and friendship with Reel Big Fish, Powell had relationships with many people in the Orange County scene. Save Ferris quickly gained popularity and made the leap to headliner status, angering more established bands. "There was a sort of bro-type attitude: 'We've been around longer than you have,'" says Powell. "I was like, 'We're selling more tickets than you are, so I'm sorry, you have to open for us.'"

Without any distribution, *Introducing . . . Save Ferris* earned the band airplay on KROQ and sold in the neighborhood of 20,000 copies. Somewhere along the way, the group applied for a national Grammy Showcase competition for unsigned bands. After winning round one in L.A., Save Ferris flew to New York City, where they took first place in the finals and made a big impression on David Massey, senior vice president of A&R for Epic Records. In a 1997 interview with the *Los Angeles Times*, Massey said he signed Save Ferris "with no hesitation whatsoever." "That was one of those spontaneous things," he added. "They simply drove the crowd wild." Powell is a little more cynical. "No Doubt was doing really well at the time, so all of these A&R guys had very little creativity," says Powell. "They were looking for the next female in ska or whatever."

■ ■ ■

By the time Save Ferris released their Epic debut, *It Means Everything*, in September 1997, Reel Big Fish had made a huge splash on radio and MTV. In fact, Reel Big Fish's Mojo debut, *Turn the Radio Off*, reached its peak position of #57 on the Billboard 200 in September '97, just as Save Ferris were getting ready for their turn in the spotlight. *Turn the Radio Off* had been out since August 1996, but it took the single "Sell Out"—which also reached its chart peak in September '97—to push the band over the top.

Reel Big Fish recorded *Turn the Radio Off* with two producers, Mojo label boss Jay Rifkin and John Avila, ex-bassist for ska-influenced New Wave rockers Oingo Boingo. The sound they achieved—particularly for the horns—has a plasticky, vacuum-sealed quality that's slightly cartoonish yet punchy as hell. It's exactly what the music demanded. Rifkin and his engineer used heavy digital compression—which makes loud parts quieter and quieter parts louder—and virtually no reverb. Another thing the band did was use stereo recording to double the horn lines. The musicians would play their parts for one channel, then do it again for the other. Except they weren't great at playing along with themselves, so they created an unintentional chorus effect. "It's all the mistakes we made that give it a cheeky personality," Barrett says.

Cheekiness abounds on "Sell Out," which reached #10 on Billboard's Modern Rock Tracks chart and became the group's signature song. It's about quitting your crummy fast-food job to sign a record deal, which is exactly what happened to Barrett. He gave his notice at Subway right after the band signed with Mojo. But he actually wrote "Sell Out" before Reel Big Fish had a deal. He was speaking his dream into existence—and commenting on some scene politics he didn't much care for.

When Barrett wrote "Sell Out," Dance Hall Crashers had just come out with 1995's *Lockjaw*, their first album for MCA, and their first without the horn section they'd employed early on. "Some people in the scene were like, 'They're sellouts—they don't have horns anymore,'" Barrett says. "I like the band, though. It's a great album. They're just trying to do their thing." Barrett penned "Sell Out" with the intent of "poking fun of the elitist scene" that would diss bands like DHC for breaking the accepted ska rules of conduct. That was the idea, anyway. Barrett admits the lyrics are vague and very much open to interpretation. The video confuses the issue further. In the clip, evil record company men lure Reel Big Fish away from their burger-flipping day jobs and force them into jumpsuits stamped with the words "ska band." If the lyrics justify shaking hands with a major, the video makes it seem like surrendering your identity to a soulless corporation.

"When I look at it, it doesn't really make any kind of statement either way," Barrett says. "It's just like, 'Sell out with me. Oh yeah.' What a stupid song."

Turn the Radio Off isn't just about being in a ska band and wrestling with what level of financial compensation you therefore deserve. There are also crazy-bitter breakup songs like "All I Want Is More," which had been titled "Fuck Yourself" on *Everything Sucks*, and "Skatanic," a chilling metal-ska rager that finds Barrett's protagonist outside his ex's house, screaming "Fuck you, bitch, I love you!" Some of the lyrics are slightly problematic by twenty-first-century standards, and even Barrett admits they make him cringe. But he says the songs shouldn't be taken as misogynistic. He was writing about specific relationships he'd been through, not women in general.

"I was a 19-, 20-year-old kid singing whatever shit popped into my head," Barrett says. "I didn't think about the long term. Like, 'Oh, someday people will be analyzing this, living their lives by them.' I was just trying to write some lyrics, because that's what you do when you make up songs. . . . I'm like 45, and my whole life is this band. That's how I make my living. And now [people are] like, 'So what do you mean by this? Is this how you live your life?' No, none of that stuff. I was an angry young kid. I had problems. Now I'm just a happy old man."

There's less anger and more doofy humor in "She Has a Girlfriend Now," featuring guest vocals from Monique Powell. Barrett patterned the song after the 1985 Fishbone classic "Lyin' Ass Bitch," only he changed the story to be about a guy whose ex has come out as a lesbian. "She Has a Girlfriend Now" suggests Barrett had some self-awareness regarding the inadequacy of his male protagonists elsewhere on the album. Explaining her new lifestyle, Powell's character declares, "Guys don't do no more for me."

FIG.5 Aaron Barrett shreds for the masses on the 1997
Warped Tour. Photographer unknown.

But examining *Turn the Radio Off* through the lens of adulthood is a foolish endeavor. The music is ebullient and silly and designed for teenagers, who ate it up. In November 1997, some 15 months after its release, the album was certified gold. (As of November 2019, it had sold 724,000 copies, according to Nielsen Music.) That was largely due to "Sell Out," which Barrett remembers being released as a single on the same day in the spring of 1997 that the Mighty Mighty Bosstones dropped "The Impression That I Get."

"I remember going, 'Oh man, that [Bosstones] song is so much better!'" Barrett says. "But I think it was lucky for us that it did come out the same day, and not later, 'cause it might not have done as well."

■ ■ ■

Fresh off their Epic deal, Save Ferris recorded *It Means Everything* with English producer Peter Collins, whose résumé included Bon Jovi, Suicidal Tendencies, and Indigo Girls. The album features five songs from *Introducing*, five new originals, and one '80s cover that would define their career.

"Come On Eileen," the sole American hit for Dexys Midnight Runners, wasn't that left-field a cover choice for a ska band. Formed in 1978, Dexys played '60s American soul with U.K. punk power. They were operating parallel to bands like the Specials and Madness, whom Dexys opened for on 1979's 2 Tone Tour. "Come On Eileen" appears on Dexys' 1982 sophomore album, *Too-Rye-Ay*, a departure from the heavy-duty brass of its predecessor, *Searching for the Young Soul Rebels*. This time around, England-born, Irish-blooded front man and mastermind Kevin Rowland was forging a new Celtic soul sound. Banjos, violins, and accordions mixed it up with the trombones and saxophones. It's all there on "Come On Eileen," which topped the Billboard Hot 100 for one week in April 1983.

"Come On Eileen" is about trying to get laid. As Rowland told *The Guardian* in 2014, the character of Eileen was a "composite, to make a point about Catholic repression." He might've gotten that point across a little better had he not written such a supremely catchy and bizarre song.

The numerous tempo changes and killer chorus melody ensure that most listeners are too preoccupied with the music to worry about the lyrics. And besides, Rowland's yowling falsetto on the verses is nearly impossible to decipher. Even the members of Save Ferris didn't know what the heck Rowland was singing. "It always seemed like a weird, cool song to me when I was a kid, but I had no idea what it meant," Mashburn told *Billboard* in 1997. "Once we saw the lyrics, it was like, 'Wow, this song has an odd message.' It really is a 'come on' song. He's basically just conning a girl into sleeping with him."

Powell sings the tricky verses more clearly than Rowland, and yet people still didn't catch on. None of the articles written about Save Ferris circa 1997 make note of the fact that Powell is singing about seducing another woman—and that's precisely the kind of thing that would've gotten people going back then. Even with Powell's enunciation, the lyrics remain secondary to the barrage of hooks. The horn section takes all the familiar violin parts, and the band beefs up the Dexys arrangement, betting on nostalgia to draw people in.

"Come On Eileen" had sentimental value to Powell, who came up with the idea of covering the tune. "That was one of the songs from my childhood that I would hear on KROQ and see on early MTV," she says. When the song was chosen to be the album's lead single, the band felt some trepidation. There's a novelty factor that comes with doing a cover, and besides, you don't make as much money. "But we were like, 'If this is a song they're gonna pick up, and it's gonna register in people's consciousness, then it'll hopefully lead to a second single,'" Powell says.

"Come On Eileen" reached #26 on Billboard's Modern Rock Tracks chart and landed the band on MTV. There was a follow-up single, the bittersweet swing-ska cocktail "Goodbye," and while it fared nearly as well on the Modern Rock Tracks chart, reaching #32, it made nowhere near as lasting an impact as "Eileen." For all intents and purposes, Save Ferris became a one-hit wonder, just like Rowland's overall-clad crew.

The image of Save Ferris presented by "Come On Eileen"—that of a perky party band with a foxy, carefree frontwoman—doesn't tell the whole story. *It Means Everything* veers off in some unexpected directions, despite the band's strict adherence to a formula of horns and offbeat guitars. "Lies" is a sultry reggae jam dressed up with elegant strings—you can almost picture James Bond easy-skanking with a martini in hand. That one was co-penned by Mashburn, the band's chief songwriter, and Powell, just like closer "Everything I Want to Be," an inspirational duet about following dreams other people discourage. "It means everything / it means *something* to me," Powell sings in the bridge, her voice spiking with a millisecond of defiant anger nobody associates with Save Ferris.

One thing—or person, rather—that many people did associate with Save Ferris was Gwen Stefani. During the band's heyday, Powell was constantly hit with comparisons to the No Doubt singer. Both were attractive young women fronting ska bands from the same geographic region. Beyond that, they're very much their own artists. Powell is a trained singer who commands attention with the sheer power of her voice. Stefani is more a vocal stylist; her arsenal of shrieks and pouts makes her magic on the mic. If the comparisons irked Powell in the '90s, she made peace with them in time.

"We were influenced by the same lifestyle. And, of course, our music is gonna sound the same," Powell told *Houston Press* in 2003. "And Gwen and I were the only two chicks coming out of the scene, so they would compare her to me and compare me to her. It's totally not even a big deal. I love that band."

■ ■ ■

Save Ferris and Reel Big Fish toured heavily behind their breakout albums and even hit the road together in 1997. When it came time for both bands to record their follow-ups, ska's window of coolness had slammed closed. The savvy move would've been to abandon the horns and jumpy guitars. Neither band did—not entirely.

Reel Big Fish labored over 1998's *Why Do They Rock So Hard?*, recording with producer John Avila during breaks between tours. It's still very much a ska album, with horns and upstrokes all over the place, but over the course of the 16 tracks, the band also tries some new things. "The Set Up (You Need This)" is poppy alt-rock with horns. "Big Star" is a somber acoustic ballad that morphs into a punk song accented by plinking piano. "We Care" is an epic power ballad complete with a guitar solo that would make Poison's C. C. DeVille proud. "We got real experimental, 'cause we had a successful album, so we had a good budget to mess around a lot," Barrett says.

What many of the songs have in common is a sour outlook on life in a famous band. On "The Kids Don't Like It," Barrett complains about how fans don't appreciate the group's artistic growth. He's even more defensive on "Down in Flames," which addresses both the industry turning its back on ska and elitist ska kids rooting for Reel Big Fish to fail. "Somebody Hates Me" is pretty self-explanatory. In the span of a few years, Barrett had gone from angry, self-deprecating nobody to bitter somebody.

"I was already an insecure, weird guy," Barrett says. "So having to deal with the fame and my band becoming popular gave me even more of a complex about myself and my place in the world and the band and the scene. It made me think about all that stuff even more and go crazy about it. One little bad review, or one person saying a comment or whatever, would send me into a whole thing. That's why a lot of the songs are just complaining about—'Ah, everyone hates our band, blah, blah, blah!' And now it makes me cringe: 'Oh what a wasted awesome song!' Like, 'The Kids Don't Like It' could've been such an awesome song."

With ska's popularity on the wane, Mojo was happy to see Reel Big Fish flexing their artistic muscles. "While we were recording *Why Do They Rock So Hard?*, they were like, 'Can you give us a no-horns-at-all mix of the album?'" Barrett says. "And we're like, 'No. We are a horn band and a ska band still. We might be branching out and doing other weird things

and experimenting, but we're still a ska band, and we love playing ska.'"
While Mojo didn't push the point, the label picked the ska-free "The Set
Up (You Need This)" as the lead single.

Reel Big Fish's decision to stick with ska probably wasn't enough to
endear them to genre purists, who were always going to dismiss their music
as lightweight fluff. But their loyalty to the music is worth noting. In June
2019, Mike Park of Asian Man Records, who included Reel Big Fish on his
1995 compilation *Misfits of Ska*, tweeted in the group's defense. "People
love to hate on a band like @ReelBigFish," Park wrote. "But the truth is,
when almost every other band of the 90's ditched the genre when it was
deemed as UNCOOL, RBF was one of the very few bands still out there rep-
resenting the SKA. So today, I give my props to RBF."

Why Do They Rock So Hard? stalled at #67 on the Billboard 200—10
spots shy of where *Turn the Radio Off* crested—and failed to produce a
hit single. But the group's visibility remained high, thanks in part to the
1998 comedy *BASEketball*, starring *South Park* creators Trey Parker and
Matt Stone as a couple of dumbasses who invent a sport that sweeps the
nation. Reel Big Fish appear several times in the movie, and the soundtrack
includes their cover of the Norwegian synth-pop group a-ha's 1984 smash
"Take On Me." In concept and execution, Reel Big Fish's "Take On Me"
shares a lot in common with Save Ferris's "Come On Eileen." It's an
amped-up ska remake of a kooky '80s favorite with an iconic music video.
(Dexys had overalls; a-ha had a lady falling in love with a comic book
hero.) Although it never charted, "Take On Me" remains one of Reel Big
Fish's best-loved songs.

■ ■ ■

Save Ferris followed a long and winding road to their sophomore album,
Modified, released in October 1999. Their two years of constant touring
included a stint on the Warped Tour in the summer of 1998. While crossing the country with the "punk-rock summer camp," a couple of key things
happened. One was that Save Ferris filmed a scene for *10 Things I Hate*

About You, the now-canonical teen 1999 romcom starring Heath Ledger and Julia Stiles. Save Ferris appear in the climactic prom scene, a requisite for any teen movie taking its cues from John Hughes. It was spot-on casting, considering Save Ferris were named for a Hughes film. Powell's only regret was that Save Ferris didn't get to play on the roof of Tacoma's Stadium High School during the film's closing scene. That honor went to '90s soundtrack mainstays Letters to Cleo, who also turn up at the prom to play Nick Lowe's "Cruel to Be Kind" with lip-syncing assistance from Save Ferris.

That summer, Powell met and fell in love with another musician. They got engaged but broke up before making it down the aisle. The split left Powell to grapple with the feelings of pain and abandonment she'd dealt with since childhood. She was also suffering from some physical ailments. For years, she'd been singing around a fluid-filled cyst on her left vocal cord. Amid all the emotional turmoil, she developed a callus on the right cord that turned into a blister. This required surgery, which meant weeks of silence before and after the procedure. Being alone with her thoughts didn't help her mental state, but fortunately, the therapist she began seeing around that time did.

In light of everything going on behind the scenes, it's no surprise that *Modified* is about 75 percent less frothy than *It Means Everything*. The producer this time out was John Travis, who'd recently engineered Sugar Ray's 1997 blockbuster *Floored*. Sugar Ray, incidentally, were not a ska band in any shape or form. But the breezy SoCal vibes of their vaguely reggae-flavored hit "Fly" led to their occasional mention in newspaper and magazine articles about ska in the '90s. *Spin* writer Jane Dark (actually Joshua Clover) name-checked both Sugar Ray and fellow beachy bro-rockers Smash Mouth in his 1997 article "Party at Ground Zero," which decries the "goon ska" trend overtaking alternative radio.

Modified only features two ska songs, both hybridized outliers. On "Angry Situation" the distorted upstrokes and insistent brass recall the frenzied ska-core of Voodoo Glow Skulls. "What You See Is What You Get" alternates between ska and stomping '60s soul. The prevailing sound on *Modified* is reggae, or some variation thereof. Witness the Sublime-like bounce of "The Only Way to Be," "I'm Not Crying for You," "Your Friend," and "No Love."

The lead single, "Mistaken," is blink-182–style pop-punk sans horns. A similar sound characterizes album opener "Turn It Up," whose punky guitars are supplemented by turntable scratches from DJ Swamp, who'd also manned the decks for Vanilla Ice and Kid Rock. "One More Try" is a minute-long trip-hop teaser. "It was just a natural progression in the way Brian and I were writing," says Powell, insisting Epic never pressured them to ditch the ska.

The album ends with "Let Me In," a lushly orchestrated Mashburn-penned breakup ballad that seems to capture a lot of what Powell was going through at the time. "It was one of the nicest, kindest things he ever did for me," Powell says. "Recognizing the amount of pain that I was in every day. I couldn't stop it, and he wrote that song, and it really told me a story. I'm always gonna be grateful to him for that song. I don't know if he meant for it to be, but it was such an act of friendship and understanding when I really needed it the most."

Absent any winning singles, *Modified* managed only #136 on the Billboard 200. "*Modified* came out at a time when it was really difficult for women to have careers in the alternative industry," Powell told the *Honolulu Advertiser* in March 2002. "I feel like we're still paying a lot for what happened at that time. For lots of female-fronted bands and female musicians . . . we just stopped getting played on the radio."

Whatever the reasons for *Modified* flopping, it spelled the end for Save Ferris as a major label band: they were dropped by Epic in early 2001. The band soldiered on until October 2002, when Mashburn left, followed by Zamore and Uechi. Before completely dissolving, Save Ferris came close to finishing a third album. That's partly why Powell fought to keep the band together. "When the band broke up, I remember sitting with them and sort of pleading with them like, 'Listen, you guys. We have an album. It's almost completely done. We have the capability to be able to put some money—like real money—in everybody's pockets.'" The last gasp—for a while, anyway—came when Powell assembled a new band for 2003's For the Fans Tour.

■ ■ ■

The commercial death of ska was less a problem for Reel Big Fish than it was for other bands. Barrett and the boys continued selling out shows well into the new millennium and developed a strategy to keep fans coming back. While touring behind the less popular *Why Do They Rock So Hard?*, the group was careful to play old favorites from *Turn the Radio Off*. "Being on tour so much and wanting to please the crowd made me get good at entertaining people and reading the crowd," says Barrett.

In the meantime, the band was starting to write even more experimental songs for their next album. They were working with Val Garay, the producer behind '80s megahits for the Motels and Kim Carnes. Barrett describes Garay as "insane" but credits the Grammy winner with helping Reel Big Fish remember that simplicity is always better. Garay wound up producing the bulk of 2002's *Cheer Up!*, an album that kicks off with five horn-fueled rock songs and offers only niblets of ska thereafter. "A lot of people were shocked," says Barrett. "But a lot of people really liked it, too. For a lot of people, it was their first Reel Big Fish experience. It was a whole new generation by then." The lead-up to *Cheer Up!* brought the first of many lineup changes, as drummer Andrew Gonzalez left in 1999, followed by trumpeter Tavis Werts in 2001.

Those craving a full ska record from Barrett needed only to wait until 2003, when his side project the Forces of Evil released their first and only album, *Friend or Foe*, on Mojo. Barrett had formed the "ska supergroup" with former members of the SoCal band Jeffries Fan Club as a kind of "insurance system," according to the Reel Big Fish website. "I wanted to show people I still loved ska music, that I still liked to play it," Barrett says. When he gave the album to Mojo, the execs told him, "This should've been the new Reel Big Fish album."

All subsequent Reel Big Fish albums—five more as of 2020—lean much heavier on ska. "I figured out what I was good at doing and just did that, instead of trying to search for a new sound or something else," Barrett says. "I still experiment a little and go in different directions, but maybe I just got better at what I do. It doesn't seem like I'm reaching or trying too hard anymore."

Reel Big Fish parted ways with Mojo—which had been acquired by Zomba Recording Corp. / Jive Records in 2001—following 2005's *We're Not Happy 'til You're Not Happy*. The band later signed with the Tennessee indie label Rock Ridge Music, their home as of 2020.

With the departures of bassist Wong in 2007 and trumpeter Klopfenstein in 2011, Barrett became the last original Fish standing. He's kept the party raging with a cast of newcomers, though not without some degree of wistfulness for the past. The band's 2018's album *Life Sucks . . . Let's Dance!* features an uncommonly reflective and sentimental tune called "The Good Old Days." Barrett sings in the opening verse, "Now if you had told me that in '95 / That those were the best days of my life / I would've told you you're crazy, but look at me now / I would give anything at all to get back there."

It's a reasonable sentiment for a musician carrying on with a band 20-plus years past its commercial prime. But Barrett actually wrote the song in 2004 for the Forces of Evil. "It was already nostalgic back then, but I also realized, 'Someday, these will be the good old days,'" Barrett says, quoting the optimistic chorus. "I'm starting to get it a little bit. There's a long road ahead of me. I feel like I'm happier now than ever. I was angry and frustrated and had a lot of issues. I've worked through a lot of them."

■ ■ ■

As of 2020, Powell was also the lone original member of her band. She reactivated Save Ferris in 2013 after undergoing surgery for a degenerative spinal condition and resolving to make a comeback if the operation was a success. Her Save Ferris "reunion show" in July 2013 at the Pacific Amphitheatre didn't sit well with her former bandmates, who claimed Powell never invited them to take part. (By then, Mashburn, Zamora, Willy, and Uechi had started a new ska band called Starpool.) Powell said she did reach out, and a court battle ensued over use of the name. The whole thing wound up on TMZ—surely a first for a ska band—and in the end, Powell won the right to continue performing as Save Ferris.

The victory prompted a backlash from some fans who dubbed her new band "Fake Ferris." There was even a vicious Tumblr page devoted to discrediting and shaming Powell. Nevertheless, Powell pushed ahead with the new Save Ferris and recorded the five-song EP *Checkered Past*, released in 2017. Produced by John Avila, the collection revives the jaunty sound of *It Means Everything* while presenting a tougher, more confident Powell. Neville Staple of the Specials guests on "New Sound," a statement of Powell's hard-won confidence.

In the summer of 2019, Powell said she was proud of what she accomplished with the original band, especially in situations like the '98 Warped Tour. "I was really one girl in a sea of dudes," she says. "For me, it was about just doing it and succeeding, which was a big fucking deal for someone like me, who looked like me and acted like me and sounded like me.

"It was about having fun and being yourself and not making excuses or apologies for who you are and having a sense of humor about it. That was one thing I really liked about our scene and our bands. There was a lot of tongue-in-cheek. There was a lot of laughter and a lot of jokes and very happy, upbeat, joyful music that makes people super-happy."

CHAPTER 5

California Skaquake

It was no coincidence that most of the ska bands on MTV in the '90s came from California. The Golden State scene had been gestating for more than a decade by the time anyone east of the Mississippi heard of No Doubt or Reel Big Fish. While the East Coast was responsible for America's most important ska label, Moon Ska, and loads of trailblazing bands, California was the true incubator of the third wave.

It was partially about infrastructure. In the early '80s, cutting-edge modern-rock stations like KROQ in L.A. and KQAK in San Francisco played 2 Tone bands and the Americans they inspired. At the same time, art house theaters up and down the coast screened *Dance Craze*, the kinetic 1981 concert film featuring all the original 2 Tone bands. And let's not discount the weather: ska is beach music naturally suited for surfing and skating. Plus, sunny Southern California was a natural habitat for backyard shows and scooter rallies.

By the late '80s, bands had sprung up all over the state. There were the Uptones in San Francisco, the Donkey Show in San Diego, and Let's Go Bowling (and the Kyber Rifles before them) in Fresno. Most crucially, there was Fishbone, the Untouchables, and Operation Ivy, the three most influential American ska bands of the decade.

Fishbone formed in 1979 as a byproduct of efforts to integrate L.A.'s public schools. Each day, Walter Kibby, Chris Dowd, Kendall Jones, and brothers Philip and John Norwood Fisher were among the thousands of Black kids from South Central bused to the San Fernando Valley. There, they met a smiley local freakazoid genius named Angelo Moore and formed a genre-agnostic band reflective of their various influences. Ska was the engine of Fishbone's early sound, and there's no overstating the importance of their awe-inspiring 1985 self-titled debut EP, the blueprint for all of ska-punk.

But Fishbone were never interested in being just one thing. Even that first EP features a funky rock tune called "V.T.T.L.O.T.F.D.G.F." (Voyage to the Land of the Freeze-Dried Godzilla Fart). Fishbone's challenging catalog is stuffed to the gills with funk, punk, metal, reggae, soul, and more. Theirs is a complex, at times heartbreaking story told nicely in the 2010 documentary *Everyday Sunshine: The Story of Fishbone*. Suffice it to say there's a little Fishbone in every ska band that swam in their wake.

Right up there with Fishbone were the Untouchables, mod revivalists who fostered a community of sharp-dressed scooter kids in the greater L.A. area beginning in 1981. Racially integrated like their 2 Tone heroes, the UTs brought the ska in a big way on essential early singles "Twist 'N' Shake" (1982) and "Tropical Bird" (1983). They began incorporating more soul and funk on their 1985 debut album, *Wild Child*, and while 1988's *Agent 00 Soul* suffers from dated funk-pop production, side two remains a skanker's paradise.

Operation Ivy are directly responsible for the creation of two bands and indirectly responsible for scores more. Formed in Berkeley in 1987, Op Ivy played 2 Tone ska like a bunch of grimy street punks. The music was stark and ferocious, propelled by guitarist-singer Tim Armstrong's urgent upstrokes and front man Jesse Michaels's motormouth proselytizing. Op Ivy were all about "unity," a message heard throughout their one and only album, 1989's *Energy*.

Op Ivy split up in 1989, and Armstrong and bassist Matt Freeman went on to form Rancid, a street-punk band that crossed over to MTV and made a welcome return to ska with 1995's ... *And Out Come the Wolves*. Before starting Rancid, Armstrong and Freeman got their ska fix in a side project called Dance Hall Crashers. They didn't stay in the band long, but the Crashers carried on with new members, including front women Elyse Rogers and Karina Deniké. Over the next decade, DHC released four excellent albums, two on a major label.

Only the first Crashers LP, a self-titled effort released on Moon in 1990, is pure third-wave ska. DHC broke up after that album and reconvened in 1991 without the horn section. Their next three albums—*Lockjaw* (1995), *Honey, I'm Homely!* (1997), and *Purr* (1999)—are pop-punk with a pronounced ska influence. For whatever reason, none produced a major hit.

California affirmed its early ska supremacy on Earth Day 1990 at the Greek Theatre in Berkeley. English Beat members Dave Wakeling and Ranking Roger reunited with their former bandmates in the International Beat and topped a bill that included Bad Manners, The Donkey Show, the Uptones, Gangster Fun, and Dance Hall Crashers. Some 10,000 people showed up, including Tim Armstrong, who was there reporting for a local TV show. Footage available on YouTube shows a sea of kids dancing to a beat that most of America wouldn't learn about for another five years.

■ ■ ■

Those art house screenings of *Dance Craze* in the '80s really were vital. That's how ska-punk trailblazer Mike Park, then a high school junior in suburban San Jose, discovered the genre in 1986. Park was perplexed and intrigued by what he saw on the screen. He didn't really know what ska was. But the next day, he went out and bought *Klass*, a 1983 compilation album by Bad Manners. This purchase said a lot about who Park was and where he was going.

As evidenced in *Dance Craze*, Bad Manners were the wackiest of the 2 Tone bunch. They were led by Buster Bloodvessel, a rotund baldie with a freakishly long tongue he'd wave around like a stage prop. Bad Manners were known mostly for covers and novelty songs. "I've read stuff where other people in the 2 Tone movement, the bigger bands, kind of saw them as a joke," says Park. "Which hurt my feelings." Inspired by Buster's antics, Park would make irreverence and flat-out silliness a key part of the music he created with Skankin' Pickle, the influential ska-punk group he led from 1989 to 1995. Skankin' Pickle could be the zaniest ska band of all time—and the most serious.

Park definitely saw something wild and different about Bad Manners in *Dance Craze*, but looking back on that fateful trip to the record store, he figures there's another reason he bought *Klass* instead of something by the Specials or the English Beat. "I bet it was cheaper than the other ones," Park says. "I could totally see myself going, 'Wow, this is only $4.99 versus $9.99.'" That frugality and savviness with money would serve Park well when he started Asian Man Records, the indie label that would define his legacy even more so than Skankin' Pickle.

Soon after his 2 Tone epiphany, Park found another life-changing band in Fishbone, whose all-Black lineup pointed a way into a predominantly white punk subculture. Park was born in Seoul, South Korea, and growing up Asian American outside of San Jose, he experienced his share of racism. "Kids are brutal; they can be very mean," he told the *Los Angeles Times* in April 1998. "They'd slant their eyes up and pretend to speak Chinese to me. It's just not cool at all."

As a true believer in 2 Tone's message, Park viewed ska as entertainment and a vehicle for social change. In 1989, he formed Skankin' Pickle with some classmates at De Anza College, where he studied music. The band name—a wonderful albatross that's impossible to both forget and take seriously—was based on a doodle Park drew of a gherkin dancing the ska. The lineup included trombone players Gerry Lundquist and Lars Nylander, drummer Chuck Phelps, guitarist Lynette Knackstedt, and bassist Mike Mattingly. Park sang and played sax. The title of the group's 1991 debut album, *Skafunkrastapunk*, is an accurate description of their hyper-hybridized early sound. They started playing shows right away, not always with other ska bands.

"The ska scene really didn't like us back in the late '80s, early '90s," Park says. "It was very scene-oriented in terms of the scooter culture. We clashed because we played other styles. We were bastardizing the ska in a lot of people's eyes and ears."

Park was all for the bastardization and having a sense of humor, but he cringes when he listens back to *Skafunkrastapunk* and its 1992 follow-up, *Skankin' Pickle Fever*. For every political song Park wrote, the group recorded a jokey funk tune like "Doin' Something Naughty" or "How Funk." Skankin' Pickle had multiple singers and songwriters, and Park says it was Mattingly, the slap-happy bassist, who led them into egregious funk territory.

"Even the serious songs I wrote, I think he fucked up a lot of them," Park says. "I feel like they would have stood the test of time way better if it was just played correctly."

A lot of the music does hold up. *Skafunkrastapunk* highlight "Racist World" features original Skatalites saxophonist Roland Alphonso, whom Park met when Skankin' Pickle opened for the Jamaican legends. Park approached Alphonso about playing on his record, and the sax great asked how much he could pay. When Park said he didn't have much money, Alphonso replied, "Just give me $50." Park was glad for the bargain but surprised to learn that such an important ska figure was so hard up for cash. Alphonso arrived at the studio without having heard the song and told the band to just play the track—he'd solo all the way through. He was there for 15 minutes, long enough to weave mournful lines that perfectly echoed the song's lyrics.

Park wrote one of his finest songs, "Ice Cube, Korea Wants a Word with You," off *Skankin' Pickle Fever*, in response to Ice Cube's incendiary "Black Korea," all about flaring tensions between Blacks and Korean shop owners in Los Angeles. At one point in his song, Cube warns, "Your little chop suey ass'll be a target." This irked Park for two reasons. First, he felt like Cube's threatening language was only going to make things worse for people on both sides of the conflict. Second, chop suey is American

Chinese food, which Park explains in the first verse of his song. Later in the lyrics, Park references Public Enemy's "Fight the Power" while outlining the philosophy that would inform much of his music and activism: "Fight, fight, fight the power / Who's that? 'Cause if I knew I'd end it all like that / But I think the power's in each one's self / And if we all opened up / There would be no more mess."

Skankin' Pickle replaced Mattingly with Ian Miller for 1994's *Sing Along with Skankin' Pickle*, the best of the band's four albums. Miller had previously played in Hoodlum Empire, a San Francisco group with a cool surf-ska-punk sound and seriously warped lyrics about Charles Manson and gang wars at Disneyland. According to Park, Epitaph Records was interested in signing Hoodlum Empire when tragedy struck. Shortly after Miller left the band, lead singer Rob Rock went missing, never to be heard from again. Park had no idea Rock was suffering from mental illness (he was diagnosed with schizophrenia), and to this day, he worries that Miller's departure to join Skankin' Pickle pushed the singer over the edge.

Although it's less aggressively kooky than its predecessors, *Sing Along with Skankin' Pickle* is hardly a somber affair. Park shouts out Korean American comedian Margaret Cho ("It's Margaret Cho") and professes his love for a character on the Canadian teen drama *Degrassi Junior High* ("I'm in Love with a Girl Named Spike") on two of the more memorable cuts.

By the mid-'90s, Skankin' Pickle was drawing large audiences across the county. Without any mainstream exposure, they'd influenced newcomers like Less Than Jake and paved the way for the ska-punk revolution right around the corner. The trouble was, Park wasn't enjoying himself. He announced he was leaving as the band released its swan song, *The Green Album*, a 1996 collection of covers and previously unreleased songs. (Knackstedt and Nylander continued on with new members before retiring the Skankin' Pickle moniker in 1997.)

"I think the rest of the band were having fun," Park says. "I just didn't party. I didn't drink. I didn't do drugs. I had nothing to help cope with the stress of touring. You've got to remember, we were small in terms of comfort level. We didn't have a big staff. We never went on a tour bus. At our peak, we had a van with a trailer, and two friends would come help do merch and help roadie. The comfort level was never there, and we toured a lot before ska got big."

Ska was finally on the verge of breaking when Park launched Asian Man Records out of his parents' garage in 1996. He had some experience running a label. The first three Skankin' Pickle albums had been released on Dill Records, nominally run by the band but really spearheaded by Park. Dill had also been responsible for Less Than Jake's 1995 debut album, *Pezcore*, and the seminal ska-punk compilation *Misfits of Ska*—featuring songs by Reel Big Fish, Sublime, and the Suicide Machines—released the same year.

As ska's popularity grew, Park felt like the music was losing its connection to 2 Tone's activist roots. So in 1998, he launched the Ska Against Racism Tour, a 38-date cross-country trek featuring the Toasters, Less Than Jake, Christian skanksters Five Iron Frenzy, Japanese American ska-punks Kemuri, Mustard Plug, Blue Meanies, and MU330, who backed Park each night for a set of his own songs. "I've always been a big advocate toward anti-racist ideas or movements," says Park. "Being in the music business strictly for capitalistic gain, I felt almost like a whore. I wanted to do something more than just playing music for strictly profitable endeavors, if that makes sense. I wanted to do more."

Despite Park's best intentions, Ska Against Racism drew criticism in some circles. Debate centered on whether bands playing boisterous ska-punk to rooms full of white teenagers—many of whom only wanted to dance around to Less Than Jake—were really going to accomplish anything. If nothing else, it was a different situation than the Specials and the other 2 Tone groups had faced in late-'70s England, where the large population of Caribbean immigrants was a target of right-wing hatred. The combination of punk with Jamaican reggae and ska was inherently more meaningful in places like London and Coventry in 1979 than it was in America 20 years later.

Daraka Larimore, lead singer of the Chicago ska band the Adjusters, voiced his skepticism about the tour in a July 1998 *Chicago Reader* story titled "Ska's Lost Cause." "Not talking about racism as a system, or racism as something that you should be actively fighting against, but talking about it like, 'You shouldn't be mean to Black people,' is just ridiculous," he said. Reviewing an early tour stop for the *Los Angeles Times*, Jennifer Vineyard acknowledged that some of the bands sang about racial unity. "Still, there was no overwhelming indication, other than the bands' diverse racial composition, that this daylong concert was anything more than a kickoff to the festival season," she wrote. "The chance to revive ska's 2-Tone political slant was lost, and the carefree teens in attendance didn't even notice."

Nevertheless, the tour garnered a fair amount of press coverage and raised $23,000 for anti-racist charities. "The fact is, [ska] is white music," Park says, defending the tour. "It isn't originally, but it became popular with white kids. People are going to criticize everything no matter what. What can you do? Is it bad because they're white kids? You can't tell them racism is bad? It didn't make any sense to me. If anything, this is the market you should be talking to."

Park does admit, however, that most third-wave ska bands were not concerned with the state of the world. "I think they just wanted to play fun party music, and there's nothing wrong with that," he says. "I don't fault anybody for being fun. If everything was political, it would be a boring subject matter. There's nothing wrong with a love song or a goofy song. I respect a 'Weird Al' Yankovic song as much as I do a Bob Dylan song. Well maybe not. Well maybe I do, actually. I love 'Weird Al,' what am I talking about?"

As of 2020, Park was still running Asian Man out of the same garage. Because it was never solely a ska label, he's been able to avoid financial ruin during the genre's fallow years by releasing music by bands like Chicago pop-punkers Alkaline Trio. Park has also continued making music with various outfits, including the Bruce Lee Band and the indie-rock combo Ogikubo Station. He's something of an anomaly in the music industry: a nice guy and fair businessman whom everyone likes. In 2007, Park organized a benefit concert at the legendary Berkeley punk club 924 Gilman Street for his old Skankin' Pickle bandmate Lynette Knackstedt, who died of a drug overdose. Knackstedt had been openly gay throughout her career, and in a statement Park praised her as "a role model for many young women and men."

The loss of Knackstedt doesn't necessarily mean a Skankin' Pickle reunion is out of the question. A lot of younger ska fans never got the chance to see the band, and Park says Coachella and other festivals have contacted him about getting the old gang back onstage. It would actually be the second reunion, as Park quietly reactivated the moniker for some shows in Japan in 2015. "I still feel like I have the ability to do it," Park says. "My body hasn't broken down completely to where I can't still put on a good live show."

In September 2020, as racial unrest stoked by the Trump administration led to nationwide protests, Park teamed up with the rising ska-punk label Bad Time Records and the news outlet Ska Punk Daily to release *Ska Against Racism*, a compilation benefiting numerous charities, including the Movement for Black Lives and the NAACP Legal Defense Fund. Packed with songs by '90s faves like Buck-O-Nine and Mustard Plug and next-gen bands like Kill Lincoln and Catbite, the double-vinyl set was Park's best chance of reviving the Ska Against Racism banner amid the COVID-19 lockdown. It sold out in days, raising more than $55,000. "It's something that even during the pandemic, we can get behind," said Park. "And through the power of music, we can still make a difference."

■ ■ ■

The first time Jorge Casillas saw *Quadrophenia*, the 1979 film based on the 1973 Who album of the same name, he couldn't understand the constant fighting between the mods and the rockers. The former liked suits, scooters, and soul music. The latter dug leather jackets, motorcycles, and rock 'n' roll. Did these tribal differences really warrant rumbling on the beaches of Brighton?

As bassist for Voodoo Glow Skulls, the band he started with his two brothers—guitarist Eddie and singer Frank—in Riverside, California, in 1988, Jorge made a career of smashing together styles of music that aren't supposed to fit—namely, hardcore, metal, and ska. Voodoo Glow Skulls are legendary for creating a variation of ska that's faster and harder than anything that came before. Amid all the offbeat pummeling and superhuman horn blowing, Voodoo Glow Skulls also brought a Latin sensibility to their music that reflects their Mexican American heritage. It's a beastly racket the Casillas brothers were born to make. Within three seconds of a Voodoo Glow Skulls song coming on the stereo, you know exactly who you're hearing and what you're in for.

Jorge was just a kid when he and Eddie began making music—or rather pretending to—with drummer Jerry O'Neill, their buddy who lived nearby. The friends built a stage in Jerry's backyard and would lip-sync along to metal records before they actually set about learning their instruments. They eventually gained some proficiency on their respective noise-making devices, and around 1987, when Jorge was 15, they started playing together for real. Elder brother Frank soon joined up, lending his signature monotone machine-gun vocals, and he even vacated his bedroom and slept on the couch so the foursome would have space to practice. If that sounds like a selfless act, consider the boys' saintly parents, who allowed a teenage punk band to practice under their roof. "It was almost like a love-hate relationship," says Jorge. "They would support us in every way possible, but they didn't like the style of music we played."

In the early days of Voodoo Glow Skulls, that style was hardcore punk, one of the many genres the Casillas brothers loved. They were also obsessed with British metal icons Iron Maiden and Judas Priest. Then they got into Fishbone and the Untouchables, ska-influenced New Wave oddballs Oingo Boingo, and the 2 Tone ska of Madness and the Specials. Thanks to their parents, they had a strong foundation of '50s rock 'n' roll and traditional Mexican music. "I would just say we are a product of our environment," Frank told Diffuser.fm in 2012. "There's a mix of Black and Mexican culture that is prominent in Southern California culture in general." He added, "We were just kids who were musically confused, I guess you could say."

It took Voodoo Glow Skulls a few years to realize they needed horns to truly stir up the stew they were destined to cook. The four-piece lineup made its debut with the 1990 EP *The Old of Tomorrow*, a play on the straight-edge band Youth of Today. Although it contains three songs the band would rerecord for its first couple albums, the EP lacks the oomph provided by the horns. The only real trace of ska is "The Clash," a bouncing cover of the Clash's "Should I Stay or Should I Go."

By the time of their next release, 1992's *Rasta Mis Huevos* EP, Voodoo Glow Skulls had added Joey Hernandez on saxophone and Joe McNally on trumpet. They'd also ratcheted up the ska influences, as heard on "Mr. Bossman" and "You're the Problem." The horns gave Voodoo Glow Skulls a fresh sound that made them more popular around Southern California, but the Casillas brothers weren't exactly counting the minutes until the next ska revival.

"You had bands like the English Beat in the '80s, but I didn't really think it would come around to where it would be accepted on a commercial level again, especially when you add heavier elements to it," says Jorge. "Our band isn't really marketable to a major record label, per se. They don't know what to do with us."

One place Voodoo Glow Skulls always felt comfortable was the back-yard-party scene around Riverside. Jorge remembers one show hosted by a guy whose father owned multiple properties in the same area. The Cali punk bands Face to Face and Guttermouth joined the Glow Skulls in performing on a flatbed truck in between two of the houses. Something like 2,000 kids turned up. "And there was a tattoo artist going in one of the houses," Jorge says.

Voodoo Glow Skulls signed with the independent SoCal punk label Dr. Strange Records for their 1993 debut, *Who Is, This Is?* The title comes from a snippet of dialogue sampled from Cheech and Chong's 1978 stoner comedy *Up in Smoke*. The Cheech sample opens the LP and leads right into "Insubordination," which Eddie Casillas has called "the definitive Voodoo Glow Skulls song." It kicks off with the guitar riff from Ozzy Osbourne's "Crazy Train," then mutates into a frantic skank-fest with lyrics affirming the group's independent streak ("What do you mean I have a bad attitude / Don't get me wrong but my nature is rude") and horn riffage displaying the awesome power of the section's lungs. On *Who Is, This Is?* Voodoo Glow Skulls don't just arrive fully formed—they lay everything on the line on track one.

Who Is, This Is? also features classics like "Dog Pile," which advocates moshing over fighting; a pair of Spanish-language tunes, "Sin Berguensa (Si Habla Espanol)" and "La Migra (Mas Espanol)"; and a hardcore cover of the Beatles' "Here Comes the Sun" that somehow doesn't lose its prettiness. The album is a thrilling listen for anyone interested in what ska sounds like at maximum velocity. It reportedly sold more than 200,000 copies worldwide within a couple years of release. Ska purists weren't responsible for many of those sales.

"They didn't get it," says Jorge. "I'm not knocking traditional ska. It's not like my number one cup of tea, but I like it just as much as anything else. But with that scene, if you don't play that kind of music . . . a lot of them turn their cheek at you. We'd get messages and letters, back when fan letters were a thing, saying, 'You guys are ruining ska.'"

Voodoo Glow Skulls weren't the only ones bastardizing ska in the early '90s. They soon learned about the Mighty Mighty Bosstones, whose "ska-core" sound had a lot in common with their own horn-powered raging. Jorge discovered the Bosstones via the Converse commercial they made in the early '90s. "We were like, 'Oh cool, there's a band that's kind of similar to us,'" says Jorge. "They were already getting notoriety. All of a sudden, there was this big thing, 'Bosstones or Voodoo,' and people were trying to pit us against them. Almost like a competitive thing. We weren't really about that. Out of nowhere, the Bosstones asked us to go on tour with them, and we accepted."

Jorge credits the Bosstones, who were already on Mercury, with being super-gracious and not the least bit standoffish in the face of "competition." The two groups got along like gangbusters, and the Bosstones offered Voodoo Glow Skulls valuable advice on how to take their touring game to the next level. The tutorial came at the right time, as Voodoo Glow Skulls had just signed to Epitaph Records, the red-hot SoCal punk label founded by Brett Gurewitz of Bad Religion. Epitaph was coming off monster success with bands like Rancid and the Offspring, whose 1994 breakthrough *Smash* became the biggest-selling album ever released on an independent label.

Epitaph put Voodoo Glow Skulls in the studio with Garth Richardson, the producer behind Rage Against the Machine's self-titled 1992 debut. The result was 1995's *Firme*, a magnification of everything that made *Who Is, This Is?* so brilliant. The single "Fat Randy," a bleating sprinter with distorted upstrokes that occasionally slows to something resembling normal ska, made it on MTV's *120 Minutes*. The song is about a rather large dude who causes trouble at high school parties, and it's 100 percent based on a real person.

"He was the guy that was always fucking with people at parties, and he'd usually end up getting beat up," says Jorge. "But he was this big guy, so it was always kind of funny. He could fight, but he was always too drunk to protect himself." The key line in the song, "Fat Randy shit on my couch," is also factual. "Our trumpet player had just moved into a new condo with his new wife," says Jorge. "They had a party, and Randy was being drunk and belligerent, and they kicked him out. Later on that night, when they were all asleep, Randy went into his house and shit on his couch."

Fans need not speak English to learn the charming story of Fat Randy. That's because Voodoo Glow Skulls also released a Spanish-language version of *Firme*. The idea was partially a response to "rock en español," a then-popular industry buzzword given to rock bands who sang in Spanish.

"They had to call it a name, of course," says Jorge. "They couldn't just call it 'rock bands from Mexico,' or whatever. They put this name on it so they could market it. All these labels hired these Spanish reps, and they'd been kicking the term around. We were like, 'We sing in Spanish and English.' So Brett [Gurewitz] said, 'Oh yeah, let's try and do something with that.' We made the suggestion, 'Why don't we put out a Spanish record.' He said, 'Why don't we just do a Spanish version of this one?' So we went back in and just overdubbed the Spanish vocals."

The Spanish version of *Firme* sold surprisingly well and led some gringo punk and ska kids to expand their cultural horizons. "We had people coming up to us saying that they were starting to learn how to speak Spanish off of our record," says Jorge.

The '90s ska explosion was well underway by the time Voodoo Glow Skulls returned to the studio with Jim Goodwin, the producer behind *Who Is, This Is?*, to record their follow-up to *Firme*. Ska bands were getting played on alternative radio, and Epitaph wanted something poppy. "But we weren't that band," says Jorge. "We could write a pop-ska song in a second, and we do have those on the records, but we just weren't feeling it at the time. Everybody else was already doing that. So we were like, 'Well, let's put out a heavier record.'"

That album, 1997's *Baile de Los Locos*, led critics to brand Voodoo Glow Skulls "the Slayer of ska." In truth, it's not a huge departure from the albums that came before. The single "Bulletproof" eases off the gas pedal in spots just like "Fat Randy" does, and the instrumental "Los Hombres No Lloran" is practically traditional ska. Nevertheless, it was too hard and strange a record to land Voodoo Glow Skulls on the list of ska bands with radio hits in 1997.

Voodoo Glow Skulls finally decided to make their pop-ska album in 1998, after it would've been most useful to Epitaph. They recorded with John Avila, the producer who'd helped Reel Big Fish reach the masses with 1996's *Turn the Radio Off*. More importantly, Avila had played bass in Oingo Boingo, a band Frank Casillas cites as one of the three biggest influences on Voodoo Glow Skulls. (Fishbone and the Untouchables were the other two.)

Released in July 1998, *The Band Geek Mafia* is still very much a Voodoo Glow Skulls record, though Avila slows the tempos and sharpens the hooks. The single "Left for Dead," all about young people falling victim to drugs and violence, wouldn't sound *completely* out of place on a mixtape with songs by ska traditionalists like Hepcat and Jump With Joey.

FIG.6 Voodoo Glow Skulls go hard and fast on the 1998 Warped Tour. Photo: Bryan Kremkau / SkaPunkPhotos.com.

Plus, the album has a grand total of zero curse words. "I guess we're not as angry as we once were," Frank told MTV. "I think it's really cool that we can put out an album that has good hardcore, metal, ska and punk-rock elements, but we don't have to use bad language to get that point across. . . . Everybody gets older, you know."

Two years passed before Voodoo Glow Skulls released their fourth and final album for Epitaph. Produced by Gurewitz, 2000's *Symbolic* is "almost like a rock record" in Jorge's estimation. "We wanted to have a record with songs that have a little bit more breathing room, not so spastic," he says. A funky synthesizer cuts through "The Drop In," a braggadocious blend of ska, punk, and West Coast hip-hop. Spookier keyboards haunt "The Devil Made Me Do It," a dark song about stealing from family and neighbors to buy drugs. The disc's opening cut, "We're Back," features Guttermouth singer Mark Adkins playing a cheeseball TV news reporter commenting on recent musical trends. "The Voodoo Glow Skulls represent the zenith of the now-unpopular ska-core genre," Adkins says in the intro, prefacing some pointed lyrics from Frank: "Now that the whole third wave is gone / It's time for us to carry on / We took a break and stayed away / Now we've got a lot of things to say." The main message: Voodoo Glow Skulls invented and transcended ska-core long before the mainstream chewed it up and spit it out.

"We had such a backlash our whole career from the ska scene because we weren't this third-wave pop thing that was going on, and we weren't this traditional ska band," says Jorge. "We were just this bastard son with weird heaviness that touched on some ska. But we're fine with it. We've always liked to do our own thing. It's cool to be part of a scene, but we like to be a part of a bunch of scenes. We can go on tour with the Bosstones. We can also go on tour with Sick of It All. We could also turn around and go on tour with bands like [Mexican extreme metal outfit] Brujeria. It's because we don't really pin ourselves to one thing."

Feeling like Epitaph had lost interest in the band, Voodoo Glow Skulls left the label after *Symbolic*. They released their next three albums—*Steady as She Goes* (2002), *Adicción, Tradición, Revolución* (2004), and *Southern California Street Music* (2007)—on Victory Records, a hardcore label that moved increasingly toward emo and post-hardcore as the decade progressed. "We were on the label when it was cool, but it just seemed like they were going through the motions with us," Frank told *Coachella Valley Independent* in 2013, after the band had moved over to Smelvis Records, the California punk label founded by Elvis Cortez of the band Left Alone. Voodoo Glow Skulls made their Smelvis debut with 2012's *Break the Spell*, their most recent album as of 2020.

Voodoo Glow Skulls remained busy in the '10s, despite their lack of new releases and frequent lineup changes. Horn players came and went, and founding drummer O'Neill left in 2010. Then in June 2017, without telling his brothers first, Frank announced his retirement from the band during a show in Long Beach. Jorge and Eddie carried on with Efrem Schulz of the hardcore band Death by Stereo, and as of 2020 there was talk of recording a new album. (The band actually had a nearly finished LP in the can, but given all the personnel shake-ups, Jorge and Eddie decided to scrap all but a couple tunes and start over.)

Voodoo Glow Skulls also continued touring the world, often visiting distant lands where they were shocked to find pockets of superfans. "You have people in Poland and Russia crying because you're there playing, and they're telling you that they grew up listening to you," says Jorge. "It's kind of crazy to have dudes telling you that. I started my band when I was 15, and there's guys telling me, 'I've been listening to you since I was 17.'"

■ ■ ■

Few bands in the '90s ska pantheon had more civic pride than Buck-O-Nine. When Less Than Jake and Sublime sang about their hometowns—Gainesville and Long Beach, respectively—they offered warts-and-all snapshots of burnouts and lost souls. No Doubt suggested something wasn't right in Orange County with that rotting orange on the cover of *Tragic Kingdom*. Even the Mighty Mighty Bosstones, who named themselves after the city they so dearly loved, didn't pretend to live in some kind of paradise. Their 1991 song "They Came to Boston" is all about how insufferable college kids are overrunning Beantown.

On their surprise 1997 hit "My Town," good-time ska-punks Buck-O-Nine express nothing but love for where they're from. And why not? They're straight outta San Diego, that sunny and crime-free burgh nicknamed "America's Finest City." In the first verse, lead singer Jon Pebsworth describes strolling to the beach with a Walkman, some booze, and zero cares in the world. "My soul is sound when I'm in my hometown, yeah," he sings, ska guitar bouncing like a beachball behind him. Of all the ska songs to make a splash on MTV and alternative radio in the '90s, "My Town" is the sweetest and most joyful. It's about safety and warmth and feeling like you're exactly where you should be.

"My Town" reached #32 on Billboard's Modern Rock Tracks chart and garnered some MTV airplay. The single came off the group's third album, *Twenty-Eight Teeth*, which snuck onto the Billboard 200, peaking at #190. For Buck-O-Nine, it was the pinnacle of a steady-building, relatively drama-free career that had begun six years earlier, when bass player Scott Kinnerly began placing musician-wanted ads in San Diego papers. By early 1992, Kinnerly had found enough area ska kids to form an embryonic version of the band. Pebsworth hadn't yet joined as lead singer when the fledgling crew played its first show, opening for the Mighty Mighty Bosstones.

"They remember that Dicky told them, 'You guys are probably the worst ska band I've ever seen in my entire life,'" Pebsworth says, referring to Bosstones front man Dicky Barrett. "I brought that up to Dicky [recently] and said, 'Do you remember saying that?' He's all, 'Nah, I don't remember saying that. Sounds like something I would say, though.'"

Buck-O-Nine's days of sucking didn't last long. Pebsworth soon replaced the original singer, and trombonist Dan Albert and trumpeter Anthony Curry—both veterans of the local reggae scene—joined founding saxophonist Craig Yarnold to flesh out the horn section. Those changes cemented a lineup that would forge a winning ska-punk sound at a time when everyone else was playing grunge. It was the perfect band for Pebsworth, who'd been obsessed with 2 Tone since he bought *One Step Beyond* by Madness in sixth grade. Pebsworth learned about ska from a local high schooler who'd already gone full mod.

"He would ride a Vespa around the neighborhood, and he had all the mod and ska patches all over his trench coat," says Pebsworth. "We were just all like, 'Dude, that guy is fucking so cool!' We got close enough to him to see what those patches said, and that was the most distinct one, Madness."

In addition to Pebsworth's 2 Tone heroes, Buck-O-Nine drew early influence from the Bosstones and Operation Ivy. The less-than-virtuosic vocalists leading both groups convinced Pebsworth—whose singing experience was limited to screaming in local thrash outfits—that he was cut out for the job of lead singer.

Pebsworth found a voice that was thin and snotty yet endearing, like if Bill from *Bill and Ted's Excellent Adventure* decided to start a ska band. He could carry a tune, and just as importantly, he could string some lyrics together. At his very first rehearsal with the band, Pebsworth fitted some words he'd scribbled in his notebook to a piece of music the group had written with its original lead singer. The result was "New Generation," a rare semi-political song for a band whose giddy party music would attract a large contingent of SoCal skaters and surfers.

"New Generation" appears on Buck-O-Nine's 1994 debut album, *Songs in the Key of Bree*, released on the San Diego indie label Immune Records. The album is fast and punchy, loaded with grabby horn lines and lyrics that skew a little silly. "Few Too Many" finds Pebsworth yucking it up while a soused friend pukes his guts out. "Irish Drinking Song" is a Celtic-punk goof that would frequently get mislabeled as a Dropkick Murphys song in the Napster era. "I Don't Wanna Be No (J.B.J.)" lets guitarist Jonas Kleiner throw down some hair-metal licks before Pebsworth takes the mic and starts dissing Jon Bon Jovi.

The album also includes "I Can't Believe," a stab at 2 Tone–style anti-racist messaging that's better judged on sincerity than on anything else. Given their 2 Tone, reggae, and punk roots, not to mention their mixed-race lineup (trumpeter Curry is Black), Buck-O-Nine identified strongly with the concept of "unity," even if they rarely sang about it explicitly.

Prior to the album's release, Buck-O-Nine was drawing 800–900 people per show in San Diego and beginning to tour throughout California and the Southeast. After the LP dropped, Buck-O-Nine joined up with St. Louis ska-punk trailblazers MU330 and embarked on their first-ever national tour. After returning home, Buck-O-Nine caught the ear of Curtis Casella, founder of Taang! Records, the label behind the first two Bosstones albums. Casella had recently moved his operation from Boston to San Diego, and when he saw Buck-O-Nine live, he was floored by their cover of the Misfits' horror-punk classic "Teenagers from Mars." He offered them a deal—so long as they promised to record that cover.

Casella got his wish, and "Teenagers from Mars" wound up on Buck-O-Nine's sophomore effort, 1995's *Barfly*, a collection originally slated to be an EP of covers. The group had recently landed a high-paying corporate gig that required them to play for three hours, and since they didn't have that many originals, they learned a bunch of old favorites, including Musical Youth's early-'80s reggae smash "Pass the Dutchie," the Clash's rollicking ska tune "Wrong 'Em Boyo" (itself a cover originally done by the Jamaican group the Rulers), and Operation Ivy's "Sound System." All those covers make *Barfly* something of a novelty album, though Buck-O-Nine also deliver some spirited originals, the most prescient being "On a

Mission," wherein Pebsworth sings, "I want to rise from my seat / Don't want to be held down / I want to get off the couch / I want to find a new sound."

Buck-O-Nine's mission was well-timed, as the "new sound" of ska was beginning to inch its way toward the mainstream. *Barfly* dropped in October 1995, the same month No Doubt released *Tragic Kingdom* and Rancid cracked the Top 10 on the Modern Rock Tracks chart with "Time Bomb." On the strength of their Taang! releases, Buck-O-Nine began hearing from label scouts like Tom Sarig from TVT Records. TVT launched in 1985 as a vehicle for *Television's Greatest Hits*, a wildly popular album of classic TV themes. The New York City label subsequently shifted to alternative with a series of adventurous late-'80s releases, the most notable being *Pretty Hate Machine*, the debut album by Nine Inch Nails. Feeling minimal "punk-rock guilt," as Pebsworth calls it, Buck-O-Nine signed with TVT and set about making their next album with no creative interference from the label.

With ska suddenly sellable, Buck-O-Nine knew this was their chance to make an album that could push them to the next level. But as they hit the studio with producers Neill King and David Kershenbaum, they tried not to think about where the right single might get them. "We saw this was an opportunity to be able to take our time and really think about our songwriting and the lyrics and how it sounds," Pebsworth says. "Tones and choruses and harmonies and those types of things were a priority. It wasn't about, 'Oh yeah, we're going to be big—MTV and this, that, and the other.' We tried to keep that stuff in the reality-check zone."

Buck-O-Nine definitely weren't gunning for the radio with "My Town." It's track 13 of 14 on *Twenty-Eight Teeth*, and that's because nobody in the band thought it was particularly special. In terms of potential singles, Pebsworth favored album opener "Round Kid" or "Jennifer's Cold," a sarcastic song about a girl who thinks the world should stop because she has the sniffles. Neither has the heart of "My Town," a song born largely from homesickness. "At that point, we had toured so much," Pebsworth says.

"It's nice to be home, especially when you live in San Diego. It's always like, 'Ah, thank goodness.'"

In the "My Town" music video, the Buck-O-Nine boys jog and skate through San Diego en route to the beach, where all their buds are waiting. As the clip gained traction on MTV and the single made headway on alternative radio, Buck-O-Nine found themselves in some unfamiliar situations. Pebsworth remembers being paralyzed by the red light of MTV's cameras when the band sat down to be interviewed by Matt Pinfield on *120 Minutes*.

Twenty-Eight Teeth also includes a cover of Joe Jackson's 1979 New Wave nugget "I'm the Man," suggested by producer King, who'd started in the business working as second engineer for Madness and Elvis Costello. "I'm the Man" is written from the POV of a marketing genius who's sold the world the Hula-Hoop and the yo-yo and a heap of other products nobody needs. Pebsworth says they covered the song purely because they were fans, but when he sings lines like "Right now, I think I'm gonna plan a new trend," it's tempting to read Buck-O-Nine's version as a sly commentary on ska's sudden commodification.

By 1999, the industry had moved on to other sounds, and so had Buck-O-Nine. *Libido*, their follow-up to *Twenty-Eight Teeth*, includes forays into rock, reggae, and even soul. There's just a handful of ska tracks. Pebsworth admits that, subconsciously, the band was reacting to ska's downturn in popularity. At the same time, they were four albums and eight years into their run. They were ready to see where else their songwriting could go. That's what the album's closing track, "Pigeonhole Disease," is about.

"It was like, 'We don't want to be stuck in this thing,'" Pebsworth says. "Whether it's sinking or not, we're proud to be a part of the third wave of ska. We take that as a badge of honor. But we also felt like, 'Well, we don't want to just be that. We want to stand on our own, just be Buck-O-Nine.'"

Libido didn't repeat the success of *Twenty-Eight Teeth*, and by 2000, dwindling crowds meant Buck-O-Nine could no longer afford to tour full-time. The band went into what Pebsworth dubs "semi-retired status," where they remain as of 2020. They've released two twenty-first-century albums—2007's *Sustain* and 2019's *Fundaymental*—and continued a light touring schedule that lets everyone live their grown-up lives for most of the year. Amazingly, they've remained such good friends that bassist Scott Kinnerly, the guy who started the band back in 1991, is the only member of the classic lineup not featured on *Fundaymental*.

"We love it still, being able to go out and play shows," Pebsworth says. "We just came back from Japan for Chrissake. Who would have ever thought that?"

■ ■ ■

After Rancid booted down the door for ska-punk with "Time Bomb" in 1995, it was only a matter of time before another band snuck past the gate-keepers with a skankable hit. The first to strike weren't the Bosstones, who were between albums, or No Doubt, whose string of 1996 radio triumphs were of a decidedly non-ska variety. Instead, it was an L.A. group that seemingly came out of nowhere and claimed they weren't ska in every interview where the subject came up.

Goldfinger's "Here in Your Bedroom" peaked at #5 on the Modern Rock Tracks chart in June 1996, about seven months after "Time Bomb" went off. In the music video, bleach-blond lead singer John Feldmann sports a black suit and skinny tie and skanks alongside a couple of central-casting rude girls atop a checkered floor. The song itself is Rancid-lite: expertly crafted pop-punk with ska verses and an undeniable hook. Longtime ska heads had reason to be suspicious, especially if they knew anything about Feldmann's past. But Goldfinger never presented themselves as anything other than what they were: a pop-punk band whose tunesmith front man had a thing for ska.

Feldmann grew up in Northern California, and in 1983, at the age of 15, he saw the English Beat with Bow Wow Wow at the Greek Theatre in Berkeley. Not only was it his first concert, but during the show, he got a kiss from a girl named Chrissy. "It was the best time," Feldmann told KROQ in 2019. "That was the catalyst for starting my band: how do I make a band that's a cross between NOFX and the English Beat?" He didn't tackle this puzzle right away. Around the time of his ska-show smooch, Feldmann learned bass and formed a Social Distortion–influenced punk band called Family Crisis that played with Bad Religion and 7 Seconds. Feldmann's next band, IMRU, dealt in "post-punk Cult-style music," as Feldmann told the zine *Sink Hole* in 2001.

Those first two bands make sense in the context of Goldfinger. Feldmann's third one doesn't. In the late '80s, he moved to L.A. and started Electric Love Hogs, a funk-metal outfit that was discovered by Mötley Crüe drummer Tommy Lee, who co-produced the band's 1992 self-titled debut album. "We'd play with our shirts off and instigate circle pits, all that shit," Feldmann told the website Louder in 2016. "We fucking owned it in L.A. But the songs were terrible, and I still can't listen to them to this day."

The band's 1992 single "Tribal Monkey" is, indeed, terrible. In the music video, Feldmann jumps around in a Tool T-shirt and screeches like Vince Neil while the band wails away like bootleg Chili Peppers. Electric Love Hogs were dropped by London Records after that album, and that's how Feldmann wound up at the L.A. punk clothing store NaNa, selling shoes and plotting his next move.

After the demise of Electric Love Hogs, Feldmann and some of the other members carried on briefly as Eel, a short-lived group that included bassist Scott Shriner, who would join Weezer in 2001. Around this time, Feldmann began demoing some punky new tunes that didn't fit the funk-rock mold. In 1993, he sent a demo with half Eel material and half featuring his pop-punk stuff to buddy Todd Sullivan, the A&R rep for Geffen who signed Weezer. "He called me immediately after getting that cassette and said, 'Dude, you've gotta focus on side B. Let go of this other thing—it's your past,'" Feldmann said.

Following Sullivan's advice, Feldmann formed Goldfinger in early 1994, a pivotal year for pop-punk that saw the release of Green Day's *Dookie*. Feldmann recruited fellow NaNa employee Simon Williams on bass, Darren Pfeiffer on drums, and eventually Charlie Paulson on lead guitar. In a 2017 interview with the reggae-rock website The Pier, Feldmann said his initial concept was for Goldfinger to have a "mod element" and draw from the Police and '80s New Wave. He concedes it wound up morphing into "Bad Religion meets the Specials."

Goldfinger spent their first year playing regularly throughout California with groups like blink-182, the Skeletones, and Buck-O-Nine. One day, Patrick McDowell, A&R rep at a new label called Mojo Records, stopped into NaNa. Feldmann sold him a pair of Doc Martens and slipped a demo cassette into the shoebox. McDowell took the tape back to Mojo founder Jay Rifkin, whose business partner was Hans Zimmer, composer of *The Lion King*. It was obvious Feldmann could write songs, and the erstwhile metal funkster landed a $10,000 publishing deal.

During sessions for Goldfinger's self-titled 1996's debut album, Rifkin was nominally the producer, but Feldmann says the Mojo boss knew nothing about punk rock or making albums. That left Feldmann free to experiment and make a record with some interesting sonic quirks, like a snare drum that sounds like a tennis ball going *pong!* off a racket. The band worked at Hans Zimmer's studio and used whatever fancy gear the film-score maestro handed down. "There was an innocence to making that record that didn't exist moving forward because we really didn't have a leader," Feldmann told Fuse in a twentieth-anniversary retrospective.

Goldfinger is often regarded as a canonical '90s ska-punk record, but as Feldmann rightly told Fuse, the album is only 20–25 percent ska. "King for a Day" is a mellow reggae groover that hulks out with a punk finale. "Answers" is an angry skanker with a shout-along chorus. "Pictures" a fairly pure ska song with an unexpected metal breakdown. All three tracks feature horns by Hepcat saxophonist Efren Santana along with Dan Regan and Scott Klopfenstein of Reel Big Fish, whom Feldmann had brought to Mojo. There's also a minute-long reggae goof called "My Girlfriend's Shower Sucks."

The highlight, of course, is "Here in Your Bedroom," a sensitive ska-punk dude's version of the Shirelles' 1960 classic "Will You Love Me Tomorrow." Feldmann wrote the song about a girl who worked in the dress department at NaNa. After crushing on her for months, he finally hooked up with her on December 31, 1993. Feldmann barely slept that night and woke up right before his sister was due to arrive for a New Year's Day visit. "I wrote 'Here in Your Bedroom' from like 9:00 a.m. to 9:08," Feldmann said. "It took me eight minutes to write the whole song. It was inspired by all this passion and pent-up crush energy, and I wrote that song about this girl and about the next day—'Will you still feel the same?' Then my sister was there, I hadn't seen her in a year . . . there was a real emotional energy."

Those five ska/reggae offerings are surrounded by supremely catchy, albeit juvenile, pop-punk songs that would've resonated with teen Green Day fans experiencing their first breakups. "For me, I don't know anything about politics and I'm not interested," Feldmann told the *Los Angeles Times* in 1996. "I'm interested in more personal problems." If "Here in Your Bedroom" hadn't become a hit on KROQ and caught on nationally, it's easy to imagine Goldfinger might've instead broken through with "Mable," a puppy-love punk song complete with dick jokes.

Goldfinger toured like mad in 1996, playing 385 shows (apparently a Guinness World Record) and opening for No Doubt and the reunited Sex Pistols. When they returned with their terrific 1997 sophomore album, *Hang-Ups*, the ska trend they'd helped propagate a year earlier was reaching its peak. Goldfinger had just the right record for the time. A loose concept album maintaining romantic relationships via telephone, *Hang-Ups* is a cavalcade of hooks with offbeat guitars on seven of its 14 tracks. Feldmann was inspired by Elvis Costello and the Beatles, and lead single

"This Lonely Place" is a pop-reggae confection indebted to the latter's "Getting Better." "This Lonely Place" reached #14 on the Modern Rock Tracks chart in October 1997, as ska's banner year came to a close. Fishbone front man Angelo Moore adds soulful vocals on the straight-ahead ska tune "Carlita." Opener "Superman" is a zippy ska earworm that enjoyed a second life two years later, when it was included in the popular video game *Tony Hawk's Pro Skater*. Without being released as a single, "Superman" became Goldfinger's signature song.

There was more ska to come on 1999's *Darrin's Coconut Ass*, a stopgap covers EP recorded mostly live at an Omaha studio. Goldfinger rework songs by the Police, the Specials, and Peter Tosh, but Feldmann was losing his taste for offbeat guitars. Goldfinger's next album, 2000's *Stomping Ground*, is blunt radio-punk with shades of hard rock. "When we recorded those first two discs I was listening to my old ska records like crazy," Feldmann told *Sink Hole*. "I listened to that stuff so much that I got sick of it. Dude, I was over it. I told everybody we got to go back to rock, and that's what we did with *Stomping Ground*."

In the twenty-first century, Feldmann found a second career as a producer, songwriter, and A&R rep for labels like Maverick and Warner Bros. Working with groups like Good Charlotte and the Used, Feldmann again adapted to changing alt-rock mores (or jumped the bandwagon, depending on your viewpoint) and helped define pop-punk and emo for the MySpace generation. He even took gigs with pop acts like Hillary Duff, Ashlee Simpson, and guitar-packing heartthrobs 5 Seconds of Summer. According to his 2019 website bio, Feldmann has "contributed to the sale of more than 34 million albums."

As Feldmann's production workload grew, Goldfinger became a secondary concern. The band continued making punk albums with flashes of ska through the '00s but took a nine-year recording hiatus after their sixth studio LP, 2008's *Hello Destiny*. . . . Feldmann rebooted the brand in 2017 with *The Knife*, essentially a solo album made with all new side players, including Travis Barker of blink-182 (and costumed ska heroes the Aquabats) on drums. It was Goldfinger's most ska- and reggae-centric album since *Hang-Ups*, and the following year, Feldmann owned his ska legacy by teaming with Barker to launch Back to the Beach, a two-day SoCal festival featuring the Mighty Mighty Bosstones, Fishbone, the Suicide Machines, Mustard Plug, Save Ferris, and Less Than Jake, among others.

Back to the Beach came at the start of a year in which the Bosstones debuted their own summer ska party, the Cranking & Skanking Fest, and the documentary *Pick It Up! Ska in the '90s* was fully funded on Kickstarter in its first week. Optimistic ska fans began fantasizing that third-wave nostalgia meant a fourth wave was coming. But 2018 was fundamentally different from 1997. Twenty years later, a weekend of frivolous skanking was less a reflection of the culture than it was an attempt to escape its ugly realities.

"Living in the era that we do, everything is mumble rap or SoundCloud rap," Feldmann told *OC Weekly*. "Then, there's Donald Trump, and it's like, how have we all not killed ourselves? We need this. We need to be able to laugh, dance, sing and have fun."

CHAPTER 6

One Nation Under Ska-Punk

The term "ska revival" never really made sense in America. Outside of certain areas, the genre didn't make much of a stateside impression during the original Jamaican or 2 Tone eras, so most teens who discovered ska in the '90s came in fresh, with no preconceived notions about how the music should—and more importantly shouldn't—sound. Fans riding the third wave were receptive to all manner of mutations and bastardizations, most of which fell under the umbrella of "ska-punk."

Ska-punk is America's contribution to the ska story. It often came from the suburbs, the land of baggy shorts and baseball caps. The guitars crunched and the grooves were seldom smooth, but this stuff spoke to '90s kids in a way purist ska rarely could.

■ ■ ■

It figures Less Than Jake wrote songs about losers, freaks, and suburban angst. The band's two founding members hail from the cultural wastelands of New Jersey and Florida. Making fun of their swampy, mall-filled home states would've been a cinch, but Less Than Jake had the intelligence and empathy to look past stereotypes and chronicle what they actually saw happening around them. They also had the goofy sense of humor to cover the occasional TV theme song.

On their string of superb '90s releases, which includes two albums on Capitol Records, Less Than Jake created frenetic ska-punk anthems about small-town kids screwing up and questioning their places in the universe. Drummer and primary lyricist Vinnie Fiorello based these characters on himself and people he knew growing up. The vocals of guitarist Chris DeMakes and bassist Roger Lima are raw and defiant, and the ska upstrokes come scuzzy and hyperactive, erasing nearly all traces of Jamaica.

Despite the often-depressing subject matter, Less Than Jake's songs are energetic enough to have inspired wild live performances featuring costumed mascots, confetti cannons, and toilet-paper guns. Generally speaking, Less Than Jake in the '90s were serious chroniclers of adolescent turmoil on record and clownish party dudes onstage. Reconciling these two contradictory sides was and is totally optional for the band's legions of fans.

Less Than Jake's roots trace back to Port Charlotte, South Florida, where DeMakes grew up and Jersey-born Fiorello moved with his family as a teenager. In high school in the early '90s, the pair bonded over punk rock and started a band, Needless Guilt, followed by another one, Good Grief. Neither really made it beyond the garage. Because Good Grief's bassist and second guitarist worked full-time and lived 30 minutes away, DeMakes and Fiorello would get together by themselves to work on songs. Fiorello was a rarity: a drummer who could stop hitting things with sticks long enough to write lyrics—and thoughtful ones at that. DeMakes had a knack for killer chord progressions and sticky melodies. "We would do these little jams, and I was like, 'OK, there's something here,'" DeMakes says.

After graduation, DeMakes moved north to Gainesville to attend the University of Florida. Fiorello followed a year later. By that time, the pair had recorded demos of four songs that would appear on early Less Than Jake releases: "Lucky Day," "Good Time for a Change," "Process," and

"Black Coffee on the Table," later retitled "Black Coffee." All four are speedy and sincere punk tunes concerned with growing up and feeling lost. They're solid first stabs at songwriting from two guys who would soon have an original sound to match their point of view.

Less Than Jake played their first show in July 1992 and added bassist Roger Lima and saxophone player Jessica Mills not long after. "When [Jessica] got in the band, that was the start of messing around with ska," DeMakes says. "She was way into ska, as was Vinnie. I was more into the punk stuff." The idea to get a horn section actually didn't come from ska. DeMakes and Fiorello were big fans of the trombone-packing U.K. punk band Snuff. But as Less Than Jake began playing more and more ska, the horns made even more sense. Other influences included Operation Ivy and the Mighty Mighty Bosstones, two of the only bands on Less Than Jake's pre-Internet radar mixing ska and punk with anything like the same energy.

Less Than Jake became a five-piece in July 1993 with the addition of trombonist Buddy Schuab. Now they were a punk band with two horns and ska tendencies in a town that hadn't heard anything like this before. "There were people that got it immediately," says DeMakes. "Then there were the punk purists, and then there were the people that didn't get it at all. You've got to remember, we were in redneck Florida. If it wasn't for the college, Gainesville would just be another country-bumpkin town in North Florida."

With Fiorello handling the bulk of the lyrics, Less Than Jake began churning out songs that naturally tended toward serious topics. While they wrote a handful of joke songs, like "Johnny Quest Thinks We're Sellouts," the vibe was closer to social commentary. "We always prided ourselves on that," says DeMakes. "It's like, 'OK, we have this happy music, but there's this serious tone to the lyrics.' On paper, it shouldn't work, but it does." Once they got in front of an audience, Less Than Jake became a different band altogether. "We never talked about politics," DeMakes says. "We were a party band. If you give us a half hour, we're going to raise hell the whole time we're onstage."

In August 1994, Less Than Jake opened for the Mighty Mighty Bosstones in Tampa. It was a pivotal moment for the ska-punk upstarts. By that point, Less Than Jake had been touring for a couple of years throughout Florida, playing to 200 or 300 people max. The Bosstones gig drew 1,000 kids eager to hear punk rock with saxophones and trombones. "That was the start of thinking, 'Wow, maybe we could take this outside of the state of Florida and see what happens,'" says DeMakes.

The following summer, Less Than Jake embarked on their first national tour. They did 48 days and dropped their debut album, *Pezcore*, along the way. Released on Dill Records, the label run by Mike Park of Skankin' Pickle, *Pezcore* is among the most important ska-punk albums of the '90s. Highlights include "My Very Own Flag" and "Growing Up on a Couch," non-ska horn-core anthems about feeling alienated and realizing everything on TV is bullshit, respectively. "Shotgun" is so damn happy you barely realize it's about suicide. *Pezcore* ends with "Short on Ideas / One Last Cigarette," a fusion of two songs that sums up the album in four minutes. The first 1:47 is "Short on Ideas," a wounded punk rumination on how there's nothing new in the world, just different names for things we'll never understand. That bleeds into the tattered ska of "One Last Cigarette," the diary of a wound-up kid—maybe the same guy contemplating science and religion on "Short on Ideas"—walking the railroad tracks at 4:00 a.m., feeling like he's "about to crack."

On that first U.S. tour, Less Than Jake were thrilled to learn they weren't the only ones who'd thought to cross Green Day with the Specials. They made friends with Slapstick in Chicago, the Impossibles in Austin, and Supermarket All-Stars in Houston, among others. "When we would run into them, it would be like we were finding long-lost brothers," Fiorello said on the podcast *Turned Out a Punk*. "'You get what we're doing. You get it!'"

By March of 1995, Less Than Jake had roused the interest of Capitol Records A&R man Craig Aaronson, whose first signing at Capitol was Jimmy Eat World, the Arizona emo-rock outfit that would break through with *Bleed American* in 2001. After months of courtship, Less Than Jake signed in late 1995 for $100,000, a pittance by '90s major-label standards. Although the band had always been staunchly DIY, DeMakes had no qualms about joining the big leagues.

"I wanted to sell as many records and get on as many magazine covers [as possible] and be *that* band," DeMakes says. "I wanted to make as much money as I could. This is what I had set out to do. I have never been shy about saying that." Besides, Less Than Jake had been screwed over by enough handshake deals with tiny punk labels to know that "indie" doesn't necessarily mean "morally virtuous." "At least with Capitol," DeMakes says, "we knew how we were getting fucked."

Less Than Jake were riding a mini-tide of ska-punk bands signing with majors. Around the same time, the Suicide Machines linked up with Hollywood Records, and Goldfinger jumped on Mojo, an indie with distribution through Universal. "Too many people had heard about [ska]," DeMakes says. "Too many 2,000-seat venues had sold out across the United States at that point for people not to notice. The A&R people and the people at the record labels were starting to pay attention to it. Ultimately it becomes a numbers game: 'How many of these records can we sell?'"

Less Than Jake made their Capitol debut with *Losing Streak*, released in November 1996. Produced with little studio gloss by Michael Rosen, who'd helmed metal albums by Testament and Mordred and engineered Rancid's . . . *And Out Come the Wolves*, *Losing Streak* stands as the most ska-centric album in Less Than Jake's catalog. On all but four of the 16 tracks, DeMakes's antsy, rubber-wristed strumming drives the action.

The anxious pacing and no-frills production fit nicely with songs about disaffected everymen ("Happyman"), youth violence ("9th and Pine"), closed-mindedness ("Just Like Frank"), and the need to rise above where you're from ("Shindo," "Never Going Back to New Jersey"). Lead single and album opener "Automatic" is cold water in the face for anyone moving blindly through life. Alas, "Automatic" is a little too ragged and urgent to have done battle with Reel Big Fish's glossier "Sell Out" on the radio, and it failed to make even Billboard's Modern Rock Tracks chart. *Losing Streak* fared slightly better on the whole, reaching #18 on the Heatseekers Albums tally, reserved for emerging artists.

Less Than Jake's best chance at a hit might've been "Dopeman," a catchy little explanation of the societal conditions that lead people to become drug dealers. The band approved a now-dated '90s remix, complete with regrettable turntable scratching, and filmed a silly music video set in a roller-skating rink. Rerun from the '70s sitcom *What's Happening!!* makes a cameo. It was such a stupid-funny concept that Sugar Ray ripped it off for their "Every Morning" clip in 1999. And yet MTV wouldn't play "Dopeman." Fiorello told the website Noisey in 2015 that MTV "had issues with the lyrical content," but DeMakes says that's not true. "MTV didn't play it because it wasn't a hit," he says. "'Dopeman' is a terrible song. It was never one of my favorites. I wrote it, so I can say that. The version on *Losing Streak* is passable, but the remix we did, I was never into it."

DeMakes says the high percentage of ska songs of *Losing Streak* had nothing to do with Capitol urging Less Than Jake to follow the ska trend. They'd written the bulk of the songs while touring behind *Pezcore*, and they were simply feeling the offbeat guitars. While crossing the country in support of *Losing Streak*, Less Than Jake began writing material for *Hello Rockview*. It would be their first album without Jessica Mills, who quit in 1997 to focus on teaching.

Hello Rockview would feature a drastic reduction in ska and an uptick in songwriting complexity, as the band experimented with intricate harmonies and tempo and key changes. It all came together in the studio under the watchful eye of producer Howard Benson, who'd worked with hard rock bands like Bang Tango and Motörhead. A keyboard player and composer, Benson put his head down and helped Less Than Jake perfect their arrangements. He also recorded with Pro Tools, a then-emerging technology that allowed him to use Auto-Tune on everything from the vocals to the horns. Pro Tools would become the industry standard, and according to Benson, *Hello Rockview* was one of the first albums made on the digital platform.

As the music bounded forward, Fiorello was feeling reflective. His lyrics trace his journey from Jersey to Florida to the endless highway he traveled with Less Than Jake. What emerged was a concept album about his youth. Its name comes from the Rockview State Correctional Institution in Pennsylvania, which Less Than Jake would drive past when playing State College. "It always struck me as a funny thing in that these suburbs, this is what locks us into who we are and who we're going to be," Fiorello told Noisey in June 2015. "So *Hello Rockview* is like a 'hello' to this prison of suburbia and my struggle to get out of that." In the CD booklet, the lyrics are presented as a comic book illustrated by illustrator Steve Vance in the style of 1950s *Dick Tracy* strips. Vance's cover artwork features an unhinged suit-clad suburban man leaping into his swimming pool while his wife looks on with a tray of martinis.

Before releasing *Hello Rockview*, Less Than Jake headlined the Ska Against Racism Tour in the spring of 1998. The trek caught flak in some circles, as critics accused the bands of glossing over the politics supposedly fueling the whole thing. DeMakes admits that he didn't do much preaching, but that's because set times were tight and Blue Meanies drummer Bob Trondson took the stage right before Less Than Jake each night and gave a short, thoughtful speech about the corrosive effects of racism. "I thought we raised a lot of awareness," says DeMakes, who voiced his commitment to the cause in the countless interviews he did surrounding the tour. "I thought as a united front, we all did say something." If anything, DeMakes says, Ska Against Racism was preaching to the choir. "Most of the thousand people that were there every night weren't racist," he says. "They were ska kids."

A lot of those ska kids bought *Hello Rockview* when it hit the streets in October 1998. The album finally vaulted Less Than Jake onto Billboard's Modern Rock Tracks chart with "History of a Boring Town," a three-minute distillation of the LP's main themes. It's a major-key ska-punk tune about townies downing drinks and reminiscing about the past in hopes of forgetting how trapped they feel. Had Bruce Springsteen spent the early '80s listening to the Specials and Descendents, this is how "Glory Days" would've sounded. The single reached #39 on Modern Rock Tracks, and *Hello Rockview* became the first of eight (as of 2020) Less Than Jake albums to make the Billboard 200, peaking at #80.

The fact that Less Than Jake never had a big radio single during ska's golden year might've helped the band in the long run. Because they hadn't attracted much of a crossover audience, they didn't lose many fans when the trend died down in 1998 and '99. "We just kept doing our thing," says DeMakes. "We didn't have that albatross over our head of 'You sold 1.5 million albums the last time, and now you only sold 200,000.' We kept selling 200,000 or 300,000 records every record. It wasn't bigger; it wasn't smaller."

Less Than Jake parted company with Capitol while finishing their third album, *Borders and Boundaries*. In the three-plus years since the band signed with the label, nearly everyone they'd worked with—from A&R man Aaronson to the marketing team—had left. Capitol had a new president, the pop- and R&B-focused Roy Lott, and he gave Less Than Jake two choices: they could release their next album on Capitol and get little in the way of promotional support, or they could take the album and go elsewhere. Less Than Jake split and released *Borders and Boundaries* on the California punk indie Fat Wreck Chords, which had rejected the band's demo years earlier.

More touring followed, and the band underwent some lineup changes. Baritone sax player Derron Nuhfer, who'd been on board since 1995, gave his notice in 2000. He was replaced by Pete "JR" Wasilewski, formerly

Less Than Jake bassist Roger Lima lets his hair down at NYC's Roseland Ballroom, March 12, 2002. Photo: Bryan Kremkau / SkaPunkPhotos.com.

of Connecticut ska kings Spring Heeled Jack. In 2001, trombonist Pete Anna quit, leaving the two-man horn section (Schuab and Wasilewski) that was still in place as of 2020. This five-man lineup made its debut on 2003's *Anthem*, which marked the start of Less Than Jake's second stint on a major. Craig Aaronson had taken a job at Warner Bros., and he signed the band for a second time.

Less Than Jake recorded *Anthem* with producer Rob Cavallo, best known for his work on Green Day's 1994 opus *Dookie*, as well as their follow-up albums. Six years removed from the ska explosion of the '90s, Less Than Jake enjoyed the biggest success of their career: *Anthem* reached #45 on the Billboard 200, and the single "The Science of Selling Yourself Short" made #36 on the Modern Rock Tracks chart. *Anthem* remains their best-selling album in America, and it was instrumental in breaking Less Than Jake in the United Kingdom.

As of 2020, Less Than Jake have released four more studio albums and various EPs. They still tour the world, albeit with a familiar face missing behind the drum kit. Fiorello announced in October 2018 that he was retiring from the road, though not from the band. In a tweet the following September, Lima clarified that Fiorello wouldn't be involved with the writing or recording of new music. Fiorello's departure couldn't have been easy for anyone, but two decades into the twenty-first century, DeMakes is more than satisfied with Less Than Jake's status as ska-punk elder statesmen. "I'm stoked that, 27 years in, our band is still able to do this for a living, still able to have fun doing it," he says. "If anyone wants to call us a legacy act, bring it on! Those records from the past, they touched people in a way that they still want to come see the band. That's pretty cool."

■ ■ ■

Being a ska-punk band on a major in the '90s had its pros and cons. On the one hand, a label like Hollywood Records could get your album in stores and help out with radio and MTV airplay. Unfortunately, the suits might require you to make music videos and play lame radio gigs. That's where things started to turn sour for the Suicide Machines.

In early 1997, the Detroit ska-punks found themselves in a demolition-derby arena somewhere near Utah shooting a video for "S.O.S.," a standout track on their Hollywood debut, *Destruction by Definition*, released the previous November. The Suicide Machines were on tour at the time, and the plan was to film all night, then drive to L.A. to play a free outdoor show at Tower Records for KROQ. Even though the band didn't *hate* the video concept—cars spray-painted with words like "fear" and "greed" smashing into each other, bringing to life the song's theme of humanity on the brink—they didn't exactly love it, either.

"To loosen ourselves up, we drank 40s all night," says lead singer Jason Navarro. "There were 40s of Olde English everywhere, because we were getting hammered."

Navarro was boozing in part to ease the pain of his shin splints, which must've been flaring like mad as he and the band (minus drummer Derek Grant, who bailed on the whole thing) jumped around all night miming "S.O.S." They only slept a couple hours, then drove to the KROQ show. Less than enthused about playing a parking lot on a sweltering afternoon, Grant wrote "KCOCK" on his chest, and the band blazed through an abbreviated six-song set at grind-core speed. Then they told the crowd to go into Tower Records and steal whatever they wanted.

KROQ, the most powerful alternative station in the country, was not amused—and they didn't forget. The following year, Navarro says, the station refused to play "Give," the lead single off the Suicide Machines' sophomore album, *Battle Hymns*. The incident poisoned the well with alternative radio and marked "the beginning of the end," in Navarro's estimation, of the band's relationship with Hollywood. More than 20 years later, Navarro doesn't regret that act of career suicide, though he admits there was no reason for the band to behave like it did. But that's part of what distinguished the Suicide Machines in the world of '90s ska-punk crossovers: they didn't give a fuck.

The Suicide Machines always considered themselves a punk band first. They were born in the green-and-orange glow of a 7-Eleven in Livonia, Michigan, a largely white suburb 15 miles from Detroit. The 7-Eleven was the social hub for local teen punks in the late '80s, and Navarro was among the young loiterers. One day in 1989 or '90, he met a new store employee named Dan Lukacinsky, a slightly older punker who'd attended shows at Graystone Hall, a notorious all-ages hardcore venue. Navarro had chickened out of going to see Agnostic Front at Graystone right before it closed, so he knew Lukacinsky was legit.

Navarro and Lukacinsky were fans of Dead Kennedys and the Detroit hardcore band Negative Approach. At the same time, Navarro was discovering Fishbone, the Specials, and Operation Ivy. He made a tape for Lukacinsky, who figured out how to play ska chords on his guitar. Lukacinsky promptly asked Navarro, who'd played bass in local hardcore outfits, if he wanted to start a band. Navarro accepted but found it difficult to sing and play walking bass lines at the same time. So he handed off his instrument to skating buddy Jay Brake, who along with drummer Stefan Rairigh completed the original lineup.

It was 1991, and the band called itself Jack Kevorkian and the Suicide Machines, a reference to the controversial Detroit pathologist whose "suicide machines" helped more than 130 patients die painlessly through injections of carbon monoxide. (They dropped the Kevorkian bit a few years later, when people started turning up to their shows expecting to see "Dr. Death" himself.) Navarro and Lukacinsky honed their ska chops by watching local bands like the Exceptions and Gangster Fun, and in 1993, with Grant now behind the drums, the group made its debut with *The Essential Kevorkian!* The cruddy-sounding six-song cassette reveals a love of Operation Ivy and a distaste for white-bread suburban living. "Society is smothering me," Navarro declares on the mangy skanker "Bonkers."

Navarro had reason to be mistrustful of suburbia. He bounced around as a kid and lived for a time in Detroit, where his mother met a Mexican man who became his adoptive stepfather (hence the last name Navarro). By the time the family settled in Livonia, Navarro had two younger half sisters whose Mexican appearance made them targets of hatred. "We got 'Spics Spread AIDS' stickers stuck on our mailbox and white-power literature stuck on our door all the time," says Navarro. "I just thought, 'How could anyone do this to us?' Who would hate a little kid?"

With their agitated ska-punk songs, the Suicide Machines slotted neatly into a progressive Detroit scene that didn't discriminate on the basis of genre. There weren't all that many ska bands in town, so the Suicide

Machines played with hardcore, hip-hop, and even funk acts. "If you had some sort of DIY ethic, or some sort of social ideas or political ideas, you were playing together," says Navarro.

That policy held when the Suicide Machines began touring nationally around the time of their second cassette, 1994's *Green World*. However, they occasionally met fellow ska-punk bands along the way, like the Rudiments from California's East Bay. The Suicide Machines (now with bassist Royce Nunley) and the Rudiments teamed up for 1995's *Skank for Brains*, a split CD featuring 10 songs by each band. The CD made its way to the offices of Hollywood Records, where A&R man and producer Julian Raymond overheard it playing in a colleague's cubicle. Raymond sensed something special about the Detroit crew and phoned up Lukacinsky's house. Raymond asked to come see a show, but since there were none on the docket, he flew to Detroit to watch the band practice in Lukacinsky's parents' basement. "I remember almost hiding behind this pole by our PA, because I didn't even want to look at him," says Navarro. "It just felt so weird. He was like, 'You know what? There's a bunch of songs I really like by you guys.'"

If there were any doubts about Raymond's character, they disappeared after he met up with the band on their joint 1995 tour with Buck-O-Nine. In Atlanta, thieves broke into the Suicide Machines' van and made off with nearly $2,700 in cash, plus all of Grant's clothes. The band drove to their next gig in Baltimore with their window missing, only to find that the promoter hadn't actually promoted the show. "There were like seven people," Navarro says. "Two of those people were Julian and his wife. And the promoter's being a jerk, and the bar owners are being jerks. So we start hiding our shit everywhere. We'd take shits, and we were smashing it in the ashtrays. We played like lunatics that night anyways, because that's how we always played, crowd or not. Julian was just like, 'You guys are fucking crazy.'"

Raymond took the band food shopping and bought Grant a new wardrobe. Then he offered to fly the group to L.A. to record four songs he would present to the label. If Hollywood didn't sign the Suicide Machines, Raymond would secretly pass them the tapes, so they'd have four professionally recorded songs for their next 7-inch. The band accepted and soon found themselves with a record contract. They hired a manager and lawyers and still signed what Navarro calls "the worst seven-record deal."

"We were just drunk and doing drugs and like, 'Fuck yeah, whatever,'" Navarro says. "We didn't really understand the scope of it. Because we were so stuck in the DIY punk world, none of it made any sense to us." Navarro doesn't remember feeling any punk-rock guilt about signing with a major. The worries began after the ink had dried and people started calling them sellouts, even in Detroit. This despite the fact that the Suicide Machines were harder and more political than all the other ska bands going mainstream. "We didn't expect a backlash," Navarro says. "And we totally got one."

Whatever people may have thought, Hollywood had zero influence on *Destruction by Definition*, recorded with Raymond as producer. Seven of the tracks were rerecordings of *Skank for Brains* songs, including the standout "New Girl," written by Lukacinsky. Navarro credits the guitarist with penning the three best songs on the album: "New Girl," "Break the Glass," and "No Face," which reached #31 on Billboard's Modern Rock Tracks chart and garnered MTV airplay. The latter two are spastic ska-punk tunes with fidgety cross-stick and hi-hat work from Grant and lyrics that look inward to speak about larger problems facing alienated young people. That same songwriting approach drives deep cuts like "Too Much," "Islands," and "Insecurities," creating a politically charged album that doesn't actually say much about politics.

"I don't know any other way to write, and neither did Dan," Navarro says. "We're not trying to tell stories like Johnny Cash. We're looking in at ourselves and how we approach the world . . . and maybe if I write the way I feel about things, other people are going to attach themselves and understand, because they're thinking the same things."

Navarro and Grant wrote the album highlight "S.O.S.," a more outward-looking song about ignorance and intolerance building up and reaching a boiling point. There's distortion on the slashing ska guitars and an urgent organ solo prefacing the final chorus—one last "call to action" before humankind blows itself up. *Destruction by Definition* features some comic relief in the form of "Vans Song," which dates back to 1994's *Green World*. It's a punky reggae trifle about how Vans are cheap and comfortable and therefore superior to all other footwear. Vinny Nobile of Bim Skala Bim and later Pilfers underscores the message with his signature elephantine trombone.

Destruction by Definition sold well and became one of the era's defining ska-punk albums. Navarro estimates it moved more than 500,000 units, though he doubts the label even knows for sure. (Nielsen Music has the sales at 263,000.) "Hollywood Records is such a mess," he says. "They don't even have any clue of what they do. And they've changed people so many times." After the debacle with the "S.O.S." video and KROQ event, the Suicide Machines purposely began burning bridges with Hollywood. It began with 1998's *Battle Hymns*, which they wrote in two weeks and recorded in just a few days. According to Navarro they hadn't seen any of the $280,000 they were given to record *Destruction by Definition*, and since the budget was going to be the same for the follow-up they decided to record as quickly as possible and pocket all the leftover money. They also wrote the "fastest, craziest punk songs in the world," giving Hollywood few options for singles.

There are only two songs with anything close to a hook. One is the opening track, "Someone," an anxious tangle of ska and punk about feeling alone in a hateful world. "Give," the single KROQ wouldn't play, is a poppy ska reminder to properly vet your friends. All told, there are skanking guitars on about half of the album's 20 proper tracks. The other half is brutal hardcore that required Navarro to scream his guts out in the studio. After the rest of the band laid down the backing tracks in two days,

Navarro sang half of the album in one day, blowing out his voice in the process. He went back to Raymond's house and recuperated by downing rum and watching conspiracy videos. Then he went back and finished the remaining vocals in another daylong session.

Battle Hymns sold roughly 32,000 copies its first month, according to Nielsen Music—a flop by Hollywood standards. Navarro admits that half the album simply isn't very good. And yet the prevalence of ska songs kept the Suicide Machines popular among the checkerboard set. Navarro may identify more with the punk scene, but the fact remains that his band released two ska-heavy major-label albums in the '90s. They'll forever be associated with bands like Reel Big Fish, even though they came to ska from a vastly different place.

"Detroit was still completely fucked in 1995," says Navarro, thinking back on abandoned buildings and pervasive unemployment. "We grew up around the crack and heroin epidemic, which ran so rampant in Detroit, it destroyed it. We weren't living in a tropical paradise with fucking palm trees, and *life's not so bad*, you know what I mean? Whereas bands like— I'm only assuming, which might be completely wrong—Reel Big Fish were living in that kind of world. We were the exact opposite of that. That's why our music was the way it was—just because of our surroundings."

Grant left the band after *Battle Hymns*, and new drummer Ryan Vandeberghe walked into what Navarro calls a "stormy situation." Lukacinsky and Nunley were at each other's throats, and Navarro was too busy dealing with the loss of his first son to make an attempt at fixing things. He backed off and left the bulk of the songwriting to Lukacinsky and Nunley, who took the group in the unexpected Beatles-gone-punk direction heard on 2000's widely derided *The Suicide Machines*.

The infighting got worse during sessions for 2001's *Steal This Record*, a return to punk the band recorded piecemeal, since nobody could stand being in the studio with each other. Nunley jumped ship after that album, and having fulfilled their Hollywood contract, the band signed with the

L.A. indie SideOneDummy. Invigorated by the change of label and opposition to the Bush administration, the Suicide Machines ended their initial run with *A Match and Some Gasoline* (2003) and *War Profiteering Is Killing Us All* (2005), foamy-mouthed punk assaults with flashes of ska.

The group split up in 2006, then reformed sans Lukacinsky in 2009. The guitarist issued a statement blasting the so-called reunion and claiming he was never asked to participate. Amid other musical projects, Navarro carried on playing live with the Suicide Machines throughout the '10s and released a new album, *Revolution Spring*, in 2020. For the comeback LP, Navarro avoided writing the kinds of political diatribes fans might've expected in the age of Trump. Navarro says it's more an album about values that ought to be "common sense" to people but somehow aren't.

"I've flipped in my old age, because I'm a bit of an activist these days and actually doing shit instead of just pointing fingers and bitching about it," Navarro says. "That speaks to my lyrics on this record. It's just like, 'Hey, man, use your fucking brain and your heart.'"

■ ■ ■

One night in 1992, three ska bands met in a cornfield in Lawrence, Kansas. This was the unlikely location of the Outhouse, an infamous punk club in the middle of nowhere that hosted groups like Nirvana, Fugazi, Fishbone, and Ice T's Body Count from 1985 to 1997. Billy Spunke was lead singer of Blue Meanies, one of the ska outfits booked to play there on the evening in question. Driving to the club through miles and miles of corn, the Chicago native thought maybe his band had been duped.

Not only was it a legit gig, but in Spunke's estimation, it was a historic show in the history of third-wave ska. With their spicy puree of punk, funk, jazz, klezmer, polka, metal, and more, Blue Meanies existed on the outer fringes of ska. That made them natural allies of fellow misfits MU330 and Skankin' Pickle, the other two acts on the Outhouse bill. "We met them and loved them as people," Spunke says. "It would drag us into the community of ska. Probably because we liked them so much, we were like, 'All right well we should always throw a little ska into most of our songs.'"

Throughout the '90s, Blue Meanies played just enough ska to warrant the tag. They even took part in 1998's Ska Against Racism Tour. But they pushed the music as far as it could go and still be vaguely recognizable as ska. Other bands like Voodoo Glow Skulls played fast and hard. Blue Meanies played fast and hard and *weird*, switching between several incongruent styles in the span of single songs. This earned them a national following and, at the very end of the '90s, a short-lived deal with MCA Records. They used the opportunity to release 2000's *The Post-Wave*, an album that's more palatable (and less ska) than their previous two LPs but uncompromising in the political subject matter that also set Blue Meanies apart from most third-wave groups. A year later, this strange and wondrous chimera of the third wave was gone.

Named for the music-hating baddies in the 1968 Beatles cartoon film *Yellow Submarine*, Blue Meanies formed at Southern Illinois University in Carbondale in 1991. They were all fans of Fishbone and the Red Hot Chili Peppers, plus hardcore punk and the 2 Tone ska of the Specials and the Selecter. Bass player Jay Vance became the main songwriter, though the nascent Meanies established a rule that would last throughout their 10-year run: everyone could contribute. "That's what led to songs never staying cohesive as far as one genre," says Spunke. "You'd throw everything in there, and then it got so chaotic. But everyone was equal."

While at Carbondale, Blue Meanies recorded their debut, *Peace Love Groove*, a live album showcasing the band's funk leanings. It was released on No Record Co., a fictitious label the Meanies invented so clubs would take them seriously. Amid all the bass slapping, the Meanies make time for one ska tune, the Eastern European–sounding "Grandma Shampoo," about washing your hair with your grandparents' ashes. Throughout the performance, Spunke works the mic like a campus revolutionary well-schooled in the ways of Jello Biafra. The anti-racist funk workout "Brother Free" offers an early glimpse at where Spunke was coming from politically.

Spunke's left-wing politics weren't informed by punk and hardcore. He was reared on classic rock before discovering Dead Kennedys. Spunke attributes his worldview to growing up the son of a blue-collar gas-company worker in inner-city Chicago. The neighborhood taught him about the value of hard work but also the prevalence of racism in American society. That would become a major theme in his writing.

After graduation, Blue Meanies got serious, moved to Chicago, and took on some new members, including keyboardist and songwriter Chaz Linde. They became more cohesive, and the funk elements mercifully melted away. By their next album, 1995's *Kiss Your Ass Goodbye*, Blue Meanies had evolved into a pulverizing seven-headed, two-horned (trumpet and sax) monster with boundless energy. Vance, still the primary songwriter, was sacked before the sessions but flew to St. Louis to record his parts. The prevailing sound is wild-eyed ska, with frantic guitar upstrokes slicing through standouts like "It Doesn't Matter"—all about the pointlessness of subcultures and religion and most everything else in life—and "Johnny Mortgage," a grim picture of middle-class struggles. On the gnashing punk track "Average American Superhero," Spunke describes the kind of beer-swilling workaday racists he saw in his neighborhood growing up.

Before *Kiss Your Ass Goodbye* came out in early 1995, Blue Meanies broke up for a few months. Spunke moved to New Orleans but returned to Chicago as the band again took on new personnel, including drummer Bob Trondson and bassist Dave Lund, both of the Wisconsin ska band Weaker Youth Ensemble. The Meanies were back and better than ever.

With ska beginning to generate mainstream buzz, Blue Meanies nearly got called up to the majors. Terry Ellis, co-founder of Chrysalis Records and the man who launched Billy Idol's solo career, was interested in signing the Meanies to his Imago label. For one reason or another, it didn't work out. There were also conversations with Hollywood Records, home of the Suicide Machines. The Meanies were all set to fly out to L.A. for a meeting when the deal fell through. MCA also had the Meanies record some demos that didn't lead anywhere.

Although the Meanies didn't land a major label deal during ska's breakout year of 1997, they toured with many third-wave heavyweights, including Reel Big Fish. "What [kids] would see when they saw us was just terrifying," Spunke says. "We were loud, extremely fast, and we probably weren't smiling. But there was a small section of each one of those audiences that was drawn to that. They were like, 'Wow I guess there's more to the ska movement than just this happy-go-lucky thing.'"

Only the most adventurous ska fans would've been ready for the band's next album, *Full Throttle*, released in 1997 on the indie label Thick Records. "*Full Throttle* is a very angry record," says Spunke. "It was about what was happening not only politically or socially around the world, but within that scene. We were like, 'OK, we could write an easy ska song, or we could just go full tilt and go faster and harder and more angry.'"

If a lot of '90s ska was a reflection of groovy times in America, *Full Throttle* was a reminder of all the rotten stuff going on below the surface. Nearly every track goes like hell and changes direction multiple times. The album opens with "The 4th of July," an incendiary thrasher about the erosion of American ideals. "Send Help," the closest thing to a pure ska track, is a tirade aimed at those who sit back and talk while the nation's problems get worse. "Smash the Magnavox" blames TV for destroying American families. "The Great Peacemaker" is a commentary on youth gun violence set to demonic circus music.

The relentless attack of *Full Throttle* doesn't leave much room for ska. But Blue Meanies never said they were a ska band. They didn't let that stop them from joining 1998's Ska Against Racism Tour with their buddies Mike Park and MU330. Blue Meanies were one of the bands that made a point of saying something about racism every night. Bob Trondson would take the stage right before Less Than Jake's headlining set and extend a spoonful of medicine in between buckets of sugar. A couple months after the tour, Spunke was quoted in the *Chicago Reader* story that criticized the tour for not putting enough emphasis on the message. "God, I hate to say this," Spunke told the paper, "but it was almost like the racism part of this tour was just a marketing tool."

Spunke says he never meant to diss Park, a true believer in equality whose heart was unquestionably in the right place. "However, when you do Ska Against Racism at that time . . . you're bringing out people who were part of the ska third wave, and this whole phenomena of ska," Spunke says. "They were really just coming out to have fun. A lot of times, I think the message was forgotten about." Which isn't to say it was a total loss. "It was good for us to try to deliver that message every night, even if people didn't want to hear it all the time," Spunke says.

Blue Meanies toured for 250 days to support *Full Throttle*. By 1999, they'd reached a crossroads. It was getting too expensive for seven musicians, plus a merch guy and soundman, to survive on the road. That's when MCA stepped up and provided a lifeline. For years, the Meanies had been friends with Rick Bonde, founder of the Tahoe Agency, an influential talent booker whose '90s clients included Sublime, blink-182, and Skankin' Pickle. MCA had hired Bonde as a talent scout, and he suggested signing Blue Meanies.

"It was a last-ditch effort: 'This has to happen now, or we just can't do it,'" Spunke says of the deal. The Meanies had already resolved to start writing more cohesive songs, and to achieve this goal, they invited Mark Goldenberg—a producer and session guitarist who'd played with everyone from Linda Ronstadt and Peter Frampton to Eels—to visit their basement practice space and help with the writing process. The first thing Goldenberg did was make them turn down the volume, so everyone could hear what everyone else was doing. "We then began to think about space in songs," Spunke says. "Like, 'Oh we don't necessarily need to be so dense all the time. We can serve the song better if we listen to each other.' It was a huge moment for us."

All the hard work and song-doctoring yielded *The Post-Wave*, a terrific album of catchy organ-driven, horn-flecked punk tunes about environmental degradation ("Chemicals"), white flight and opposition to forced school bussing ("We're All the Same"), and the vapidity of television ("TV Girl"). The slurping hi-hats on "Mama Getting High on Chardonnay," the Meanies' update of the Rolling Stones' "Mother's Little Helper," *almost* evoke ska, but the album is utterly devoid of offbeat guitars. That was kind of the point.

"We were stepping out of that genre again," Spunke says. "But at the same time, I thought we were leading the genre, too. We were saying, 'OK, let's all move forward. All of us, all the bands, let's develop our sounds and not be afraid to grow and try new things.'" *The Post-Wave* was produced by Phil Nicolo, one half of the Butcher Brothers, the Philly duo that oversaw three tracks on the Mighty Mighty Bosstones' 1994 album *Question the Answers*.

Shortly before *The Post-Wave* hit shelves, Bonde had a falling-out with MCA. Blue Meanies were suddenly left without a champion at the label, and midway through a national tour MCA pulled all support. Blue Meanies finished the trek knowing full well that when it was over, they'd have to go back to booking tiny shows and struggling to make a living. In other words, they knew it was the end.

Before officially calling it quits, Blue Meanies issued a statement facetiously thanking MCA for spending $500,000 on *The Post-Wave*. The money went to new musical gear and a sweet RV the band still owned. The Meanies even got back their master tapes and reissued *The Post-Wave* on Thick. "It's as if we walked into the jaws of the dragon's lair, extracted its golden tooth, and walked away unscathed," the letter reads. Only that was the end of the quest.

Since splitting up, Blue Meanies have re-formed several times, including two appearances at Riot Fest in Chicago. Spunke says future reunions remain on the table, even though the Meanies are spread out across the country. "The less we play," Spunke says, "the bigger the crowds are."

■ ■ ■

In 1998, the alternative rock station in Grand Rapids, Michigan, would play the hell out of the Mighty Mighty Bosstones, but it wouldn't touch Mustard Plug, hometown heroes who'd been squeezing out tangy ska-punk jams since 1991. Nevertheless, the station invited Mustard Plug to contribute a song to a compilation CD they were putting together. Rather than waste a new original tune on a cheesy radio comp, Mustard Plug offered a cover of "The Freshman," the stone-faced and serious alt-rock crossover smash (#5 on the Billboard Hot 100, #1 on Modern Rock Tracks) by fellow West Michigan natives the Verve Pipe.

Lyrically, "The Freshman" is a double whammy of abortion and suicide, and The Verve Pipe original rocks with the post-grunge somberness those topics require. Mustard Plug's version isn't exactly cheery, but it's done in a ska-punk style that can't help but lighten the mood. "We weren't sure if the radio station would just be totally offended or not, but we also didn't really care that much," says Mustard Plug lead singer Dave Kirchgessner.

As it turns out, everyone loved it, including the Verve Pipe. Mustard Plug could've easily reissued their then-most-recent album *Evildoers Beware!* with "The Freshman" included to drum up sales. Instead, they opted to press up 1,000 copies of a CD single with "The Freshman" and their own song "You," hoping radio stations would spin the latter. The plan didn't work, and more alternative stations, some as far away as Phoenix, began playing "The Freshman."

"Coming from a punk-rock background and having this sense of integrity, for lack of a better word, we didn't want to be known as this gimmick band that played someone else's song," says Kirchgessner. So Mustard Plug never made a music video or approved a wider release of "The Freshman." The song faded away in a matter of months, and Mustard Plug missed their chance to pull a Save Ferris and see how far a ska cover of a popular song might take them. "It's one of those things you look back on like, 'Wow, did we make the wrong decision?'" Kirchgessner says. "I don't know."

In the late '90s, Mustard Plug were about as popular as a Midwestern ska-punk band with a ridiculous name and zero radio or MTV presence could be. *Evildoers Beware!* sold something like 100,000 copies in its first year, Kirchgessner says, and Mustard Plug headlined shows across the country. They'd won fans the old-fashioned way, beginning with their very first shows in 1991. Kirchgessner formed the group with guitarist Colin Clive, whom he met going to punk shows in the late '80s. When they both discovered ska—2 Tone, Skankin' Pickle, Michigan's own Gangster Fun— they resolved to start a band after college.

There was no ska scene to speak of in Grand Rapids, so Mustard Plug scammed shows however they could. Kirchgessner was dabbling in concert promotion, and he'd bring bands like Skankin' Pickle and Canada's King Apparatus to town, then stick Mustard Plug on the bottom of the bill. Mustard Plug soon built up a following, thanks in part to a high-energy live show that made ample use of props. "It was a huge change compared to the other bands that were around at the time, which were really depressing grunge and industrial stuff like Nine Inch Nails," says Kirchgessner. "We rebelled against that and were goofy and lighthearted and fun."

With no ambitions beyond playing around town, Mustard Plug's next step was to document their first batch of songs, lest they be lost to the sands of time. The seven members jammed themselves into the basement studio of a local producer who usually made metal records and emerged with 1992's *Skapocalypse Now!* The self-released 10-song cassette comes out skanking with "Brain on Ska," Mustard Plug's love letter to a scene that's all about "simply havin' fun and unity." The track is bright and elastic, powered by a sense of joyful irreverence that carries through to highlights like "We Want the Mustard" and "Summertime," a song the group promoted with a cheapo music video that somehow went into rotation at local teen hangouts.

Skapocalypse Now! was a test run for Mustard Plug's CD debut, 1993's *Big Daddy Multitude*, released via a licensing deal with Moon Ska Records. Kirchgessner knew Moon boss Rob "Bucket" Hingley from back in his days working for the campus radio station at Michigan State. He once visited New York City for the CMJ Music Marathon and made a trip to Moon headquarters, a place he imagined would be a giant warehouse but was actually Bucket's tiny apartment.

The type of deal Moon offered bands was perfect for Mustard Plug. They'd get the benefit of Moon's national distribution, and if they wanted to take the record elsewhere later on, they'd be free to do so. Plus, there was also the legitimacy that came with being on Moon, which was to ska in 1994 what Sup Pop was to indie. "At that point, if you were a ska fan, you pretty much picked up anything Moon would put out," Kirchgessner says.

You could tell *Big Daddy Multitude* was going to be worth your $10 just by looking at the cover, a close-up photo of a dude's face completely covered in mustard. Because nearly every track is a novelty song, nearly every one stands out. Opener "Skank by Numbers" is a handy four-step guide to enjoying yourself at a ska show. "Ball Park Skank" is "Casey at the Bat" told in ska form, with a happier ending. "I Made Love to a Martian" is about making love to a Martian. Best of all is "Mr. Smiley," the chilling tale of a seemingly normal dude who snaps and murders his family. Clive made the story up, basing the homicidal character on the creepy old man in *Home Alone*.

Big Daddy Multitude arrived before Reel Big Fish, Less Than Jake, or Slapstick released debut albums. Mustard Plug were innovators, though fans who got into ska later might not have recognized them as such. "If you listen to us in the context of what was going on in '97, we didn't sound that pioneering," says Kirchgessner. "But if you listened to us in the context of like '92, it was kind of out there."

With ska gaining traction across the country, Mustard Plug toured nationally behind *Big Daddy Multitude* and banked some money to fund their next album. They recorded at the Blasting Room, the Colorado studio founded in 1994 by Bill Stevenson and Stephen Egerton of the enduring L.A. pop-punk band Descendents. During their 10 days in Colorado,

Mustard Plug learned of an imminent Descendents reunion, and in October 1996, when Descendents headlined a week of shows at the Whisky a Go Go in Los Angeles, Mustard Plug were tapped to open one of the nights. Several label scouts turned up, and the group signed with the SoCal punk label Hopeless Records for their just-finished album.

That album, *Evildoers Beware!*, is Mustard Plug's high-water mark, a far more focused and mature album than the previous two. "Some of it's growing up, and some of it's taking yourself a little bit more seriously, whether that's good or bad," Kirchgessner says. Opener "Box" looks at the ways people wall themselves off from the world. "Suburban Homesick Blues" veers again toward social commentary, as Kirchgessner pities an old friend who's settled down and chosen a life of conformity. The album closes with perhaps Mustard Plug's greatest and best-known tune, "Beer (Song)," a scream-along anthem whose "Don't let 'em take it away!" chorus lets you insert your own "it" every time. "It's not so much about beer," Kirchgessner admits. "The theme is more staying up through adversity, that sort of thing."

Evildoers racked up six-figure sales and became Hopeless's biggest record to date. Mustard Plug hit the road hard, playing 161 shows in 1997 and 121 in 1998, the year of "The Freshman." Some of those '98 gigs were part of the Ska Against Racism Tour, which Kirchgessner considers a massive success, despite criticism it was mostly white kids turning up. "That's one of the disappointing things about the way the ska scene evolved in the late '90s: It became primarily white bands playing to white audiences, which is really different than the ska that I grew up on and loved, the 2 Tone stuff," he says. "I don't think the ska scene has ever been less than open to other people of different sexes and genders and races. I think it's more a reflection on American society in general." As for charges the tour was "preaching to the choir," Kirchgessner argues that sending an anti-racist message to white dudes in their early 20s was extremely worthwhile. "I wish it was more diverse, but I guess that's the whole point of it," he says. "You've got to start somewhere."

MUSTARD PLUG

P.O. Box 1440
Grand Rapids, MI 49501
Booking:Dave
(616) 774-7152

FIG.8 "This is your brain on ska!" Mustard Plug, 1993.
Photo: Amy Young.

Mustard Plug managed one more album before the close of the decade, 1999's *Pray for Mojo*. It was another exercise in *Evildoers*-style semi-seriousness, and this time there was even a political song, "Throw a Bomb," about how misguided losers become weapons of mass destruction. The message is pretty obvious—violence is bad—but the band purposely omitted the song when performing in Oklahoma and Hiroshima, places still traumatized by bombings. Japan was one of 12 countries Mustard Plug visited in 1999, even as ska's popularity took a nosedive and *Mojo* sold only half of what *Evildoers* had.

"During the '90s, the media was trained to go from one fad to the next," Kirchgessner says. "It started with grunge. Then punk, and Green Day is the next big thing. Then, all of a sudden, ska is the next big thing. Then it was, 'Well, we decided it's going to be swing revival.'"

As ska bands nationwide fired their horn sections, got funny haircuts, and transitioned to emo, Mustard Plug stayed the course. Maybe they were saved by their modest Midwestern values. They never wanted to be superstars, so when that option was off the table for ska bands, they never thought of chucking their trombone. "I would question, a lot of the bands that moved from ska to emo, how much they really liked ska in the first place," Kirchgessner says.

Mustard Plug have released three twenty-first-century albums that range in spiciness from honey (2002's *Yellow #5*) to yellow (2007's *In Black and White*) to Dijon (2014's *Can't Contain It*). They gradually decreased their touring but played no fewer than 33 shows in any year from 2000 to 2019. The band members have families and full-time jobs but also enough fans in America and in places like Australia and Japan to warrant booking short tours when everyone's schedule allows. "People have accepted that they're not going to make money off the band—that helps a lot," says Kirchgessner. "If you're not in the band for the money, you're in it for fun. So, as long as it's fun, you keep going."

CHAPTER 7

Old's Cool

Not every American ska band in the '90s tested positive for mutant punk genes. Some were staffed by musicians who started with 2 Tone and traced the music back to Jamaica. Existing mainly on the coasts, these new traditionalists faced a difficult challenge: playing authentic '60s ska while maintaining honesty and originality.

Trad bands paid attention to fashion and tended to draw members and fans from ska's three main affiliate subcultures: mod, rude boy, and skinhead. Less outwardly aggressive than distortion-loving ska-punk outfits, old-school ska groups had their own built-in, understated toughness. Their grooves had stood the test of time, and they wouldn't be swayed by fads.

■ ■ ■

It was 1986, and the 321 Club in Santa Monica was jammed full of Fishbone fanatics. Singer and saxophonist Angelo Moore took the stage and started the show by blowing the foghorn-like opening notes of "Ugly." The crowd swayed, and a local teenager named Greg Lee was literally lifted off his feet. "I was kind of freaking out, because I didn't know what was going to happen," Lee recalls. "Then the song broke in, and everybody went nuts. I was like, 'This is what I'm doing from now on.'"

Lee did devote his life to ska—just not the kind that might cause bodily harm. A few years later, in 1989, he and some buddies formed Hepcat, a band interested in preserving the proud island grooves of the Skatalites, the Wailers, Desmond Dekker, the Paragons, and other ska, rocksteady, and reggae masters of the '60s and '70s. Throughout the '90s, on albums like their 1997 instant classic *Right on Time*, Hepcat were a refreshing antidote to every hybrid band treating ska like a novelty. Boasting two charismatic Black lead singers—Lee and Alex Désert, who'd perform synchronized dance moves when not harmonizing on the breeziest melodies the third wave ever carried in—Hepcat were, in a word, cool. This was no easy feat for a '90s ska band.

Hepcat's aesthetic revealed a deep appreciation for and understanding of Jamaican music. Lee's sister gave him a copy of the mega-selling Bob Marley hits package *Legend* when he was in middle school, but his first exposure came much earlier. He was born in Huntsville, Alabama, about 90 minutes from Sheffield, where his father worked as a producer and engineer at the famed Muscle Shoals Sound Studio. "My dad was always having things to do with music," says Lee. "Quite a few of the artists were Jamaican. Whenever they would play, I thought it sounded like circus music, so I fell in love with it."

When he was three months old, Lee moved with his mother to Los Angeles. That's where he'd absorb *Legend* in his formative years in the mid-'80s and begin to follow breadcrumbs from Marley to other essential artists. "When you find reggae, little by little, you piece the puzzle together," Lee says. "You do long drives to reggae festivals and clubs and restaurants with reggae bands that you're not old enough to get into, but you stand outside. I kept bumping into people dressed in black and white and ties and parkas and riding scooters."

Through these SoCal mods and rudies, Lee found 2 Tone, Fishbone, and the Untouchables. He was so into the scene that he convinced his guidance counselor at Granada Hills High to let him transfer to nearby John F. Kennedy High School. Lee said it was so he could participate in their outstanding ROTC program, but that was bogus. "There was, like, rude boys and mods and punks, and they had dances every Thursday in the middle of the school with DJs," Lee says. "It was a totally happening school."

At JFK, Lee met Deston Berry, who would become Hepcat's founding keyboard player. The first band they started together was called the Sharpeville Six, named for six South African protestors sentenced to death for the murder of a deputy mayor. The Sharpeville Six played in the punky 2 Tone style that Lee was growing tired of. Increasingly, when he'd go see bands like No Doubt and the Donkey Show, he only cared about the DJs spinning traditional ska in between sets. That gave Lee the idea for his next band. "I wanted stuff that people could dance to with their girlfriend," he says. "They'd want to dress up nice and come to a show and know that it'd be safe enough they could actually dance."

The drumming in such a band is key, and Lee took a gamble on Greg Narvas, a Filipino American skinhead he'd seen play in a local oi! band. And then there was Désert, whom Lee met at a Toots and the Maytals show at the Hollywood Palladium. Désert had grown up in New York City and graduated from the School of the Performing Arts, aka the *Fame* school. He moved to L.A. to pursue acting and wound up scoring roles in films like *Swingers* and *High Fidelity* and TV series like *Boy Meets World* and *Becker*.

Also in the fold were bassist Joey "Pepe" Urquijo, alto saxophonist Raul Talavera, and guitarist Lino Trujillo. The band's original ambition was to play one backyard show at their friend Rami's house. It would be just like early No Doubt gigs, when the DJs spun old-school goodness in between sets, only this time, *they* would be the ones providing the vintage Jamaican bounce. They rehearsed five songs, one of which might've been "Earthquake and Fire," the finest track they would record for their debut album a few years later. Driven by a bittersweet horn line and soulful melody, "Earthquake and Fire" is sexy and mature and very impressive for a teen ska band. "That song helped us realize that we could write a song that sounds like what we want," says Lee. "We've been on the trip to perfect it ever since."

Although the bulk of the group was still in high school, Hepcat began playing hip L.A. clubs like the King King, the converted Chinese restaurant on La Brea that served as clubhouse for neo-swing originators Royal Crown Revue and Jump With Joey, peerless sonic mixologists who stirred up their Jamaica ska with Latin music and jazz. The first time Hepcat met Jump With Joey, bassist and bandleader Joey Altruda offered to produce the band's debut single for his Laughing Pussy label. The result was a charming 1990 7-inch whose up-tempo A-side, "Nigel," gives Désert plenty of opportunity to try his faux-Jamaican accent.

Lee remembers Hepcat's King King days as "magic," even though he and his bandmates were too young to be allowed inside. "We'd hang out in the alley singing a cappella and set up the drum kit," Lee says. "We'd be out there for hours waiting, and some guy would open the door, 'OK, you guys. You're on in five minutes.' Then we'd play and they wouldn't pay us anything and they'd treat us like shit. But we were stoked. In the audience was Joe Strummer, Boy George, Dan Aykroyd, Kenny Loggins. Everybody was at this club."

Around the same time Lee and his friends were trading 2 Tone for trad, Dave Hillyard, saxophonist for the Donkey Show, found himself similarly disillusioned with modern ska. Hillyard quit the group, went back to school at UCLA, and hung up fliers seeking musicians interested in starting a group influenced by ska, reggae, and jazz. The only person who responded was Hepcat bassist Urquijo, and soon Hillyard was in the band.

For as much as Hepcat studied their Skatalites, they were never going to play exactly like their heroes. They weren't as good, for one thing, and they weren't Jamaican jazz cats inventing new sounds as their nation gained independence. Even if they weren't tainting their ska with slap bass and metal guitars, Hepcat were SoCal kids. "Ska was doing its magic again. It was hybridizing. Mixing," Hillyard writes in the "Story of U.S. Ska" series he posted on his MySpace blog in 2008. (It was later republished with permission on the website Lawless Street.) "This time we were adding Latin touches. Swing. Jump blues. Jazz. The early '90s was a big time for lounges and lounge music in L.A., so we probably picked up on that too."

Hillyard eventually moved to New York City to be with his girlfriend. Although the relationship didn't last, he ended up joining the Slackers, a wannabee 2 Tone crew he'd help transform into one of the finest ska outfits of all time, so it wasn't a total loss. He stuck around in Hepcat just long enough to play on the band's 1993 debut, *Out of Nowhere*, released on Moon Ska, the label run by Rob "Bucket" Hingley of the Toasters. The deal was brokered by Hepcat's manager, Elyse Rogers of Dance Hall Crashers, who were also on Moon. "We were stoked," Lee says. "We weren't all big fans of the Toasters, but we'd been to a few Toasters shows. To be the first band on that label doing what we were doing was kind of a big deal."

Out of Nowhere is among the freshest and most joyful ska debuts of the decade. Lee and Désert fall effortlessly into the roles of amiable lovermen as the rhythm section glides from ska to reggae to rocksteady, with a dash of swinging Latin jazz on "Skavez." The album opens, fittingly, with "Dance wid' Me," Hepcat's invitation to a scene that'd spent too long in the mosh pit.

Ironically, dancing to Hepcat would prove difficult for fans in some parts of the country. While touring the Midwest with Dance Hall Crashers in 1994, Hepcat were offended by the fans who would stand like statues during their performances. Lee famously declared "Fuck the Midwest!" in a radio interview, which prompted the DJ to explain something: people weren't dancing to Hepcat's '60s ska because they didn't know how. Lee and Désert rectified this by choreographing dance moves for the edification of their audiences.

As they honed their stage act, Hepcat were also gaining strength in the songwriting department. That was reflected in the title of their next album, 1996's *Scientific*. "We spent Saturdays and Sundays all day at my house working out these songs, and they just kept coming together," Lee says.

FIG.9 Alex Désert and Greg Lee put on a dance clinic at the New England Ska Festival in Westford, Massachusetts, August 22, 1998. Photo: Bryan Kremkau /SkaPunkPhotos.com.

"Mixing the red beaker with the blue beaker, and it became green. Suddenly it's like, 'Eureka, we did this.' Every day, there were like 12 eurekas."

Scientific arrived on BYO, the SoCal punk label run by Shawn and Mark Stern of Youth Brigade. By this time, Dance Hall Crashers had split from Moon, but Lee says that wasn't the reason Hepcat decided to change labels. "[BYO] are local heroes as far as the punk scene goes," says Lee. "We all looked up to those little guys for a long time. When they approached us, it was like, once again, we get to be the first band [doing our style of music] on this label that's established itself. It will allow us to do our music. Sure."

BYO's "do your thing" attitude was just what Hepcat needed at the time. The group stretches out on *Scientific*, using the 16 tracks to bounce from exuberant ska ("Bobby & Joe") to mellow reggae ("Black Sky") to Jump With Joey–style loungy exoti-ska ("Solo"). "Dollar Dance," a terrific instrumental penned by guitarist Trujillo, gives the band's new horn players, tenor saxophonist Efren Santana and trumpeter Kincaid Smith, space to show their stuff. The music is jazzy yet friendly and begging to be heard by a larger audience.

Enter Tim Armstrong and Epitaph Records founder Brett Gurewitz, who approached Hepcat in 1997 about joining the newly formed Hellcat label. According to Lee, Gurewitz didn't just see Hepcat as another potential signing. He sealed the deal by explaining Hepcat's place in his grand vision for Hellcat. "Epitaph was like, 'We want to make a music category at every record store. It's not ska. It's not world music. It's something else. We've got to come up with that name, and we want you guys to be the first band in it,'" Lee says.

Whatever this new category was going to be called, it would comprise old-school ska and street punk, the main styles heard on Hellcat's widely distributed 1997 label sampler *Give 'Em the Boot*. Hepcat are represented on the CD with "I Can't Wait," the tastiest track off their 1997 Hellcat debut, *Right on Time*. Lee originated the song himself but struggled to finish the progression. "The guys in the band were like, 'Dude, I don't know about this song.'" That's when Lee phoned Chris Murray, a Canadian ska vet who'd played in the popular '90s band King Apparatus before going solo with 1996's lovely acoustic LP *The 4-Track Adventures of Venice Shoreline Chris*. The two finished the song in 15 minutes, and when Lee showed it to the band, they flipped. "Then the writing on a different level began," says Lee. "I think they realized they had to listen to me in a different way when I was trying to lead them through the creation of a song."

Hepcat weren't just writing better songs. They were feeling a new sense of confidence since Gurewitz started landing them gigs with artists like the Allman Brothers, Taj Mahal, and Prince. "At the time, there was not a whole lot of crossover like that, particularly with ska bands," Lee says.

"We owe that to Tim and Brett and Elyse for putting us out in front of these people. When we did a couple of these things, we would look back at Dance Hall Crashers and think to ourselves, 'They couldn't have done that.' We'd look at Bad Religion and think, 'They couldn't have done what we just did. We just did it and came out with flying colors. Everybody's walking away with a T-shirt. People are trying to figure out where we're going to play next.' It was a big deal."

Along with stronger songs and skyrocketing confidence, Hepcat had the perfect producer for *Right on Time*: Andy "Stoker" Growcott, who played drums in Dexys Midnight Runners and the English Beat offshoot General Public. Lee told Stoker he wanted the booming pop-reggae sound of Culture Club's "Do You Really Want to Hurt Me," and the Englishman delivered in a big way. "I Can't Wait" was intoxicating enough for Heineken to license the song for a commercial, and it's not even the most likable track on the album. That would be "No Worries," which makes "Hakuna Matata" from *The Lion King* sound like a murder ballad.

When neither "I Can't Wait" nor "No Worries" blew up on radio or MTV, Lee couldn't have cared less. "We'd hear these guys get on the radio, and we really didn't like them anyway," Lee says of the day's major-label ska acts. "We're all really good friends now. But at the time, they were on the other side of the world playing ska, to us. Even Reel Big Fish from Orange County, when somebody would suggest we play together, we were like, 'Yeah, not so much. We're not into slapstick and humor. We're into having fun and bringing a certain level of class and seriousness to what we're doing. I don't think we really mesh.'"

One thing that did earn Hepcat news coverage on MTV.com was the East Coast versus West Coast ska battle instigated by "Open Season . . . Is Closed," the final song on *Right on Time*. It's an answer to the title track off the Stubborn All-Stars' 1995 album *Open Season*, in which Jeff "King Django" Baker declares himself the greatest ska DJ, or toaster, and challenges anyone to prove him wrong. "Open Season . . . Is Closed" was

Désert's idea—he's the one on the mic calling Django a "braggadocio dingo from the East Coast." Django quickly fired back with "Hepcat Season," and while the whole thing was supposedly in good fun, it quickly turned into a headache for Lee. That's because not long after *Right on Time* came out, Désert left the band to focus on the sitcom *Becker*.

"It put me in the unenviable position of having to answer for that all the time," says Lee. "We'd go to the East Coast, and it's like, 'Oh my god, this fricking Django thing again.' Then Django got a little huffy there for a minute. I'm like, 'Dude, you need to slow yourself down. Talk to Alex.' It didn't get to the point of fighting or anything. It was just tedious and droll. It's like, 'Dude, why are we doing this? Just play your music. We'll play ours.'"

With Désert out of the picture, Lee became sole front man for the band's next album, 2000's slower and moodier *Push 'N Shove*. It was a slog to make, as Lee had never dreamed of being a lead singer. "That changed the whole scope of what Hepcat was doing," he says. "Hepcat was made to be lovers rock and ska, strong in the harmonies, but with full character up front. It's not meant to be a single rock star band." There were eight songs intended for the album that Lee simply couldn't muster the will to sing.

At the same time, the band had added a couple of new players who thought Hepcat were the next No Doubt and started acting like prima donnas. Lee refuses to name the musicians but says their expectations about where Hepcat were headed created "a huge miscommunication" regarding the band's mission. "That miscommunication nearly led to the ending of Hepcat," he says.

Hepcat essentially broke up in 2000, as Lee moved to Costa Rica and everyone else focused on other projects. Hepcat might've stayed dormant, Lee says, if not for the damn Internet. "Once the Internet popped up, [the others] were getting messages to me in my little plot of land in the middle of nowhere: 'Dude, they're asking us to play this show and asking us to play that show. Would you be down to fly back to L.A.?' I'd be like, 'Fly back to L.A.? I live in the fricking jungle. Why would I ever do that?'"

But Lee did start flying back, and Hepcat resumed sporadic touring in 2003, with Désert once again joining Lee up front. As of 2019, Lee estimates the group has three albums of material saved up, though they've yet to finish the follow-up *Push 'N Shove*. If and when an album emerges, it might come out on Hellcat—or it might not. "They want us to go with them and make a record, but they also understand that the times have changed," Lee says. "We could easily go somewhere else and do it. We could easily release a whole bunch of singles. They leave it wide open. I appreciate that."

Lee's main concern is the same as it's always been: making good music. From time to time, his friends in the Slackers ask him when the new album is coming. "Alex put it best: 'We prefer quality over quantity,'" Lee says. "It might have been taken as a slight on [the Slackers], but it isn't a slight. I think their records are good.

"I just want to focus on making the perfect cake. I don't want to kick out a bunch of cakes that nobody likes. Or that some people like and other people just stay away from altogether. Every time something comes out, I want it to be a special thing."

■ ■ ■

Vic Ruggiero started wearing porkpies when he was 10. The Bronx native with the accent to match grew up digging Motown, doo-wop, and Humphrey Bogart, and he liked hanging out with his grandfather. Everywhere he looked, his male role models rocked stumpy-brimmed hats, so why shouldn't he? "My dad made fun of me about it," says Ruggiero. "He'd be like, 'What are you, 60 years old over here? Put on a baseball cap.'"

Fans of the Slackers, the New York City ska band Ruggiero has fronted since 1991, will have no trouble picturing these father-son exchanges. Ruggiero is the resident old soul of third-wave ska. As far back as 1996's *Better Late Than Never*, a teaser of a debut that only hints at the musical complexity and depth of feeling the Slackers would achieve on later albums, Ruggiero croons like a wounded nighthawk with a rumpled suit and fistful of wilting flowers. He's your classic troubadour, the closest ska's ever had to a Bob Dylan, Tom Waits, or Leonard Cohen. Once the Slackers found the right personnel to create what they call "Jamaican rock 'n' roll"—a '60s-centric sound rooted in Kingston but not stuck there—they made two of the finest ska albums of the '90s or any other decade: 1997's *Redlight* and 1998's *The Question*. They're timeless, grown-up albums that transcend the label "'90s ska."

It took awhile for the Slackers to get there. When Ruggiero assembled the group in the early '90s, he was a psychology major at New York University whose musical influences had jumped from punk rock to 2 Tone when he discovered the Specials in high school. For this rebellious and progressive son of a police officer, politics were central to ska's appeal. "I felt like, 'Great, it's not this vapid scene that's not talking about anything that matters,'" Ruggiero says. "You could get out there and say some real shit."

In the earliest incarnation of the Slackers—referred to in hindsight as the Nods, though they were always billed as the Slackers—Ruggiero played guitar and did his best to mimic his 2 Tone heroes. The Nods made caustic, choppy, horn-free ska with a strong political bent. The lineup included bassist Marcus Geard, who'd played in Sic and Mad, a punk group Ruggiero founded with his buddy Happy in the late '80s. On drums was Luis Zuluaga, who'd rocked with Ruggiero in another short-lived group called the Raybees. The trio became a five-piece as Geard brought in guitarist T. J. Scanlon and Ruggiero enlisted Marc "Q-Maxx 420" Lyn, a singer and toaster he worked with at a gourmet Manhattan deli.

The Nods symbolically became the Slackers a couple years later with the addition of Jeremy "Mush One" Mushlin on trumpet and Dave Hillyard on saxophone. After stints with the Donkey Show and Hepcat, Hillyard moved to New York City in 1992 to be with his girlfriend. One day, that girlfriend happened to strike up a conversation with Ruggiero's old buddy Happy in Tompkins Square Park. Happy invited Hillyard to attend a Slackers rehearsal, and voilà, Dave was in the band. Hillyard and Mushlin introduced Ruggiero and his crew to improvisational jazz and dub reggae, respectively. The old Nods songs began disappearing from the set.

"In the '90s, the aesthetic of bands was to be every band in one," Ruggiero says. "As many influences as you could possibly list on your band description, the better. You couldn't just be a rock 'n' roll band. You had to be rock 'n' roll / funk / New Wave / jazz / new jazz / bebop / experimental. It gave you more bang for the buck. I was like, 'Great, now the Slackers can also play instrumentals; we take jazz solos.' We didn't know how to play for shit back then, but it was an option."

One band in New York City with a similar appreciation for '60s ska and jazz was the Scofflaws. Ruggiero was impressed by their suave, suited-up look, which reminded him of *The Blues Brothers*, a big influence on his personal style. Scofflaws bassist Victor Rice wound up producing *Better Late Than Never*, released on Moon Ska Records. The album collects the first batch of songs Ruggiero wrote for the new and groovier Slackers. He'd recently broken up with his high school girlfriend, Sarah, and for the first time, the rabble-rousing ex-punk found himself writing love songs.

The most notable, "Sarah," is among the saddest and greatest ska songs of the '90s. Ruggiero had moved over to keyboards as part of the band reorganization, and he opens the song with some bittersweet jazz piano. Then comes this ice pick of an opening line: "Mother says 'You turn my food to poison' / To my father on a cold Thanksgiving Day." From there, as Mushlin riffs on the mournful trumpet hook and the band vamps along like after-hours lounge cats, Ruggiero describes losing the only girl in the whole miserable world who made him feel OK. By the end of the song, he's reduced to muttering, "Oh Lord, I had such plans for us."

"I learned somewhere along the line that people would tell if you were full of shit," says Ruggiero. "So you might as well just go through all the gory details and see if it works." Vic and Sarah wound up becoming close friends. She still turns up at the occasional Slackers shows, telling people "I'm *the* Sarah."

Better Late Than Never also showcases Ruggiero's sense of humor in the form of "Pedophilia," a rousing ska song that's become the band's perennial concert closer. "Well, mama, some old man's looking at your baby / And your baby, she's looking good," Ruggiero sings, working his wily charms even while coming off like a total sketchball. "When you're a young guy, you can make jokes that you can't make as an old guy," Ruggiero says. "We couldn't release a song called 'Pedophilia' at 50 years old. That was [about] the irony of meeting some girl's mother and feeling gross."

Around the time of *Better Late Than Never*, the Slackers became friendly with the Skatalites. "They were really sweet," Ruggiero says. "They were that kind of band that would take young guys under their wing if they felt like we were fans and trying to do the thing." That's how the Slackers got Skatalites vocalist Doreen Shaffer to sing on the album's penultimate track, a cover of the '60s R&B chestnut "Our Day Will Come." Shortly before the recording session, Ruggiero spoke to the Jamaican legend on the phone and asked what key she felt most comfortable singing in. She said "D," but Ruggiero heard "G," so that's the key the band used to record the backing track.

"We're playing in the key that's a fifth away from where her key is, so she sang it really strange," Ruggiero says. "I think she was annoyed with us for doing that. She was like, 'Oh man, I couldn't even sing it right. I wanted to sing with you guys.'" Shaffer's performance is nevertheless brilliant, and the slight reaching you hear in her delivery suits the song's yearning lyrics. "Vic Rice was like, 'I think it's even better in a way, because you guys have Doreen singing in a way that she doesn't sing normally. You got another voice out of Doreen,'" Ruggiero says. "I think she's such a good singer that she can do absolutely anything."

Better Late Than Never features trombone from Jeff "King Django" Baker, a longtime musical associate of Ruggiero's (and bandmate in the side project Stubborn All-Stars) who arranged an interesting musical adventure for the summer of 1996. Django had played with Rancid, who needed ska musicians to accompany them on 1996's Lollapalooza Tour. Django suggested they hire Ruggiero and Hillyard, and the three NYC ska luminaries spent the summer touring America with Soundgarden, Devo, the Ramones, and Metallica. As a newcomer to the music industry, Ruggiero found it fascinating to talk shop with these veterans. He discovered that many were more complex than their public personas suggested. This was especially true of Rancid singer and guitarist Tim Armstrong, a grizzled punk lifer with a spider web tattoo atop his noggin.

"He's very thoughtful," says Ruggiero. "If he's intimidating, it's more because of his musical knowledge and the breadth of his capability." Ruggiero struck up a friendship and songwriting partnership with Armstrong and co-authored three songs for Rancid's sprawling 1998 triumph *Life Won't Wait*. He and Armstrong also recorded a whole album under the name the Silencers. The idea for the LP—which has never been released—was to have different singers, including Armstrong's then wife, Brody Dalle, hop on tracks laid down by an all-star band including Ruggiero, Armstrong, Hillyard, and Vandals drummer Josh Freese. That the album has never surfaced is one of the "biggest frustrations" of Ruggiero's career. "I haven't heard [the recordings] in 20 years, but in my memory, they're some of the best things that I ever played on," Ruggiero says.

The Slackers were among the first bands signed to Hellcat Records, the Epitaph imprint founded by Armstrong in 1997. Joining Hellcat meant leaving Moon Ska, and it was not an amicable split. The band felt Moon had given them a lousy deal, and what's more, they believed the label was losing credibility after some less-than-stellar releases. It was time to move on, and hotly tipped Hellcat seemed like the perfect move.

With the band another year tighter and Ruggiero's songwriting improving seemingly by the day, the Slackers returned to Coyote Studios in Brooklyn, where they'd recorded *Better Late Than Never*, and made

Redlight, a stunning improvement on all fronts. The album opens strong with the steaming-hot ska instrumental "Cooking for Tommy," a tribute to Skatalites saxophonist Tommy McCook. It's one of two Hillyard compositions on the record, the other being "I Still Love You," a clever faux-breakup song aimed at America and its false promises. (This would become a common device in the Slackers catalog—any song you think is about a girl is probably about the government.)

Ruggiero penned another all-time classic in "Married Girl," a fusion of ska and Latin boogaloo with film-noir lyrics about adultery and murder. Another standout, the twinkling reggae jam "Rude and Reckless," opens with Ruggiero relaying some words of wisdom from his straitlaced policeman father: "Do as you must." It's a phrase that surfaces in at least two other songs Vic's written over the years, so it clearly made an impression. "He often gave lectures that came straight out of Catholic school," says Ruggiero of his old man. "They would say, 'God, country, and family.' And that's the order it came in. If ['do as you must'] wasn't a phrase he used all the time, it was definitely a theme: 'Hey, you're not supposed to do what you *want* or what you *like*. You do what you must do.' Otherwise, you're a schmuck—that was the next half of the conversation."

The Slackers toured for nearly a year behind *Redlight* and returned to the studio ready to push things forward again. In the interim, they'd picked up Glen Pine, a terrific trombonist, singer, and songwriter whose big strapping voice contrasted nicely with Ruggiero's Bronx rasp. It all came to fruition on *The Question*, 19 tracks of old-school ska, rocksteady, reggae, and dub informed by soul, jazz, '50s rock 'n' roll, boogaloo, and more. *The Question* is one hour and eight minutes in a murky underground world where everything's going to hell but a killer band is onstage singing your pain. There's a ripping instrumental ("Motor City"), a calypso-ska showstopper (Pine's "Mountainside"), and moments of profundity to ponder after you've finished dancing ("Knowing" and "Have the Time"). "*The Question* was really us," says Ruggiero. "It was like we found our voice."

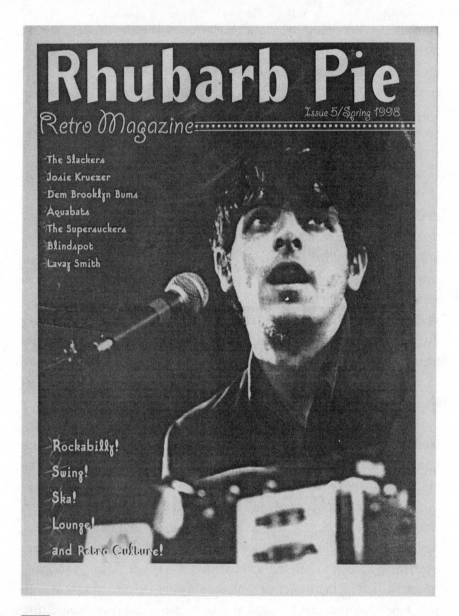

Vic Ruggiero on the cover of the California ska/
swing zine *Rhubarb Pie*, 1998. Photo: Teague Schneiter.
Courtesy of Jes Reiter and Katie Ioffe.

Redlight and *The Question* arrived during the peak years for ska's mainstream popularity and sounded nothing like the records getting love on MTV and alternative radio. "People talk about these days as being the great days of the ska or whatever," says Ruggiero. "We were out on the road. We were busy. We were getting our sound together." The Slackers were friends with the Pietasters and MU330 and a few other bands, but by and large they had no idea what was going on with the ska-punk explosion. "We didn't want to play that music," says Ruggiero. "It wasn't for spite or anything. It just wasn't attractive. We felt like it didn't suit us."

Three years would pass before the Slackers' next album, 2001's *Wasted Days*, a kind of darker sequel to *The Question*. Two years later, in the aftermath of 9/11, they returned with the meditative *Close My Eyes*, the only type of album that would've made sense at the time. By the end of the decade, the lineup had been whittled down to Ruggiero, Geard, Hillyard, Pine, guitarist Jay Nugent, and drummer Ara Babajian. The sextet continues releasing worthy albums and, more importantly, touring the world. For as great as the Slackers are on record, their enduring legacy is that of a live band that moves bodies across continents, year after year. It was after ska's boom that the Slackers found their loyal audience, and Ruggiero says it's not ska kids coming to the shows anymore.

"Their friends might've been the ska kids, or their kids might've been the ska kids," Ruggiero says. "We've got people's parents that stuck with us over the years, that are like, 'I dropped my kids off at a show, and I came back, and you guys were playing, and I thought, man, this band's great.' So now we got some 70-year-old lady that still comes to the shows, because she's like, 'This is great.' You know?"

■ ■ ■

Around the time he made *Open Season*, the excellent 1995 debut album by his supposed side project Stubborn All-Stars, Jeff "King Django" Baker had some frustrating conversations with a would-be manager. Stubborn All-Stars were signed to Profile Records, best known for breaking Run-DMC,

FIG.II Slackers horn players Glen Pine (trombone) and Dave Hillyard (saxophone) are truly one with the people. Photo: Imelda Michalczyk.

and the label was trying to hook Django up with a manager who worked with emo bands. "They were trying to push us in that Reel Big Fish direction," says Django. "They were taking me to see all the ska bands that were around at that time. All the California bands and stuff. And I was trying to explain to them, 'Yeah, this isn't . . . It's got the same name, but it's not the same music. Don't you guys notice?'"

All through the '90s, as leader of two bands—Skinnerbox and Stubborn All-Stars—and head of Stubborn Records, Django repped hard for the real stuff: Jamaican ska, rocksteady, reggae, dub, and dancehall. The streetwise Brooklyn native was a purist who proved you could make modern-sounding music without completely forsaking a genre's core elements. He even recorded a klezmer-ska album in honor of his Jewish heritage.

As a prolific singer, songwriter, DJ, producer, studio owner, and label boss, Django positioned himself at the center of a mini-universe of great music. If there were a Mount Rushmore of '90s NYC ska—a public works project *clearly* deserving of taxpayer dollars—he'd be up there with Bucket, Vic Ruggiero, and maybe Victor Rice of the Scofflaws or Coolie Ranx of the Toasters and Pilfers.

Although he would become associated with authentic Jamaican music, Django discovered ska like everyone of his generation: via 2 Tone. A friend took him to Bleecker Bob's record store in Greenwich Village in 1979 and pointed him toward "The Prince," the just-released debut single by Madness. Django spent the next couple of years absorbing everything 2 Tone and doing his homework on the music's roots. In his mid-teens, he discovered NYC reggae radio and began frequenting Jamaican record shops deep in the heart of Brooklyn.

While attending Hunter College High School on the Upper East Side of Manhattan, Django began DJing—as in toasting over beats—at parties. He'd rhyme on reggae backing tracks spun by DJ pal Marvin Young, soon to be known to the world as Young MC, the rapper behind the 1989 smash "Bust a Move."

Django started NYC's first ska zine, *Rude Awakening*, in 1984 and interviewed artists like Rob "Bucket" Hingley, who would become a mentor. "I was a high school kid," says Django. "He was a grown man with a job and his own apartment and his own band. Whenever I had questions or anything, he was always very forthcoming and very helpful."

The next step was for Django to start making music. In his first year at the University of Massachusetts at Amherst, he co-founded Too True, a band that recorded just one song, "Free South Africa," which appears on Moon's 1986 compilation *N.Y. Beat! Hit & Run*. Django had begun teaching himself trombone, and after graduating and moving back to the city, he joined the NYC reggae and ska band the Boilers. This gave him an opportunity to write songs, a craft he learned by messing around with a piano and figuring out how to fit chords with melodies.

In late 1988, as the Boilers were falling apart, Django founded Skinnerbox, his primary band—though not his most famous—for the next decade. His original idea was to play "jump blues, Jamaican boogie, traditional ska, and dub reggae." But the lineup he put together included musically advanced and adventurous guys like Brandt Abner, a keyboardist with a scholarship to the New School. *Special Wild*, a collection of Skinnerbox output from 1989 to 1994, presents a band skilled in nervy 2 Tone ska ("Addiction"), Sly Stone–esque soul-funk ("Right Side"), and loungy jazz ("Danny's Duelin'"), among other styles. Eclecticism wasn't the reason Skinnerbox remained largely a New York phenomenon, though. It's because they literally remained in New York, favoring local gigs over touring. When Django finally decided he wanted to take the show on the road after the release of 1997's terrific *What You Can Do, What You Can Not*, his bandmates were resistant, and Skinnerbox split up.

Years earlier, before releasing their 1993 debut, *Tales of the Red*, Skinnerbox were being courted by a label that was making all kinds of promises. "Nothing was really happening—it was just a lot of smoke getting blown up our ass," says Django. "It kept dragging on and dragging on, and we were just like, 'You know what? Screw it. Let's just do this ourselves.'" And so Django founded Stubborn Records, a label that would specialize in new bands doing traditional Jamaican music. It was a natural move for Django, who idolized Coxsone Dodd and Prince Buster, Jamaican producers who also ran their own labels.

In 1994, Stubborn released *Old's Cool*, a four-song EP by a new outfit called Stubborn All-Stars. Assembled by Django, it was a murderers' row of NYC ska heavies, including Victor Rice, Insteps drummer Eddie Ocampo, and Vic Ruggiero, aka Sir Lord Sluggo. The record opens with a gorgeous Django-penned love song, "Rise to Find You," followed by a couple of novelties. "Judge Knotte," a takeoff on Prince Buster's "Judge Dread," stars saxophonist El Wood as the title character, a tough-but-fair magistrate presiding over the "International Court of Subculture." Judge Knotte orders a bandwagon-jumping wannabe rude boy to learn his ska history by listening exclusively to the Skatalites and Prince Buster. He hands down a tougher sentence to a racist, homophobic skinhead, sending him off to a hippie commune to learn bead-making.

Old's Cool also features "Open Season," Django's most infamous track. "This is an invitation to all self-proclaimed ska dons," he says as the start of the song, a five-minute boast-fest dedicated to his lyrical prowess. It's Brooklyn street-kid bluster filtered through a deep appreciation of Jamaican DJ culture. The idea was to provoke answer records, and within a few years, Django got his wish.

Two weeks after *Old's Cool* dropped, Django received a call from Profile Records. Just like that, Stubborn All-Stars were signed to the massive indie label's rock subsidiary, Another Planet. Django drafted even more heavyweights to play on 1995's *Open Season*, a '60s ska album that could've only been made in the '90s. Guests include original Skatalites tenor saxophonist Roland Alphonso, Fishbone keyboardist Chris Dowd, and even Bucket. Dave Hillyard shows up on four songs, and Jayson "Agent Jay" Nugent, later a Slacker, holds it down on guitar. The "hit," insofar as it got played on *MTV Skaturday* a couple years later, was "Tin Spam," a song whose opening line illustrates Django's worldview: "They don't make them like the used to in this cold and plastic time."

Around this time, Django met with that manager who wanted him to play more in the poppy ska-punk style of Reel Big Fish and their ilk.

Although they shared a common label, "ska," Django felt like his music had nothing to do with the stuff starting to make its way to MTV. "It's all rock music—it's not really ska music, and it confuses me as to why they persist in using that name for it, because there's literally zero ska in the ska," Django says. "It has offbeat or upbeat guitar, but that's probably the least distinct element of legitimate ska music. To me, the drums and the bass are probably the most defining elements of ska. The upbeat is intrinsic to it, but that's in polka as well. That's in Irish music. That's in Eastern European dance music. It's in almost every dance music in the world. Why? Because it makes you dance."

There was at least one group with genuine ska knowledge taking the music mainstream: Rancid. When they came through New York to promote 1995's . . . *And Out Come the Wolves*, they issued a call for a punk-rock trombonist to join them onstage. Django, who'd played with NYC hardcore vets Murphy's Law, got the gig and gave Tim Armstrong a copy of *Open Season*. Armstrong loved it, and Rancid hired Django, Hillyard, and Ruggiero to join them on Lollapalooza in the summer of 1996. That same year, Rancid and the Stubborn All-Stars teamed up for "I Wanna Riot," a snarling ska stomper with horns galore that appeared on the soundtrack for *Beavis and Butt-Head Do America*.

Django downplays the excitement of that period. He says Lollapalooza was musically pretty boring, since Stubborn All-Stars only played on a few songs every night, and he's lukewarm on the *Beavis and Butt-Head* track. Unlike Ruggiero, who formed a fruitful songwriting partnership with Armstrong, Django never really connected with the Rancid singer. "He was always way more than fair with the money," Django says. "I have nothing bad to say about Epitaph or Hellcat as far as that kind of stuff goes. I just felt disappointed in the phoniness on a personal level."

Armstrong and Rancid bandmates Lars Frederiksen and Matt Freeman nevertheless contributed vocals to three songs on *Back with a New Batch*, the 1997 sophomore set from Stubborn All-Stars. In the two years since

Open Season, major label Arista had begun to purchase Profile Records, and Another Planet founder Fred Feldman started a new label, Triple Crown, where Stubborn All-Stars landed. Despite a minuscule promo budget, the self-help single "Pick Yourself Up," featuring all the Rancid guys, plus Dicky Barrett from the Bosstones, earned some MTV airplay. Arriving at the height of ska's popularity, *Back with a New Batch* bucked trends and skewed toward rocksteady and reggae, offering further education for young fans devoid of roots.

Also in 1997, Hepcat accepted Django's "Open Season" challenge and released "Open Season . . . Is Closed." The track is a showcase for Hepcat singer Alex Désert, a New York City native whom Django knew from high school reggae parties back in the day. "Live not in fear of the braggadocio dingo from the East Coast," Désert says on the song. On the day *Right on Time* came out, Django bought the CD, assembled a band, and recorded a response, "Hepcat Season."

Django had 7-inch copies ready when Hepcat pulled into NYC on their tour. As he tells it, he went to the show with his compatriot Rocker T and challenged Désert to a freestyle showdown. They laid it on pretty thick. "I remember Alex was like pacing," says Django. "I was like, 'What's up, buuuuddy! You gonna battle me tonight onstage in front of everybody? He's like, 'No.' And I'm like, 'What do you mean, no? You're talking all this shit on your record. How are you going to not battle me now?' He goes, 'I don't know how, man.'"

Django says he backed down after Désert agreed to give him props on the mic that night. The whole episode was probably less confrontational than it sounds. "We were always friends before that, and we've been friends since that," Django says. That night, he gave Désert an autographed copy of "Hepcat Season." It read, "To Alex, it's a love thing, Django."

A different type of love inspired the album that would become Stubborn's biggest seller. In 1997, Feldman from Triple Crown asked Django if he'd be into making a Christmas album. Django declined, on account of his Jewishness, and a couple weeks later Feldman came back with another idea: a Jewish ska album. Django ran with the idea and produced 1998's *Roots & Culture*, a melding of Jamaican music and klezmer sung almost entirely in Yiddish. Django tapped his parents and other family members to provide background vocals, and the sessions brought back warm memories of his grandmother, who used to sing him Yiddish lullabies. Given the close connection between Rastafarianism and Judeo-Christian traditions, *Roots & Culture* wasn't that much of a stretch, and the music—ska and reggae with clarinets and violins—is surprisingly accessible for Gentiles. The album ends with the English-language song "Slaughter," all about Django's grandfather, a Holocaust survivor who was like a second father to him. The final minute of the song is just two words repeated over and over: "Never again."

Stubborn All-Stars had always been a difficult proposition, since everyone in the group was on loan from another band, and by the end of the decade it had become untenable. They managed one more album, 1999's *Nex Music*, recorded for Stubborn Records at Version City, Django's dingy basement studio on East 3rd Street. Described by Django as their "weird record," *Nex Music* is a lo-fi collection of late-night mood music, with bits of French jazz and tango spicing up the usual Jamaican flavors. The band was progressing—toward what we'll never know.

"People had their own agendas," Django says. Indeed, Victor Rice moved to Brazil, Agent Jay eventually joined the Slackers, and Roman Fleysher, who played tenor sax on *Nex Music*, became a Mighty Mighty Bosstone. (Django hooked that up when the Bosstones called him up looking for a sax player.) "If I were to pick my exciting band today, it wouldn't be the same people," Django says. "Not for any personal reason. Just situationally."

There was talk in the '90s of Stubborn All-Stars releasing something on Hellcat, but it never came to pass. However, Django did contribute to Hellcat's catalog with 2001's *Reason*, a left-field album of punky reggae, dancehall, and hip-hop. Tim Armstrong was supposed to produce, Django says, and when that didn't happen, Lars Frederiksen was going to take his place. In the end, much to his disappointment, Django produced himself. "It's really hard sometimes when it's all on you, and you have to have the vision for everything: the songwriting, the performances, the style, the recording style, the mixing, the mastering," he says.

That same year, Django moved his Version City operation to New Jersey. He's continued playing with various bands and releasing music on Stubborn ever since. As of 2020, he was leading the King Django Band and serving as musical director for New Jersey ska-oi! heroes Inspector 7. While the twenty-first century is a rough time to own a record label, Django doesn't pine for the '90s, when ska's popularity had little effect on Stubborn's sales.

"I don't think that what we were doing was a part of that," Django says of the '90s ska boom. "It just confuses people about what ska means. Two people can say they love ska and hate each other's music. One of them is right and the other is misinformed. When you say 'ska,' most people are really turned off to that. They think it's a bunch of children dressed in checkerboards and bright colors playing shitty child's music. That's not ever what it was for us. It made it harder to be taken seriously."

CHAPTER 8

East Side Beat

Rob "Bucket" Hingley likes to joke that if the Immigration and Natural-ization Service knew what a socialist he was, they never would've let him enter the United States in 1980. Fortunately for America's capitalist over-lords, Bucket wasn't *that* kind of revolutionary. Over the next two decades, as the leader of Moon Ska Records and its flagship band, the Toasters, the expat Englishman devoted himself to the development of ska in America. Bucket's admirers would cite his communal bands-helping-bands philos-ophy as one reason he was able to create a New York City scene and grow Moon from a one-man bedroom operation to one of the most important labels the genre has ever known.

Bucket's critics—members of bands who left Moon on bad terms, and there were a few—might question that utopian assessment of his business practices. Either way, there's no denying that Moon was a major driver of the '90s ska explosion. The label gave No Doubt their first appearance on record and launched the careers of numerous crucial bands, includ-ing Hepcat, the Slackers, the Pietasters, and Dance Hall Crashers. All of these groups wound up leaving Moon for bigger labels, and in 2000, as ska's popularity returned to pre-boom levels, Bucket closed up shop, sig-naling the end of the third wave.

At its peak, Moon Ska had its own East Village storefront, a subsidi-ary label for emerging artists called Ska Satellite, and a sizable catalog of releases that could be found in stores across the country. Toasters records typically sold 60,000–100,000 copies, according to former Moon director or marketing and communications Steve Shafer, while popular releases by smaller bands might move 20,000 units. This was unthinkable success for a label that Bucket formed out of necessity in 1983, when no other record companies would take a chance on ska.

Bucket didn't come to America to play music. He worked for the U.K. comic book retailer Forbidden Planet, which sent him to New York City to train employees at the new store at East 12th Street and Broadway. He was supposed to stay six months. Back in England, Bucket had played guitar in the ska and reggae bands I-Witness and the Klingons and experienced the tail end of 2 Tone. He'd been hooked on ska ever since he bought a copy of Millie Small's 1964 smash "My Boy Lollipop" when he was nine. Bucket decided to start a band in New York after going to see the English Beat at Roseland Ballroom in 1981 and feeling disappointed that only 150 people turned up. For this comic book store manager, the Roseland moment was tantamount to Bruce Wayne watching his parents get killed. As the legend goes, Bucket vowed then and there to make breaking ska in America his life's mission.

The first step was forming a band—one of the first to play ska in America, it turned out. Bucket recruited coworkers from Forbidden Planet, and after going by various names, including Not Bob Marley, he settled on the Toasters. It was a nod to the original mic-rocking DJs from Jamaica, not the kitchen appliances. Plus, everyone in the band enjoyed the occasional pint, so there was a nifty double meaning.

Forbidden Planet's clientele included English rocker Joe Jackson, who'd dabbled in reggae and ska on his 1980 album *Beat Crazy*. Jackson and Bucket struck up a friendship that grew into a long-standing musical partnership. Using the name Stanley Turpentine to avoid contractual issues with his label, Jackson produced the Toasters' self-titled 1985 debut EP, later retitled *Recriminations*. At this point, the five-person lineup was horn-free, though Jackson blows some sweet melodica on the reggae cut "Run Rudy Run." On the other three songs, the Toasters offer a punky New Wave vision of ska with cool flashes of rockabilly guitar from Bucket.

The Toasters was issued on Moon Records (not yet Moon Ska), as were two seminal '80s compilations: *N.Y. Beat! Hit & Run* (1986) and *Skaface* (1988), a national comp that includes "Everything Wrong," a tentative first step at songwriting by No Doubt. However, the first two Toasters albums, 1987's *Skaboom!* and 1988's Joe Jackson–mixed *Thrill Me Up*, were not originally Moon releases. They came out on Celluloid, the French/American label Bucket made a deal with after experiencing distribution failures on his early Moon titles. Celluloid even created a special imprint for the Toasters called Skaloid.

During these years, the Toasters expanded and transformed their sound, adding a horn section and the Unity 2, a vocal duo comprising Sean "Cavo" Dinsmore and Lionel "Nene" Bernard. Bucket has called the Toasters "the missing link" between 2 Tone and the American third-wave ska of '90s, and *Skaboom!* and *Thrill Me Up* support this archaeological metaphor. Both are super-upbeat, danceable albums sprinkled with social commentary. "Decision at Midnight," a standout from *Thrill Me Up*, name-checks Operation Pressure Point, an NYPD initiative targeting street-level dealers.

Thrill Me Up reached #54 on the CMJ college music chart, and in 1989, the Toasters scheduled their first U.K. tour. Months before the planned trek, the Unity 2 left to sign with Warner Bros. Bucket found a substitute in the young dancehall DJ Coolie Ranx, and the U.K. wound up being a huge success. Upon their return to New York, the Toasters signed with the powerful talent agency Falk & Morrow and began touring the States more regularly.

Unfortunately, right after *Thrill Me Up* came out, Celluloid folded and failed to pay royalties on either Toasters LP. Wary of being at the mercy of another label, Bucket secured a new deal through RED, an independent distributor owned by Sony, and began building up Moon Ska as its own entity. In 1990, the Toasters finally released their first official album on Moon, *This Gun for Hire*, a radio-ready anomaly in the band's discography. The disc includes the calypso-pop earworm "Paralyzed" and "Roseanne," a combination of ska and acid house. According to Steve Shafer, who joined Moon Ska around this time as director of marketing and communications, *This Gun* was tailored for the major labels who were starting to take an interest in the band.

Shafer's ramped-up promotional efforts were well timed, as Moon was hitting its stride with a series of essential third-wave releases. In 1990, Moon dropped the self-titled debut by Dance Hall Crashers, a perky Berkeley unit formed from the ashes of Operation Ivy and fronted by two female singers. The following year brought two more classic debuts: Let's Go Bowling's *Music to Bowl By* and an eponymous opening salvo from the Scofflaws. Hailing from Fresno, California, and Long Island, New York, respectively, Let's Go Bowling and the Scofflaws were jazzy quasi-traditionalists who formed in the '80s and honored their '60s Jamaican roots while maintaining a sense of modern irreverence.

Shafer's first hint that ska might go mainstream came in 1992, when a producer from *USA Up All Night*, a late-night cable series that played trashy B movies, booked the Scofflaws and the Toasters to appear on a special New Year's Eve show. The groups performed snippets of music on a stage flanked by dancers, *American Bandstand*–style. "For like the next year, I had people calling me," Shafer says. "It was like almost every ska kid in the United States saw it. That really made us sit up and say 'wow'— they were out there."

Also in 1992, the Toasters released their fourth album, *New York Fever*, a return-to-form after the pop experimentalism of *This Gun for Hire*. The cover features gritty cartoon depictions (some of them crude stereotypes) of the various characters you'd have encountered on the New York subway during the early '90s. As the title track reminds us, this wasn't a pretty time for the city. Vocalist Cashew Miles sings of being broke and depressed, "dodging bullets on the street." Behind him, the music skanks along happily, just as it does on "Ploughshares into Guns" and "History Book," songs about American warmongering and the lingering effects of colonialism.

Shafer got another clue that ska might break in February 1993, when the Toasters joined the Skatalites and Bad Manners in headlining a "Skalapalooza" show at the Ritz, the former site of Studio 54. Also on the bill were the Scofflaws, Philadelphia's Ruder Than You, and the Skunks from Washington, D.C. The show sold all 2,500 tickets and led directly to that fall's Skavoovie Tour, America's first ska package tour. Featuring the Toasters, the Skatalites, the Selecter, and the Special Beat (comprising members of the Specials and the English Beat), Skavoovie packed houses from coast to coast, indoctrinating scores of newbies.

Then in January 1994, *Billboard* ran a front-page story titled "Hunt for 'Next Big Thing' Unearths Ska Underground." Bucket and Joe Gittleman of the Mighty Mighty Bosstones were among the artists interviewed for the piece, which curiously makes no mention of No Doubt, who'd already released their Interscope debut. "It put the scene on the major label radar," Shafer says. "There was this buzz. And even though [the majors] ended up promoting bands who weren't really ska bands, they were able to capitalize on that buzz."

Moon continued bringing the goods through '93 and '94, releasing more iconic debuts. There was *God Bless Satan* from NYC's premier Satanic ska-jazz-punk band, Mephiskapheles, and *Out of Nowhere* by L.A. trad-ska kingpins Hepcat, who would switch over to the SoCal punk label B.Y.O. for their 1996 sophomore set, *Scientific*. Hepcat were managed by Elyse Rogers of Dance Hall Crashers, another group that left Moon after one record. In Shafer's opinion, some of the West Coast bands had unrealistic expectations about what a small indie like Moon could deliver, and that led to tension and ultimately bad blood. "We couldn't pay money to have a professional person service a record to the much bigger mainstream modern rock stations," says Shafer. "We could never do the more pay-to-play stuff. It was a big thing for us to be able to do a regular monthly ad in *Alternative Press*. That was almost upper limits."

Dance Hall Crashers became the first band signed to (510), an MCA affiliate founded by Green Day's managers, and Hepcat inked a deal with Tim Armstrong's Epitaph subsidiary Hellcat Records, which built a nice little collection of former Moon bands. Hellcat also snagged the Pietasters—Washington, D.C., soul-ska troublemakers who found their niche with the 1995 Moon release *Oolooloo*—and the Slackers, who dropped their excellent Moon debut, *Better Late Than Never*, in 1996.

Neither the Pietasters nor the Slackers split easily from Moon. The Pietasters had signed a two-album deal with the label, and according to front man Stephen Jackson, they felt they'd fulfilled their contract by releasing *Oolooloo* and the 1996 live album *Strapped Live!* Bucket argued that *Strapped* didn't count, Jackson says, but in the end, Moon worked out a deal with Hellcat that allowed the Pietasters to move on.

Somewhere along the way, though, things turned ugly. Shafer says the Pietasters accused Moon of shortchanging them on royalties, seemingly to justify the Hellcat move. Shafer says the band's lawyers and accountants checked the books and found nothing out of order. While Shafer suspects the audit was motivated more by the Pietasters' management than by the band itself, he describes the episode as especially disheartening. "If they'd just come and said, 'Hey, we have this opportunity to go to the next level,' we would've been sad, but I don't think it would've been a huge thing."

Jackson says the money dispute happened after the Pietasters signed with Hellcat, and their lawyers noticed that Moon's royalties didn't jibe with extrapolations based on the sales of their Hellcat debut, *Willis*. Jackson says Moon offered to let them review the books, but those wound up being boxes of files in a garage. The expense of sifting through everything would've outweighed the contested royalties, Jackson says, so the two parties agreed on a settlement. By all accounts, Jackson and Bucket have since patched things up.

Things weren't much better with the Slackers. "They were a hard band to deal with," says Shafer. "They were incredibly talented, but there was never a good relationship." Asked about the Moon split, Slackers front man Vic Ruggiero says his band got "the simplest, worst deal" possible from Moon. "We were like, 'Cool. We're going to get ripped off. We'd rather make a record than not,'" Ruggiero says. "We took it for face value. When Hellcat came along and offered us something, Moon suddenly tried to keep us. We were like, 'Hey, you never did nothing for us, so why would you want to keep us? From what I gather, you could give a shit whether we are alive or dead, so let us go to a label that gives a shit about us.'" Luckily, Ruggiero says, the Slackers had never signed a contract.

It wasn't all bad between the Hellcat and Moon camps. Shafer remembers a meeting that took place between Bucket, Armstrong, and Rancid guitarist Lars Frederiksen. Armstrong apparently expressed his admiration for Bucket and shared the story of how Operation Ivy sent Moon their demo back in the day. (Bucket passed because he had no money to press anything, Shafer says, and because Op Ivy's ska-punk was ahead of its time.) "Tim was very much like, 'You've been there. You were forging this path, and we are one of the beneficiaries of that, and we want to pay it back,'" Shafer says. Armstrong proposed doing a split Toasters/Rancid 7-inch, Shafer says, but Hellcat never followed through.

"It would have been beautiful," Shafer says. "All the Hellcat stuff sort of rubbed us the wrong way, but that would have repaired things. We would much rather have been collaborative. One of the founding principles [of Moon] was always, 'We want to work together so everybody gets something out of this.'"

In the early days, Moon favored simple single-page licensing contracts that Shafer describes as "very artist-friendly." As the label grew, Moon began advancing bands money for recording sessions and music videos. That led to increasingly complex deals that further tainted Moon's relationships with some artists. "We were fronting a lot of money," says Shafer. "Then bands have to sell a lot of records to recoup. It got stickier and stickier. We were inching toward a more major-label model, which we probably shouldn't have."

As Moon signed and lost bands, the Toasters kept rolling. If they weren't New York City's best ska band throughout the '90s, they were certainly its most reliable. Coolie Ranx stepped up to the mic on 1994's *Dub 56*, a solid album of bright, mostly up-tempo ska songs with shades of soul and R&B. Ranx shines on the standout "Legal Shot," a reggae banger he'd remake with Pilfers, his supergroup featuring Bim Skala Bim trombonist Vinny Nobile, for their 1999 Mojo Records release *Chawalaleng*.

With 1996's *Hard Band for Dead*—another slick and satisfying album featuring guests like founding Skatalites saxophonist Lester Sterling and "Godfather of Ska" Laurel Aitken—the Toasters made the jump to MTV. Shafer added "music video director" to his list of Moon duties by filming a grainy black-and-white clip for "2-Tone Army," the album's anthemic opening cut. MTV premiered the video on *120 Minutes* in October 1996.

By this time, the Toasters had generated some major-label interest. According to Shafer, David Silver, vice president of A&R at Mercury Records, home of the Bosstones, was a huge Toasters fan who'd catch the band live whenever they were in NYC. That led to some promising talks in 1995. "[Silver] was like, 'Listen, I want to bring the Toasters to Mercury. We've had such great success with the Bosstones, we think we can repeat that with you,'" Shafer says. There was even a meeting with Mercury president Danny Goldberg, who apparently made an offer to the band and the label. (Goldberg says he doesn't remember courting the Toasters or Moon, but he concedes he was a busy man in the '90s.) According to Shafer, Mercury wanted to take over the manufacturing and distribution of the Moon Ska catalog.

Having been burned in the past by failing distributors and the collapse of Celluloid, Bucket wasn't willing to bet Moon's entire future on Mercury. Much to the surprise of Mercury's execs, Shafer says, Bucket backed out. "The Toasters could have gone to the next level, but to have it linked with somebody that could just kill everything else that we worked so hard for was too much," Shafer says. "It was heartbreaking, because by that point, I had this realization we couldn't take bands beyond the point we had gotten to. We would always be a great minor league feeder to the majors."

In 1999, there was a gigantic merger between Mercury's parent company, Polygram, and Universal. When the dust settled, Goldberg was out, and all of Mercury's artists who weren't dropped moved under the Island Def Jam umbrella. It's hard to imagine any of this would've helped Moon, though by 1999, it might not have mattered. Moon's sales began dipping in late 1997, Shafer says, and in 1998, as critics declared ska dead, chain stores began sending back boxes of unsold CDs. The back room of the Moon Records store on East 10th Street was filling up with returned product, and Shafer ceased promotional efforts. He left Moon in 1999, before the label formally closed its doors in 2000.

According to Shafer, on his last day in the office he and Moon's business manager learned that a former employee had embezzled between $100,000 and $200,000. "It was not an amount that would have saved the label, but it was just this dagger in the heart," says Shafer. In the aftermath of the discovery, Shafer says, Moon threatened to go to the district attorney, and the employee paid back most or all of the money.

The final Toasters album on Moon was 1997's *Don't Let the Bastards Grind You Down*. This time out, Jack Ruby Jr., son of Jamaican producer Jack Ruby, stepped in for Coolie Ranx, but even so, the album feels like the culmination of a trilogy that began with *Dub 56* and *Hard Band for Dead*. All three bright and sprightly albums were produced by Mathias Schneeberger, who'd mixed 1992's *New York Fever* with Joe Jackson in Berlin.

Bastards features the prophetic "I'm Running Right Through the World," a major-key high-stepper in which Bucket advises, "You won't get far if you stay where you are." The perennial road dog took that advice to the next level after Moon's implosion and moved with his wife and kids to Valencia, Spain, in the early 2000s.

In 2002, Bucket started a new label, Megalith, and sought to learn from Moon's mistakes. He told *In Music We Trust* in 2004 that he planned to sell direct to consumers via the web and rely less on independent distributors. In the same interview, he blasted the Hellcat bands for getting "sucked too much into the glory game" and losing sight of what was good for ska on the whole. "If everybody had stuck together at Moon Ska and basically said we aren't going to run for the money and we are going to keep our thing here, Moon Ska would still be around," Bucket said. "We had pumped a lot of promotional money, for example, into a band like the Pietasters, who actually when they went to Epitaph broke the contract with us—there was a potential lawsuit there that we never capitalized upon mainly because I don't believe in that sort of stuff."

Megalith has continued releasing material throughout the twenty-first century, albeit with nothing like Moon's frequency. That's not a bad thing, since one criticism of Moon's '90s run is that the label favored quantity over quality. Jeff "King Django" Baker of Skinnerbox and Stubborn All-Stars says Bucket got so busy he couldn't pay attention to everything coming out on the label. "Also, he had to fill his distribution pipeline," Django says. "He had to have releases coming out. That's the way the distribution scene worked back then."

With the rise of digital music consumption, Bucket has focused more on touring than recording. The Toasters haven't released a new album since 2007's *One More Bullet*, and while fans around the world can expect the band—that is, Bucket and some hired guns—to come through at least once a year, it's unclear whether there'll ever be a new LP for sale at the merch table.

"Music has been devalued and trivialized to a large degree, so kids now view it as being really disposable," Bucket told the Northern Irish radio show *Ska Craze* in 2016. "Instead of spending 30 grand on a record, I'd rather buy some air tickets and take the band to Australia, or take the band to South America or Japan—places we haven't played—and take the live show there so everybody can have a look and basically broaden our footprint that way."

■ ■ ■

In 1992, the Pietasters caught the first in a series of lucky breaks that—along with hard work, talent, and a penchant for raucous live shows—would make them third-wave icons. At the time, the band consisted mostly of students from Virginia Tech, where they'd formed two years earlier. Through a friend on the school's programming board, the Pietasters learned that Bad Manners, a major influence on their booze-soaked brand of party-ska, were coming to America and looking to add a tour stop in between Washington, D.C., and Atlanta. The Pietasters used their connection to book Bad Manners at Virginia Tech and install themselves as the opening act. They also supported the 2 Tone legends on the next few dates.

"We drove them around and hung out with them and took them to the airport and heard all these crazy stories," says Pietasters lead singer Stephen Jackson. All of which gave them an idea: "Let's continue to drive around and pretend like we're in Bad Manners.'"

That's basically what they've done ever since. During their '90s heyday, the 'Tasters enjoyed stints on America's two greatest ska labels, Moon Ska and Hellcat, and released a series of essential CDs. In a world of hybridized ska bands, the Pietasters found their lane by filtering '60s soul and garage rock—pet sounds of the mod subculture they loosely repped—into their rowdy anthems. They were lovable knuckleheads, well-dressed beer monsters, and keen experimenters who could energize ska-punk kids without alienating purists.

The original Pietasters members grew up in the suburbs surrounding Washington, D.C., the city the band would eventually call home. Gentrification hadn't yet hit the nation's capital, and Jackson has fond memories of going into the city as a teenager to see live music. "It was a rough place to be," he says. "But there were these nightclubs that held punk-rock shows and rockabilly shows and mod shows, you name it. You would like some chick, and she would be at a ska matinee, and you'd go to that. All the scenes intertwined."

When he started at Virginia Tech, located some five hours outside the city in Blacksburg, Jackson discovered an extension of that musically diverse D.C. scene. The informal assemblage of friends that would become the Pietasters started out doing punk covers but expanded to ska at the urging of their friend Tal Bayer, a student at nearby Radford University. The name they settled on stems from some British neighbors calling certain band members "pietasters," slang for "fat guys."

Bayer and Jackson shared front man duties, and the group played its first show at the house where Stephen lived. "We built a stage in our living room, and we would have bands come from Richmond or Roanoke," Jackson says. Other campus house shows followed, and the Pietasters happily played frat houses, rugby parties, hippie pads—anywhere there was a keg, really.

In 1993, after all the original members managed to graduate, the Pietasters released their self-titled debut album, sometimes referred to as "Piestomp." Sharing little in common with the records that would follow, *The Pietasters* is the work of a band in thrall to 2 Tone and still searching for an identity, though their remake of "Night Owl," an oft-covered R&B tune they lifted from an obscure '70s group called the Bad Habits, was a harbinger of things to come. The Pietasters learned about "Night Owl" from a couple of DJ friends, Scott Lightsey and Keith Willis, who turned them on to such vinyl treasures and helped to steer the direction of the band.

To promote the album, the Pietasters toured across the country in a $900 used school bus. When they returned home, everyone save for Jackson, guitarist Tom Goodin, and bassist Todd Eckhardt quit. Two members went to law school, and another went to grad school. Among those who hung up his black suit was Bayer, who'd been one of the main songwriters on *The Pietasters*. He may have missed his chance to become a ska star, but his was a nobler calling. As detailed in a moving 2013 story in the *Washington Post*, Bayer went on to found a rugby program at Hyde Leadership Public Charter (later renamed Perry Street Prep Public Charter) and help dozens of underprivileged Black teens excel on the field and in the classroom.

After the mass exodus of '93, Jackson and the remaining 'Tasters added some new members, including drummer Rob Covington, trombonist Jeremy Roberts, and saxophonist Alan Makranczy. The group played regularly in D.C. and toured enough to impress Bucket from Moon. "Bucket was looking for anybody that was going to put in the time," Jackson says. "We showed that we were dumb enough to get in a school bus and drive across country." The Pietasters joined the Toasters and the Scofflaws out on the Skavoovie '94 tour, and the following year they made their Moon debut with *Oolooloo*.

Produced by Scofflaws bassist Victor Rice, *Oolooloo* is a '90s ska touchstone, the point at which the Pietasters become the Pietasters. The vibe is soul-ska, and the disc includes covers of the Motown classic "It's the Same Old Song" and Tyrone Davis's 1968 smash "Can I Change My Mind," which has been recorded by numerous Jamaican artists, including legendary siblings Alton and Hortense Ellis. The Pietasters get in the loving spirit with the original "Tell You Why," wherein Jackson comes clean to his lady about how much she means to him.

Elsewhere on the album, the Pietasters don't always come across as your typical tenderhearted R&B lovermen. An air of casual sexism permeates "Maggie Mae," a tribute to an accommodating "barmaid beauty in a tight black dress," and "Biblical Sense," in which Jackson basically tells his girl he did it all for the nookie, as Fred Durst would later say. "Pleasure Bribe," about a night with a prostitute, once got Jackson maced by a PC zealot at a show in Gainesville, Florida. "Obviously, the singer is the face and delivers the lyrics, but I didn't even write the song that I got maced for," says Jackson. The irony of a moral crusader using violence to protest offensive lyrics isn't lost on Jackson. "I'm big into letting people have their say and not really attacking them for whatever they think," he says. "As ignorant or as stupid as you may think it is."

The Pietasters also caught flak for covering "Drinking and Driving," a tongue-in-cheek 1983 song by the English oi! band the Business. A version appears on the Pietasters' 1996 live album *Strapped Live!* The chorus ends with the line "Drinking and driving is so much fun," which fans naturally scream along with in concert. After a gig at Toad's Place in New Haven, Connecticut, the Pietasters received a letter from a Ph.D. at Yale University who took offense at the song. "We're obviously not encouraging people to go drinking and driving," says Jackson. "And if you have that little sense of humor, please don't ever come to see our show again."

By 1996, the Pietasters had justified their decision to keep going after that initial school bus tour. They'd shared stages with major artists and released two CDs on Moon. But it seemed like they'd hit a wall, and for a while they considered breaking up. Fortunately, Dicky Barrett of the Mighty Mighty Bosstones came to see them one night in Providence, Rhode Island, and cheered everyone up with gin and tonic. Barrett urged the 'Tasters not to quit and offered to take them along on the next Bosstones tour. That trek coincided with the colossal success of 1997's "The Impression That I Get," and once again the Pietasters had new life.

By tour's end, the Pietasters had signed to Hellcat with the understanding that label co-founder Brett Gurewitz would produce their next album. The resulting LP, 1997's *Willis*, pushes further into garage-soul territory, as the group loses the offbeat guitars on songs like "Stone Feeling" and

Pietasters trombonist Jeremy Roberts fuels the soul-
ska dance party. Photographer unknown.

"Quicksand," a cover of the 1966 garage nugget by the Outsiders. The disc
opens with "Crazy Monkey Woman," a brass-accented fuzz-punk blow-
out featuring slurry, shouted vocals from Jackson.

"It wasn't like we played or wrote differently to suit the label's input,"
says Jackson. "Brett's like, 'I'm a rock 'n' roll guy, and I can fucking make
you sound like *Raw Power*, and it will be awesome.' In the '90s, I remember getting a lot of heat from friends of ours that were into the traditional
ska. They were like, 'What is this?' It's like, 'Just fucking relax. It's an experiment, and it's awesome.'"

Willis featured plenty of ska jams, including the Gurewitz co-write "Out
All Night," about going out drinking to escape your annoying girlfriend.

"Out All Night" made it to MTV and became one of the band's signature songs, though it never charted. "That was the time for ska bands and bands that masqueraded as ska bands to be on *120 Minutes* or whatever," Jackson says. "It was fun."

That time had definitely passed by the time the Pietasters made their second Hellcat album, 1999's *Awesome Mix Tape #6*. In fact, someone at the band's publishing company asked whether they'd considered making an album without horns. Needless to say, they had not. With Gurewitz again at the controls, the Pietasters bashed out another set of hard-hitting ska, soul, and rocksteady songs, with a couple of flat-out punk tracks chucked in. Gurewitz and the band recorded at various studios in the Valley, including Sound City, where artists like Tom Petty and Nirvana made some of their best records.

"When we started playing at house parties [in college], we never had any pretension that we were going to have a record deal, let alone be in Los Angeles recording a record," Jackson says. "Every time something cool happened, it was like, 'This is fucking awesome, man. I just carried the two-inch tapes for Don Was, who's producing the Rolling Stones' new record. Keith Richards is in our mixing room right now, and I just took a piss next to Mick Jagger. This should not be happening.'"

Also during 1999, the Pietasters were given the opportunity to tour for six weeks with Joe Strummer, who'd landed on Hellcat with his new world-rock band the Mescaleros. "It was amazing, first of all, that some dopey guys from a ska band from Virginia would be out touring with this big guy," Jackson told the *Daily Progress* in 2008. "Every night he would come and hang out and have nice things to say about us, and you could tell that it was more than just 'good show,' he actually watched the set and was kind of a friend."

With *Awesome Mix Tape #6*, the Pietasters came to the end of their two-album deal with Hellcat. It was 2000, and the American ska scene looked quite different than it had when they signed three years earlier. "We weren't going to push it, and we didn't want to waste [Hellcat's] time, so we were like, 'Let's just figure out what's going on,'" Jackson says. Their next stop was Fueled by Ramen, the label co-founded by their buddy Vinnie Fiorello of Less Than Jake, for the 2002 album *Turbo*. The shows got smaller and the scene changed. "It wasn't the people you started playing to that knew all the Specials and Bad Manners albums," Jackson says. "It was just watered down."

In 2003, the Pietasters got the luckiest break imaginable for a bunch of lifelong soul lovers: they were tapped to serve as James Brown's backing band for the WHFS Holiday Nutcracker Ball at the MCI Center in Washington, D.C. The Godfather of Soul had a reputation for being a strict taskmaster onstage, docking musicians' pay for missing notes, but the Pietasters escaped without a scolding.

The Pietasters returned in 2007 with *All Day*, released on Indication Records, a label they launched through the North Carolina–based indie distributor Redeye. With a no-fuss production aesthetic reminiscent of the Slackers, who would land on Indication for their 2008 LP *Self-Medication*, *All Day* is a late-career triumph. The most telling track is "Oolooloo," named for the album that will go down as their masterpiece. The tone is somewhere between wistful and defensive as Jackson takes stock of nearly 20 years as a band: "And to the people that we've hurt along the way / If they can't take a joke, well fuck 'em anyway."

As of 2020, the Pietasters had yet to issue a follow-up to *All Day*. They continue touring, however, with Jackson presiding over a dugout of musicians that always justifies the price of admission. Jackson doesn't see this changing anytime soon. "We're still going to be driving around in circles," he says. "And we've got a bunch of new songs. We've been wrestling with the how of releasing new stuff. I'm cautiously optimistic, but I feel like we're on to something good."

■ ■ ■

To people who hate ska, every band with horns and offbeat guitars sounds like the work of the Devil. But only one genre practitioner actually claimed to be in league with Satan. That band was Mephiskapheles, and throughout the '90s, they laid waste to the scene with sulfuric avant-jazz horn sorcery and demonic vocals. As a listener, it wasn't always clear whether the correct response was to laugh or cower in fear, especially when they played their signature song, a cover of the Bumble Bee tuna jingle.

"We didn't want to be cheesy," says guitarist Brendan "Brendog" Tween, who founded the band with drummer Mikal Reich in 1991. "We didn't want to be, 'OK, rudie, everybody skank!'" Tween's cheese intolerance is understandable: he got his start in the hardcore punk band the Shaved Pigs, who released a pair of albums in the late '80s that earned some attention from tastemaking BBC DJ John Peel. After the Pigs split up, Tween moved in with Reich, and the pair worked as busboys/waiters at Panchitos, a Mexican restaurant in Greenwich Village. Their coworkers included an aspiring comedian by the name of Jon Leibowitz, soon to be known as Jon Stewart.

Reich played a lot of ska around the apartment—Specials albums and Trojan box sets—and he and Tween began attending local shows. Tween was simultaneously listening to old standbys like Johnny Thunders and the Heartbreakers, while Reich was digging alternative antagonists Butthole Surfers and Big Black. The standard post–2 Tone rude-boy thing didn't appeal to them, so they began thinking about how they might approach ska with an experimental punk sensibility.

One of the first to join them was tenor sax player and former Shaved Pigs sideman Mike Berger. During his brief membership, Berger came up with the rapid-fire horn riff for "Doomsday," Meph's eventual ticket to MTV. Later came Dave Doris, a tenor and baritone saxophonist who got the band going in some atonal directions. "We all played really over-the-top naturally," says Tween. "Even if we wanted to play like a classic ska band, I don't think we could have."

The inimitable Mephiskapheles horn section was eerie and cheery in equal measure and often sounded almost out of tune, though really they were flexing complex jazz technique. This became even more pronounced as the original horn players left and were replaced by trombonist Greg Robinson, trumpeter Osho Endo, and alto saxophonist Alexander McCabe. That was the brass pack throughout the '90s, as Mephiskapheles built an international following that continued even after ska stopped being cool. "We ended up with a bunch of jazz guys that played horns who hated ska, which probably worked to our advantage," says Tween.

The vaguely unsettling jazzbo horns complemented the band's name and overall theme. At first, the group was known as Skatterbrains, a tag they fortunately had to scrap because another band was using it. Once they hit on the name Mephiskapheles, everything fell into place. The Satanic gimmick inspired atypical ska songs, especially once Tween's former Hunter College buddy Andre Worrell, a native Trinidadian alternatively known as "The Nubian Nightmare" and "The Grand Invidious," became lead singer and ran with the concept.

Robinson, the trombonist, attributes Meph's singular sound to the character of New York City in the early '90s. Rents were still reasonable downtown, and the city was pulsing with a million different sounds. "It's hard to explain to people who weren't living here then," says Robinson, who moonlighted in a couple of swing bands. "You had the remnants of 50 years of jazz; those guys were still around and playing gigs. The Latin scene was huge. Reggae, ska. Hardcore was really happening. You hear a lot of great music from the '90s, because people were able to assimilate all kinds of diverse influences all around."

Not every song on Meph's stellar 1994 debut, *God Bless Satan*, plays with devil imagery, and that makes the album all the more confounding—and awesome. Produced by New York City underground icon Bill Laswell, who's worked with everyone from Yoko Ono to Motörhead, *God Bless Satan* certainly starts out sinister. It opens with "Mephiskapheles"

Mephiskapheles raise an unholy racket at the New
Music Cafe in New York City, 1992. Photo: John McCabe /
Mephiskapheles.

and "Satanic Debris," apocalyptic dance jams driven by Brian Martin's
anxious keyboards and upright bassist Michael Bitz's thudding low end.
The supercharged single "Doomsday," which landed on MTV, makes the
end of the world sound downright invigorating. But just when you think
you've got the lay of the fire-scorched land, there's "Saba," a sing-along
love song, and "Eskamo," the tale of an Inuit rude boy told with many a
groaner ska joke. Most puzzling of all is the closer, "The Bumble Bee Tuna
Song," an adaptation of a '70s commercial jingle.

There was a good reason for the "Bumble Bee" cover. Growing up, Tween knew one of the girls who appeared in the TV spot, and after he shared that fact with Reich—an advertising creative director in his non-Meph time—the band began messing around with the song in rehearsal. Tween tried to punkify the proceedings with a metallic intro riff cribbed right from the Shaved Pigs song "Cop Shot." Worrell's "biddly-biddly-biddly" vocals were an inside joke aimed at Rocker T, the white front man of the NYC reggae band the Skadanks, who'd make similar noises onstage. Mephiskapheles stuck "The Bumble Bee Tuna Song" at the end of *God Bless Satan* because it was basically an afterthought, and of course, it became their best-known song. As Reich likes to point out, though, it's not totally off-brand for Mephiskapheles. "It was a commercial jingle," he says. "What's more satanic than a commercial?"

Mephiskapheles released *God Bless Satan* on their own before signing a production and distribution deal with Bucket, thereby joining the Moon Ska family. The album sold well, and before Mephiskapheles got around to releasing their follow-up, ska blew up. Meph began fielding offers from larger independent labels that weren't all that enticing. Both Robinson and trumpeter Osho Endo worked at a music publishing company, so they knew how labels would screw artists out of their publishing. Robinson had also ghostwritten an encyclopedia of jazz, so he'd heard countless horror stories of artists getting swindled.

In the end, Meph thought it best to stick with Moon for their 1997 sophomore effort, the freaky jazz-punk odyssey *Maximum Perversion*. The far-out sound was a direct result of who was doing the writing. On *God Bless Satan*, Reich and Tween together accounted for about half the album. When it came time to write the follow-up, the horn players took over. Tween contributed just one song, "Turtle Soup," and Reich left the band before they hit the studio. That left the jazz contingent to concoct heady departures like Endo's "Break Your Ankle Punk," a collision of hip-hop, hard funk, and skronk that Worrell really sinks his teeth into. "Ska meets the Bronx," he taunts. "So what?"

"It's become acknowledged as a classic, but it definitely stiffed when we released it," says Robinson. "It was highly anticipated obviously because *God Bless Satan* had been a phenomenon, kind of. And so Bucket and Moon Records had given us quite a generous offer for it, and everything looked good. Then we put it out, and everybody was like, 'What? This doesn't sound anything like *God Bless Satan.*'"

That was the point: Mephiskapheles weren't trying to make a ska record everybody would like, even though it was 1997, and doing so might've made financial sense. That same year, Meph toured for three weeks with Gwar, the theatrical metal band known for its foam-rubber monster outfits and fountains of fake blood.

Meph's popularity and originality were such that even in 1999, well after ska had retreated back to the underground, the band earned a three-album deal with Velvel Records (later acquired by Koch), the label started by music business titan Walter Yetnikoff, former CEO of CBS Records. But before Mephiskapheles went into the studio with Stoker—the ex–General Public drummer who'd produced albums for Dance Hall Crashers, Hepcat, and the Specials—they underwent a massive reorganization. Tween and Bitz quit, and the remaining members pushed out Endo, who responded by suing everybody. Unable to pay replacement musicians while fighting Endo's lawsuit, Mephiskapheles called it quits.

The retooled lineup did, however, manage to finish 1999's *Might-ay White-ay*, another unexpected left turn, this time into metal territory. The group replaced Tween with two guitar players, including shredder Bill McKinney. The metal move was smart given the state of ska in 1999. "Our audiences didn't diminish," says Robinson. "It just became different people at the shows." The legal drama meant the album was pulled after the initial shipment, which is why relatively few fans heard ragers like "Swampskin" and "Cheap Thrill." For all its heaviness, *Might-ay White-ay* offers plenty of aerobic ska tunes with disquieting horn lines—Worrell's as electric as ever.

All was quiet on the Meph front until 2012, when Tween got Endo to drop his lawsuits on the eve of an acoustic reunion show in NYC. About a hundred people saw the classic-era horn section take the stage with Tween and Reich and play the old favorites. Worrell didn't participate, but soon after, he contacted Robinson about getting the band going again. They reconvened essentially the *Might-ay White-ay* lineup and have been performing ever since.

Tween says he's cool with Mephiskapheles continuing on without him and Reich, the guys who started the whole thing. "God bless 'em," he says. "Every time they play, we sell another 25 copies of *God Bless Satan*." As of 2019, Tween was more concerned with Barbicide, the new *horn-free* ska band he'd started with Reich. "We had 10 bitter years of experience with horns," Tween says with a laugh. "Horns can't do anything a good keyboard player can't." "We were joking we should call this new band 'The Devil Without Horns,'" Reich says.

CHAPTER 9

Misfits of Swing

Two of the strangest bands ever to splash down in the mainstream did so as part of the '90s swing revival. Both formed in college towns, chose outlandish three-word names, and arrived on MTV with novelty singles that were smarter than anyone realized. They were zany swing outsiders who did retro their own way, and decades later, their platinum success is a reminder of what a crapshoot alternative rock was in the years following grunge.

Cherry Poppin' Daddies could jump and jive with the best of them, as their 1997 smash "Zoot Suit Riot" attests. But you've only got a prayer of Lindy Hopping to a fraction of their catalog. On the three studio albums they released before their fluke hit, the Daddies tore through genres like they were going out of style. (In fact, most of them already had.)

Squirrel Nut Zippers, who hit it big with the 1996 calypso smash "Hell," were similarly stylistically ravenous, though their reference points were different. Whereas the Daddies dabbled in everything from swing onward—rockabilly, surf, soul, funk, punk, and ska—the Zippers seldom ventured beyond the '40s. They were more interested in hot jazz, blues, klezmer, calypso, and other prerock, prewar styles. They knew how to swing in the musicological sense, but the genre tag hardly scratched the surface of what these Southern weirdos could do.

■ ■ ■

Cherry Poppin' Daddies mastermind Steve Perry is the proverbial smartest guy in the room. The multifaceted artist and molecular biologist has always pursued his vision above all else and never made things easy for himself. Case in point: he called his band *Cherry Poppin' Daddies*, a name sure to mark him foul in polite company. Then he wrote brainy songs about sex, race, and other subjects bound to get him in trouble. This was not music for the masses—until suddenly it was.

Perry grew up in Apalachin, New York, a tiny town infamous for a 1957 police raid on a mafia meeting that resulted in 62 of the nation's top gangsters getting nabbed by federal agents. Nothing that exciting happened during Perry's youth, though he did discover skateboarding and punk rock. "It finally felt like music that felt like I did," Perry says. "You know, Elvis Costello, snotty and smart. There was irony. Music wasn't all expressions of someone's emotions or something."

Songwriting wasn't yet part of Perry's life, but running was. That's partially what brought him to the University of Oregon in Eugene, where mustachioed track star Steve Prefontaine had risen to national prominence in the early '70s. Perry soon discovered he didn't care enough about running to hang with Oregon's top athletes. Music was better—fewer ice baths, more girls.

Perry dropped out of school in 1983 and formed two bands before getting Cherry Poppin' Daddies going. (A constant in all three groups was bassist Dan Schmid, who remains a Daddy in 2020.) The first, Jazz Greats, had a punky sound with shades of the Kinks. Over time, Perry and his buddies got into the Paisley Underground bands of the early '80s, whose goal of reviving the psychedelic '60s offered a colorful alternative to the strict rules of hardcore. The jangly Paisley sound informed Perry's next band, Saint Huck, which he led for a few years before changing direction again. "What bugged me is that the music was kind of ethereal, and it wasn't antsy," Perry says. "Everyone sat on the floor."

Drawn as he was to making bodies move, Perry naturally got into Fishbone and the Red Hot Chili Peppers. Around the same time, 1987 or '88, he also sold his guitar and bought a jazz banjo. That unusual purchase was the result of his mother sending him *The Smithsonian Collection of Classic Jazz* for his birthday. At first, Perry had no use for the thing. "Then one day, I was sick of listening to whatever else I was listening to, and I put in the first cassette and heard all these curated, beautiful pieces from Louis Armstrong to modern jazz," he says. "I listened to the whole thing, and then I went back to the beginning and listened to it again.

"It had Duke Ellington's 'Ko-Ko' on there. I remember hearing that. It was a stormy day, and it just bowled me over. The harmonics of it were crazy, and I needed to do that. It was one of those moments. I went, 'Okay, I'm going to try and write this kind of jazz swing stuff.' I pictured a rebirth of swing music and punk rock, a mixture of them."

Perry's punk-swing epiphany led to his next band, originally known as Mr. Wiggles. That name was a reference to the 1978 Parliament song of the same name, and while Perry's crew supplemented its swing with plenty of funk, the tag didn't seem quite right. A few days before their first show, Perry decided they needed a new name. At the time, he was listening to records like *Early Viper Jive*, a collection of pre-swing jazz recordings of a risqué nature. One of the songs had a lyric about "cherry poppin'" something or other, and someone in the punk house where the band lived suggested the name Cherry Poppin' Daddies. Perry liked it. Everyone high-fived, and the poster for the show was made.

It's not that Perry didn't think the name would cause controversy. He just didn't care. "Our scene was alternative people," he says. "Through the '80s, you watched those movies with the guys with the popped collars and stuff like that. You didn't want to be part of the normal kind of people. You would never become popular. You just wanted to be amongst your small group of friends. You didn't want a bunch of frat guys showing up."

The name was only the beginning of their troubles around Eugene. During early shows, the band's stage props included "the Dilldozer," a riding lawnmower modified to look like a giant penis. It even ejaculated colorful liquid into the audience. This was the dawning of the age of political correctness, and people in the liberal college town soon branded Cherry Poppin' Daddies sexist and misogynistic.

"I'm glad people were talking about those kinds of things," says Perry. "I'm for the dialog. Here's the thing: if a person was a bad person, would they scream it from the rooftops? People don't do that. My point of view has always been difficult for people to understand, because coming out of the '60s, most music was considered from the point of view of the person, the authentic voice. The Bob Dylan or the blues singer who's singing from his heart. What I liked about punk rock was that sometimes it was just stories. It wasn't the [artist] in the song."

At various points in his career, Perry might've deflected criticism by simply explaining his intentions. But he believes most people consume art with their minds already made up. If they're ready to be offended, they'll find something offensive. More importantly, deconstructing a song or stage prop would defeat the purpose of creating the thing in the first place. "Anything in art, to me, has some ambiguity to it," Perry says. "Otherwise it's just an essay. I'm not interested in making an essay."

There's a great deal of ambiguity on the Daddies' 1990 debut, *Ferociously Stoned*. The album features five neo-swing tunes—"Drunk Daddy," "Master and Slave," "Dr. Bones," "Shake Your Lovemaker," and "Cherry Poppin' Daddy Strut"—that would appear on the double-platinum 1997 compilation *Zoot Suit Riot*. All five tracks are proof of just how fully realized Perry's cerebral punk-swing vision was from the beginning.

The LP kicks off with "Drunk Daddy," the sordid tale of a man who's suffered outrageous abuse at the hands of his father and now seeks revenge on the world. Perry wishes he could've imbued the lyrics with more nuance, so the protagonist wouldn't seem like purely a victim. But there's only so much you can do, even in a five-minute song. He's far happier with "Master and Slave," one of the finest songs in the Cherry Poppin' Daddies catalog. As the horns and rhythm section push you onto the dance floor, Perry spins a wild story that imagines America's failed promise as a tragic father-son parable. The Abraham we meet in the opening lines is both Lincoln and the biblical character who's game to sacrifice his boy. "You could be talking about an actual father and son not getting along or history handing a legacy to the next generation and not being very kind," says Perry. "'Master and Slave' is a song that might as well be written today."

Swing only accounts for about half of the album's original 11-song run. Perry and the gang also deliver funk rock ("Dirty Mutha Fuzz"), Oingo Boingo–style horn-laced New Wave ("Teenage Brain Surgeon"), and flashy soul ("You Better Move"). The Daddies couldn't have sounded less like the sludgy alternative rock that was exploding all over the Pacific Northwest. "The fact that we had horns in this band was my way of going, 'Hey, we're going to do our own thing,'" says Perry. "It's punk rock to be yourself and do something else."

The Daddies went even further afield with their 1994 sophomore effort, *Rapid City Muscle Car*, recorded partially in the studio they'd built for themselves. It was a concept album, the concept being that each song sounded nothing like the one before. "I was thinking in terms of James Joyce, how chapter to chapter would change in genre," says Perry.

Rapid City Muscle Car races from rockabilly to ska to psychedelia, making several memorable detours through swing-ville. One of them, "The Ding-Dong Daddy of the D Car Line," is about a no-good polygamist with a thing for rumps. "Mr. White Keys" introduces an even more unsavory character: a greedy, glad-handing sleazeball coasting on Daddy's millions. Those songs, plus "Pink Elephant" and "Come Back to Me," a Rat Pack–style croon-fest written for the 1965 Broadway show *On a Clear Day You Can See Forever*, all resurfaced on *Zoot Suit Riot* three years later.

The band went for a harder ska- and punk-influenced sound on 1996's *Kids on the Street*, an album they promoted by hitting the road with California third-wave ska vets Let's Go Bowling and Orange County upstarts Reel Big Fish. The tour was called Come Out Swingin', and around this time the Daddies' manager noticed that fans were always coming to the merch booth asking which album contained the most swing. Later that year, when the group found itself with only enough money to record four new songs, the manager had an idea: why not cut four new swing tunes, package them with 10 from previous albums, and give the fans something they'd really dig?

By this point, retro-swing scenes were thriving in San Francisco and Los Angeles. Cherry Poppin' Daddies had gone over well in both cities and performed alongside Royal Crown Revue, instigators of the entire movement. "It was like, 'Jesus Christ, we're playing similar stuff,'" Perry says of discovering RCR. "But we would still play our funky stuff and our rocking stuff, and we'd dress like a rock band. They came out in suits. They sounded like a jazz band to us, and we were kind of like a rock band. We didn't think of ourselves in the same kind of scene, really."

One of the new songs Perry wrote for the swing compilation became the title track, "Zoot Suit Riot." In sound and subject matter, it shares a lot in common with "Hey Pachuco," the Royal Crown Revue song included on the band's 1991 indie debut, *Kings of Gangster Bop*, and their 1996 major-label debut, *Mugzy's Move*. Both songs open with rolling tom-tom beats, and both concern themselves with the infamous Zoot Suit Riots of 1943.

"People in the swing scene were throwing shade at Cherry Poppin' Daddies because a lot of people felt like 'Zoot Suit Riot' was a little too close to 'Hey Pachuco,'" says Michael Moss, publisher of *Swing Time* magazine. "Myself, I wasn't in that camp. I liked what [Cherry Poppin' Daddies] did. I was more interested in modern sounds that combined swing music with modern sensibilities and made contemporary music."

Perry says "Hey Pachuco" had no influence on "Zoot Suit Riot." He never associated Royal Crown Revue's song with the Zoot Suit Riots, but rather with the zoot suit era itself, a period soundtracked by artists like Lalo Guerrero, known as "the father of Chicano music." During the '40s, Guerrero wrote swinging tunes for the pachucos of Southern California, a subculture of young Mexican Americans with their own slang and rebellious style of dress. Guerrero's small-band swing was a template for the Daddies and many bands in the retro-swing movement.

"['Zoot Suit Riot'] is a jump blues with a couple saxophones—that was what was happening in 1943 in Los Angeles," says Perry. "So it was perfect. It made sense, and as with something like 'Master and Slave,' it also pointed out subtly—which is what I wanted to do—this racist event in our history and put Cherry Poppin' Daddies on the side of the zoot suiters."

Perry envisioned "Zoot Suit Riot" as an anthem for the burgeoning swing scene. "My idea was that it was from the perspective of zooter, because that's who we are," says Perry. "We're the zoot suiters, the outcasts. We listened to this kind of music, which was Lalo Guerrero and people like that, this jitterbug music in Spanish. But then I used the Zoot Suit Riots as the setting for this thing. So it's really a clarion call for this scene and this music."

The Daddies released *Zoot Suit Riot* on their own Space Age Bachelor Pad label in the spring of 1997. The cover features Perry's zoot suited silhouette against a retro-cool lime-green background reminiscent of Jim Carrey's skin color in *The Mask*. The album quickly began selling about 4,000 copies a week, an impressive number that—along with some help from Come Out Swingin' tour mates Reel Big Fish—earned the group a deal with Mojo Records. *Zoot Suit Riot* was rereleased on Mojo in July of '97, and by August of the following year it was certified platinum. (It went double platinum in 2000.) The album peaked at #17 on the Billboard 200 and #1 on the Heatseekers Albums chart, while the single "Zoot Suit Riot" made it to #41 on the Hot 100 Airplay chart and #15 on Modern Rock Tracks.

"Zoot Suit Riot" is right up there with Brian Setzer's "Jump, Jive an' Wail" as the song people most associate with the '90s swing renaissance. It's brash and showy, with a pounding rhythm and sneering vocal from Perry that's cartoonish enough to give the song a novelty feel. The band made two music videos for MTV, both featuring swing dancers and plenty of mugging from a zooted-up Perry. (The Daddies started wearing suits after Dicky Barrett of the Bosstones jokingly told Perry that his mismatched crew resembled shipwreck victims.) Seemingly nobody in the press took issue with a white guy rocking a zoot suit and singing about a racist incident that affected Mexican Americans. Few interviewers in 1998 even mentioned the riots, perhaps because most Americans never learned about them in history class.

"Zoot Suit Riot" would definitely raise red flags in the ultra-PC twenty-first century, but Perry insists he wasn't trying to put himself in the wingtips of the embattled 1943 pachuco. "We were trying to reclaim that music that was gone to history," Perry says. "Other people were doing the same thing. People were just starting to learn Lindy Hop and stuff like that, so we were resurrecting this dead form. We were trying to raise consciousness about this great music that we'd discovered that nobody gave a shit about. I didn't think of it as, 'This is literally a guy in the Zoot Suit Riots.'"

The success of "Zoot Suit Riot" meant Jay Leno and David Letterman had to say the band's name on national television. "It was like they had a mouthful of poop," Perry told the Celebrity Cafe in 2000. "They knew that they were going to a mass audience. Jay Leno said it very quickly, 'The Cherry Popping Daddies, but it's not what you think, they're really great.' And when Letterman did it, he tried to say it fast so that nobody would notice." Everyone must've noticed Perry's energy, though, as he pulled off jump-splits, high-kicks, and Elvis hip shimmies.

Perry had taken the Daddies further than he ever imagined in that Eugene punk house nearly a decade earlier. Unfortunately, he found success pretty miserable overall. On top of playing for a lowest-common-denominator Top 40 audience that had no clue what the band was about, he faced immediate backlash back home in Eugene. "If I wasn't on the road, I'd be walking down the street with people yelling, 'You suck. Your band sucks.'" Perry suspects much of the vitriol came from young men who simply couldn't stomach swing.

"Guys don't feel empowered with swing music," he says. "There's too many rules. The girls like it, but the guys don't like it, in general. What

FIG.14 Cherry Poppin' Daddies dress for success at Bally's Las Vegas Hotel and Casino, 1999. Photographer unknown.

young men are interested in is trying to appear tough and savvy and strong, and something about swing music doesn't [do the job]. Unless you're smart, and you realize this actually *is* that kind of music. But they didn't get it."

If girls were one reason the swing thing happened, aging punks were another. "Anybody who was really into music and was in the punk scene, your tastes had to go somewhere," Perry says. "You couldn't just remain liking the same things you liked when you were 16." For a certain subset of curious listeners, swing and ska offered a chance to explore styles of music with rich histories going back decades.

"We were playing this music that had these bizarre roots," says Perry. "Ska music has roots in Jamaica and further back in New Orleans R&B. Swing music has roots in jump blues, postwar blues, and then the big band era, and you look before that in the '20s and '30s Cotton Club stuff. All that stuff is something that is fun to discover and makes you feel sophisticated."

Going into their next album, the Daddies knew they were damned if they did or didn't swing. The fad wasn't going to last, so another album like *Zoot Suit Riot* was sure to tank. On the other hand, a return to the band's genre-shuffling ways was bound to confuse fans who knew them only for swinging. In the end, the band decided to just do what they'd always done and hope for the best. On 2000's *Soul Caddy*, they serve up just three up-tempo swing jams, plus glam rock, ska, punk, surf, and more. It's as good as any of the Daddies' pre-'97 studio albums, and like all of those, it failed to chart or produce any hits.

"It was disappointing, because I thought, 'Well, people might see that this band has an art trip and can appreciate the full range of what we do,'" Perry says. "But not surprised that that didn't happen either, really." After touring behind *Soul Caddy*, Perry decided to take some time off. He'd been on the road for the better part of 15 years, and he finally had some money in his pockets. He reenrolled at the University of Oregon and finished his degree in molecular biology. Following his graduation, he worked in the school's Cresko Lab, helping to study the stickleback, a type of fish that's famous for evolving super-quickly in isolation. Sounds like Perry's type of critter.

The rigors of academia didn't keep Perry completely away from music. He released a self-titled one-off album with the glam-rock side project White Hot Odyssey in 2004. All the while the Daddies played sporadically, and in 2007 they began work on a new album. Released the following year on Space Age Bachelor Pad, *Susquehanna* is the usual genre grab bag, with a focus on tropical sounds like flamenco and soca. The following year brought *Skaboy JFK: The Skankin' Hits of the Cherry Poppin' Daddies*, a collection of all their ska material.

Cherry Poppin' Daddies will always be known as a swing band, and Perry knows that. That's why he began booking the band for corporate events and shows at performing arts centers, where fans are looking to swing dance. "Now that we've established that once again, it's like, 'Hey, if you have a show and you want to have an impressive swing band, you call Cherry Poppin' Daddies,'" says Perry. "So that's what we do, and we're glad to do it."

In 2013, the Daddies returned with *White Teeth, Black Thoughts*, their first all-swing album since *Zoot Suit Riot*. They followed that with 2014's *Please Return the Evening*, a tribute to the Rat Pack, and 2016's *The Boop-a-Doo*, a collection of swing and jazz standards. Just when it seemed Perry was content to keep swinging into his twilight years, the band dropped *Bigger Life* in 2019. Its focus on ska and punk recalls *Kids on the Street*, though the Daddies naturally had some surprises in store, such as "Schizo," an electro-funk banger reminiscent of Cameo's 1986 hit "Word Up."

"I think it's one the best records we've done," says Perry. "It's a throwback to that era, but each song is kind of labored over lyrically, and it fits together like a mural, like a dollhouse where each room has its little tableau."

■ ■ ■

The retro-swing aesthetic wasn't pegged to any single decade. It was a mishmash of mid-century American signifiers: zoot suits, Rat Pack sharkskin, wingtips, seamed stockings, fedoras, pompadours, Bettie Page bangs, Zippos, martinis, cigars, and tattoos. It strove to be slick, urban, and cool—none of which are words you'd use to describe Squirrel Nut Zippers.

Outliers in every way, Squirrel Nut Zippers were rooted in the '30s-era "hot jazz" sounds that predated big band swing. Influenced by artists like Cab Calloway, Fats Waller, Louis Armstrong, and Django Reinhardt, the Zippers made old-timey, rural, vaguely creepy Southern music propelled by banjo and trumpet. They were always in danger of being mistaken for some kind of ironic joke, especially after their unlikely chart ascension.

The Zippers will go down in history for their lone hit, "Hell," which was very much a novelty when it caught fire on alternative radio in 1997. Written and sung by multi-instrumentalist Tom Maxwell, "Hell" was bonkers in sound (calypso beat, shrill trumpet) and subject matter (the horrors awaiting sinners in the afterlife). Maxwell was inspired not just by '20s-era Trinidadian calypsonians, but also by the holy-rolling radio preachers he heard growing up in rural North Carolina. Profoundly weird and darkly funny, "Hell" defined the Zippers as far as many listeners were concerned.

But these one-hit wonders from Chapel Hill, North Carolina, weren't out for laughs—not exclusively. Smarter and more subversive than anyone realized, the Zippers viewed prewar musical styles as valid forms of expression that had been wrongly forgotten. The journey of rediscovery began in 1993, when Squirrel Nut Zippers mastermind Jimbo Mathus moved with his soon-to-be wife Katharine Whalen to an old two-story farmhouse in Efland, North Carolina. While renovating the place, Mathus and Whalen would listen to old records and make marionettes, as young Southern boho lovers do. Mathus taught Whalen to play the banjo and encouraged her singing, though she'd never done anything musical in her life. "I heard her singing on the porch one day," says Mathus. "I thought she was playing one of her Billie Holiday records. She was playing this little banjo song that I'd shown her and singing along to it. I said, 'Well shit.' I started working with her, and then I started looking at the different weirdos around town."

Mathus and Whalen began hosting Southern cooking–fueled jam sessions that included drummer (and later guitarist and saxophonist) Ken Mosher, upright bassist Don Raleigh, and drummer Chris Phillips, who played makeshift percussion involving coconut shells. In those days, the Zippers experimented with all sorts of "early creepy American music," as Mathus calls it. Much of it was stuff he'd absorbed as a kid in Clarksdale, Mississippi, way down in the Delta. His father was a bluegrass musician, and by the age of six Mathus had picked up the mandolin, a precursor to guitar and other instruments. "I grew up with my dad and my uncles, picking in fucking overalls under the tree," Mathus says. "I mean, this is real. Grandmamma playing the bass in a bonnet and shit."

Mathus moved to Chapel Hill in 1989 to meet other musicians and study up on the roots of American music. In addition to university libraries and book and record stores, he discovered retro-leaning local artists like punkabilly bashers Flat Duo Jets and string-band revivalists Red Clay Ramblers. Mathus washed dishes for money and played drums in several area bands, including local rockers Metal Flake Mother. Meeting Whalen, he says, was "the lynchpin" for what came next.

The Zippers played their first show at a Chapel Hill bistro and blew the roof off the joint. "Everybody in town showed up [wearing] old tuxedos and ball gowns," Mathus says. From that one show, the Zippers scored a record deal with local indie bastion Merge Records, who released their debut EP, *Roasted Right*, in 1994.

In the year between the EP and their 1995 full-length debut, *The Inevitable*, released on Mammoth Records, the Zippers underwent a swift metamorphosis. They added trumpeter Stacy Guess, a serious jazz student who'd played in the '80s-era ska-influenced Southern band the Pressure Boys. Tom Maxwell, who'd drummed for Chapel Hill rockers What Peggy

Wants, joined first on additional percussion but graduated to guitar and vocals when Chris Phillips decided he was going to be the sole drummer. The Zippers worked weddings and society parties while honing their sound. "We played some mountain music, we played some gospel-y type shit, we played some blues, and we played some more ragtime-y stuff," Mathus says. They finally settled on the hot sound that would be their foundation, and when Maxwell stepped up to sing they figured out quickly how to present their ragtag ensemble.

The Inevitable opens with "Lover's Lane," a frisky Mathus-penned fastie with nimble banjo and beaming trumpet. The noirish ballad "Danny Diamond" introduces the vocal stylings of Whalen, whom critics understandably likened to Billie Holiday and Betty Boop. The Zippers really unfurl the freak flag on "La Grippe"—a groaning tune about the Spanish flu that you can imagine Tom Waits singing—and "Wash Jones," an eerie sketch of a character you probably don't want your kids hanging out with. The mission statement comes on "Good Enough for Granddad," wherein Mathus declares, "All the good times that he had / If they were good enough for Granddad / They're good enough for me."

The Inevitable brought the Zippers more acclaim in their backyard and enabled them to tour out west. It was only at this point that the heretofore-isolated Zippers discovered the retro-swing scene brewing in California. When they turned up to play the Derby in L.A., Mathus was shocked to see a line around the block. "I walked in and all these people and all these crazy West Coast vintage suits," he says. "The band playing before us could have been one of the big bands. I have no idea—some jumpin', jivin', swingin' band. I was like, 'Holy shit, man.'"

In the summer of 1995, Mathus, Maxwell, and Mosher road-tripped to New Orleans, a city Jimbo had prowled in the '80s while on leave from working on barges and tankers. While in the Crescent City, the musicians visited Kingsway Studios, built in an old mansion by U2 producer Daniel Lanois. They fell in love with the place and returned in October with the full band to record their sophomore album. Absent from this adventure, however, was Guess, who'd been fired on account of his heroin addiction. He was replaced by session trumpeter Duke Heitger, who added his parts after everything else had been tracked. "We just left the holes where the solos were," Mathus says.

The Zippers made this second record, titled *Hot* and released in June 1996, in what Maxwell has called "six days of pure fucking magic." They recorded mostly live, using ambient microphones to capture the sound of Kingsway. *Hot* has a warm, homey, slightly spooky feel that's perfect for songs like the hard-swinging "Memphis Exorcism" and the doe-eyed and dainty "Prince Nez." The pick for lead single was "Put a Lid on It," featuring growling trumpets and call-and-response between Whalen and the boys. Maxwell wrote the lyrics about Guess's struggles with heroin: "Put a lid down on it and everything will be alright." (Guess died of an overdose in March 1998 at the age of 33.)

Tom Osborne, Mammoth's West Coast rep, tried pushing "Put a Lid on It" to alternative radio but realized it didn't fit. "Hell," on the other hand, seemed like a possible winner, so Osborne called an audible and talked KROQ in L.A. into giving it a try. "[KROQ] played it during the lunch drive time as a joke—this is the story, anyway—and the phones never stopped lighting up," Maxwell told *Indy Week* in 2016. Several months after the release of *Hot*, "Hell" was in heavy rotation on KROQ. Alternative stations across the country began adding the song, and overnight, everything changed for the Zippers. They'd already started recording their next album when Mammoth delivered the shocking news: "You have a hit."

Mammoth immediately put the Zippers back on the road to work the single, which peaked at #13 on Billboard's Modern Rock Tracks chart and propelled *Hot* to #27 on the Billboard 200. MTV gave ample airtime to the "Hell" music video, in which the Zippers appear on a variety show in some nightmarish David Lynch world. The band filmed the clip right after playing one of President Clinton's January 1997 inaugural balls, a gig they'd booked before "Hell" took off. In December 1997, *Hot* went platinum. Somewhere along the way, critics began lumping the Zippers in with West Coast swing bands like Royal Crown Revue and Big Bad Voodoo Daddy. In a 2000 interview with Pause & Play, Maxwell described the swing label as "a horrible, horrible ball and chain, a hideous weight placed around our necks." Mathus wasn't as irked by the association. "I don't have any bad feelings about all of that happening at that time," he says. "To me, it was always pretty cool."

In August 1998, Mammoth finally released the Zippers' third album, *Perennial Favorites*, which had been in the can for more than a year. The group had once again recorded in an old house, this one in Pittsboro, North Carolina. Mosher rented it for $250 a month, and the band fixed up the plumbing and electricity. *Hot* co-producer Mike Napolitano drove up with a bunch of vintage gear, and the group recorded much like they had at Kingsway. The sessions included new trumpeter Je Widenhouse and violinist Andrew Bird, who'd also played on *Hot*. (A few years later, Bird would become a Pitchfork-approved indie rocker.)

Having toured extensively in the year prior to making *Perennial Favorites*, the Zippers hadn't rehearsed a lot of the new songs. Yet in one two-week blast, they made their wildest, most accomplished album yet. On "Ghost of Stephen Foster," as East Indian strings give way to klezmer, Mathus imagines a conversation with the famed American songwriter behind "Camptown Races," a children's favorite that's actually about prostitutes. "Camptown ladies *never* sang all the doo-da-day, oh no no!" Mathus sings. "The Kraken" is demented cartoon music. "Pallin' with Al" is Maxwell's tribute to his greatest musical hero, Fats Waller guitarist Al Casey, whom the band had befriended.

"Trou Macacq" is another calypso, though Maxwell shifts his focus from the afterlife to the hassles that come with being a successful band here on Earth. Fearing being pigeonholed as a calypso band, Maxwell pushed back when the label wanted to issue "Trou Macacq" as the lead single. Instead, they went with "Suits Are Picking Up the Bill," a hot dance number that, along with "Fat Cats Keep Getting Fatter," might've satisfied the hardcore swing dancers increasingly turning up at Zippers gigs. In his sharp and entertaining 2014 memoir *Hell*, Maxwell calls them "swing Nazis," given their tendency to elbow their way up front and monopolize the dance floor.

"Suits Are Picking Up the Bill" missed the charts, even as Brian Setzer and Cherry Poppin' Daddies were shimmy-shaking across the radio dial. *Perennial Favorites* debuted at #18 on the Billboard 200 but fell well short of its predecessor. As of November 2019, *Perennial Favorites* had sold just 465,000 copies, compared to nearly 1.26 million for *Hot*, according to Nielsen Music. In July 1999, Maxwell announced that he was leaving. Asked why he quit in a 2014 Reddit AMA session, Maxwell said, "We were basically shot out of a cannon once 'Hell' hit, and couldn't stand the pressure really. I left because all the stuff I thought made us great musically was gone." According to Mathus, Maxwell was freaked out by success and the business aspects of being in a popular band. Ditto for Mosher, who left a few months later. "They just thought they were selling out to the man," says Mathus. "I'm thinking, 'Man, we're doing what we're born to do: be entertainers, packing the house with our music that we compose. What's wrong with that?'"

Mathus added a piano player and two new horn players, and the Zippers returned to Kingsway with some old friends—producer Napolitano, violinist Bird—to make their next album, 2000's *Bedlam Ballroom*. This time, Mathus leapfrogged two or three decades, referencing '50s rock and '60s James Brown funk-soul. But the Zippers' pop heyday had passed, and by 2006 the album had sold less than 70,000 copies. Disappointing sales were just the beginning of Mathus's troubles. In 2001, Maxwell and Mosher sought arbitration with the rest of the band over underpaid royalties. The arbitrator awarded them $345,569.74, and in 2003 the parties settled for $155,000. The lawsuit spelled the end for the band, and in 2003 Mathus and Whalen divorced.

Post-Zippers, Mathus has kept busy making solo records (more than a dozen as of 2020) and working with artists like Buddy Guy. He also founded the Delta Recording Service, a Mississippi studio that hosted everyone from Southern rappers to drum-and-fife bands to Elvis Costello, who dropped by to record "Monkey to Man" for his 2004 album *The Delivery Man*. The Zippers briefly reunited in 2007, and in 2016 Mathus put together an all-new lineup, which released the album *Beasts of Burgundy* in 2018. Mathus termed the twenty-first-century Zippers a "revival," not a reunion, and as of 2019 it was still rolling.

"I could be sitting here onstage playing Squirrel Nut Zippers music, God willing, as long as I'm around," Mathus says. "Now I'll have a kick-ass band, and we'll have that old, weird America presented onstage. Bring that joy and that freedom, just wild creativity, you know? That's something I can do forever, man. Until the Lord calls me home. That's the plan."

CHAPTER 10

Stray Cat Swings

In June 1998, Brian Setzer and his namesake orchestra released their third album, *The Dirty Boogie*, a long-awaited commercial breakthrough that yielded the omnipresent smash "Jump, Jive an' Wail" and defined the swing revival for a large segment of the CD-buying population. That summer, Setzer had a theory about why snazzy horns and jazzy beats were suddenly cool again. There was the fad aspect, sure, but beyond that, he took an almost Jungian view of America's fondness for the genre.

"I think this stuff is all in us—you might have heard swing as a kid on a Rice Krispies commercial," Setzer told the *Boston Phoenix*. "So it's in our psyche. Whereas I don't know if something like ska really is. I don't see how they're going to get ska in Iowa. But the rockabilly, the jazz, the country, the blues, and the swing is all there. It's just part of our culture."

These things are certainly part of Setzer's DNA. As every journalist in the '90s pointed out, the Brian Setzer Orchestra wasn't the pompadoured singer and virtuoso guitarist's first time at the retro rodeo. Nearly 20 years earlier—several lifetimes in popular music—Setzer and his band Stray Cats gave rockabilly a New Wave paint job and drove it straight up the pop charts. With early-'80s hits like "Stray Cat Strut," "(She's) Sexy + 17," and "Rock This Town," Stray Cats played '50s rock in a way punks could understand, much like the Specials did with '60s ska.

Setzer split up the Cats and went solo in 1984, then reunited them in '86 for a second go-round that lasted until the early '90s. The Cats circa grunge were burned out, playing to empty clubs they used to pack. Their excellent 1992 album *Choo Choo Hot Fish* came and went without anyone noticing. Setzer needed a change, and fortunately, he'd been toying with this *other* idea for ages.

Growing up in Massapequa, Long Island, about an hour from New York City by train, Setzer wasn't strictly the rock 'n' roll guy one might assume. When he began taking guitar lessons at eight, his teacher was a saxophone player who introduced him to jazz chords. His second instructor went further into the heady world of scales, modes, and standards. Setzer learned to read and write music, and though his early love for the Beatles led him to Carl Perkins and a lifelong romance with rockabilly, his tastes extended well beyond the '50s.

As a teenager, Setzer would ditch school and take the Long Island Rail Road into the city to see the Thad Jones / Mel Lewis Orchestra at the venerable jazz spot the Village Vanguard. "I was 15 and I don't know how I got in—a note from my mom?" Setzer told the *San Diego Union-Tribune*. "One night I'd be at CBGB, the other at the Vanguard. But what stood out for me was the Thad Jones / Mel Lewis Orchestra, because of their arrangements and the complexity of them. Their big band was as powerful as anything I heard at CBGB. And I heard some *really* good stuff at CBGB— the Ramones, the Dead Boys—that was pretty powerful."

Those nights at the Vanguard planted the idea in Setzer's head to pair rocking guitar with big band horns. He was further inspired by trumpeter Doc Severinsen, leader of the house band on *The Tonight Show Starring Johnny Carson*. Setzer used to watch Carson and imagine playing in front of Severinsen's horn section, something visiting rock bands sadly never did. At one point Stray Cats were slated to appear on the show and do "Rock This Town" with Doc's brass, but for whatever reason it never happened.

Then one night in 1992, while he was living in Santa Monica, Setzer serendipitously walked past the house of his neighbor, jazz saxophonist Michael Acosta. The horn man was hosting a jam session, and he invited Setzer to grab his guitar and sit in. "They had old Monk charts, Miles Davis—some pretty hard stuff that they were trying to get me with," Setzer told *Guitar Player*. "I sat in with them, and they were like, 'Gee, this guy's all right. He can play.'" Not long after, Setzer shared with Acosta his idea for a guitar-led big band, something that had never been tried before.

There were many good reasons *not* to pursue this idea. For starters, it was 1992. Grunge ruled, and the nascent West Coast retro-swing scene had yet to really take hold. Second, the classic big band configuration calls for five saxophones, four trombones, four trumpets, bass, drums, and piano. That meant coordinating the schedules of 17 musicians and paying just as many salaries on the road. Big bands are extremely unwieldy and expensive to keep running—that's one of the reasons they died the first time. Also, writing charts for 13 horn players is complicated and time-consuming, even if you have the know-how. But Setzer believed he was onto something, and with Acosta's help he put together a crackerjack band of L.A. session aces that included trombonist Bruce Fowler and his sax-playing brother Steve, both of whom had worked with Frank Zappa.

"The musicians are local, jazz, session players, like when you hear *The Lion King*, that's half my band," Setzer told MusicPlex in 1996. "When you see a Sinatra special, that's part of my band. Most of the guys prefer to stay around rather than go out on tour, because they make pretty good money around town. When you hear a little jazz combo on some toothpaste commercial, that's probably some of the guys in the orchestra!"

Only about 30 people turned up for the first Brian Setzer Orchestra show in late 1992. Undaunted, Setzer played on, and within six months, he'd earned a deal with Hollywood Records. "He's very pure about what he does," says former Hollywood president Peter Paterno in an episode of *VH1 Legends* devoted to Setzer. "He had a vision, and he executed that vision whether it was trendy or not, or happening or not. It was great, so I signed the band."

Setzer handled production on the orchestra's self-titled 1994 debut, a trial run with a handful of transcendent moments. Across these initial 12 tracks, Setzer treats his big band like a fancy new car he's a little afraid to drive. The horns don't blast like they do on later albums, and Setzer's guitar playing is uncharacteristically restrained. His covers of jump-blues great Wynonie Harris's "Sittin' on It All the Time" and British rockabilly star Vince Taylor's "Brand New Cadillac," famously done by the Clash on their 1979 album *London Calling*, are polite toe-tappers instead of the barn-burners they might've been.

Where Setzer really shines on the first album is behind the microphone. Always an underrated singer in his Stray Cats days, he croons smooth and confident on the original ballad "September Skies" and the standard "A Nightingale Sang in Berkeley Square." He's playful and relaxed on Carl Perkins's "Your Love," which he transforms into a swing-abilly hybrid with rippling guitar breaks. *The Brian Setzer Orchestra* is a promising start given that Setzer was literally in uncharted territory. "With that first record, we got signed so quick, I didn't have the songs, the charts, or anything," Setzer said. "It was kind of a swing band and the guitar wasn't really part of the band."

That would change by the time of his second album—and so would Setzer's record label. While Hollywood rolled the dice on the orchestra and even paid to keep the money-devouring ensemble on the road, turnover at the label—including the resignation of Paterno in November 1993—left Setzer in a place where he didn't know anybody. In 1995, Interscope A&R rep Tom Whalley scooped the band up, and Setzer soon found himself in the studio with Phil Ramone, the legendary producer behind albums for Barbra Streisand, Paul Simon, and Frank Sinatra. After catching the orchestra in concert, Ramone told Setzer he wanted to produce the next album. "But you need to record like you play live," Setzer remembered Ramone telling him. "If your guitar isn't blasting with you singing the way you sing, the band plays differently." In the studio, Ramone outlawed headphones for playback and instead set up a PA in front of the horn section, almost like they were making a live album.

Setzer called this 1996 set *Guitar Slinger*, an apt title given the orchestra's increased firepower. This time out, Setzer had a hand in writing nine of the 12 songs, including two penned with his good buddy Joe Strummer, formerly of the Clash. Both Setzer and Strummer had vintage Cadillacs and young children, so they'd round up their families and vacation together. One night, Strummer put pen to paper by candlelight and came up with the words to "Ghost Radio," a kind of spooky campfire story rooted in the British rocker's love for classic American imagery. Setzer fit Strummer's stylish lyrics—which shout out Bob Willis, the "King of Western Swing"—to a rubber-burning arrangement typical of his approach on *Guitar Slinger*. On standouts like "Hoodoo Voodoo Doll," "(The Legend of) Johnny Kool," and his reimagination of the Stray Cats fave "Rumble in Brighton," Setzer embraces his rockabilly past and lights a fire under the horn section.

With "Hey, Louis Prima," Setzer imagines cruising around with the titular swing king, slaying audiences wherever they go. When he wrote the line, "And wouldn't it be kinda funny / If we got outta town with all the money?" Setzer couldn't have known he'd hit the jackpot a couple years later by covering one of Prima's greatest hits. Unless he's as good at predicting the future as he is at reviving the past.

"I think I got the second [album] more in the pocket I wanted," Setzer told the *Los Angeles Times*. "The first record, which I still like, was more of a swing record. We got signed to Hollywood Records kind of quickly for that one, and I got put in the studio pretty quickly. It was like, 'Jeez, I've got to write some songs here.' The band was still new; we hadn't really become a band yet. So after we did it, it was like, 'OK, this does work, and I all I have to do now is write some really good songs, and I'm all set.'"

And yet despite promotional efforts that included a 1997 appearance on the CBS sitcom *The Nanny* (the orchestra shoots a music video at Mr. Sheffield's house), *Guitar Slinger* fell flat, just like its predecessor. But traffic was shifting on the great highway of pop, and the ex–Stray Cat would soon find a wide-open fast lane back to the top of the Billboard charts. In 1996, the movie *Swingers* came out, and the following year, on the strength of their fluke hit "Hell," Squirrel Nut Zippers went platinum with *Hot*. Also in 1997, the long-teased ska boom finally happened, further normalizing the presence of horns on mainstream radio and MTV. America was almost ready to jump, jive, and wail, and Setzer was the guy to make it happen.

For his third outing with the orchestra, Setzer made some crucial changes. "I found a slap bass player who could read music, know where the chords are going—that makes the record jump," he told the *Denver Post*, referring to Tony Garnier, a longtime Bob Dylan sideman who'd also played with Tom Waits, Chuck Berry, and rockabilly revivalist Robert Gordon, among others. Garnier replaced original Brian Setzer Orchestra bassist Bob Parr, more of a jazz guy who couldn't flog his instrument the way Setzer needed him to.

Setzer and trombonist Mark Jones, his principal arranging partner, left more space in their charts, an approach that gave the horns more bite. Then there was the method of recording. Working with producer Peter Collins, whose credits ranged from Bon Jovi and Rush to Save Ferris, Setzer tracked the rhythm section first, then added the horns. "Everything had to be *now*—no overdubbed solos, none of that," Setzer told *Guitar Player*. "If I ever second-guessed myself and thought, 'Oh, I can do the solo better,' and then tried to overdub it, it never sounded as good. There's something about the urgency of three guys rocking that you can't lose."

For all of these reasons, 1998's *The Dirty Boogie* sounds like a new band. The album is big and bright, with just the right amount of cartoonish humor and showboating. Unlike Cherry Poppin' Daddies front man Steve Perry on *Zoot Suit Riot*, the other big swing album of 1998, Setzer never challenges his audience to unpack double meanings or consider whether he's being ironic. Setzer's appeal lies in his earnest enthusiasm and unparalleled musicianship. *The Dirty Boogie* is, for lack of a better word, fun.

After stocking *Guitar Slinger* with originals, Setzer contributed only five new songs to *The Dirty Boogie*, one of which, the slinky jazz-noir standout "Hollywood Nocturne," was a holdover from the previous album. However limited, Setzer's writing in this period was strong. Opener "This Cat's on a Hot Tin Roof" is a thumping rockabilly rave-up with sizzling horn bursts. The jazzier title track features a roiling groove and cool call-and-response vocal interplay between Setzer and the band. Setzer practically sweats joie de vivre on "Let's Live It Up," promising to fly you to the moon and "hang your coat and hat upon a shooting star."

The covers are similarly well selected. "This Old House," a transatlantic 1954 chart topper for Rosemary Clooney later recorded by the likes of NRBQ and Carl Perkins, is an up-tempo boogie Setzer easily makes his own. "Since I Don't Have You," a lovesick smash for the vocal group the Skyliners in 1958, is another showcase for Setzer the crooner. "Rock This Town," Setzer's signature Stray Cats tune, races like a tricked-out fire engine, sirens wailing. "As Long as I'm Singin'" is a faithful remake of Bobby Darin's Sinatra-esque 1964 finger-popper.

On "You're the Boss," Setzer and Interscope labelmate Gwen Stefani play Elvis Presley and Ann-Margret, who originally recorded the duet for 1964's *Viva Las Vegas*. (It was left out of the movie.) Setzer and Stefani hadn't met prior to the session, and while they never sound as if they're about to rip each other's clothes off, like Elvis and real-life flame Ann-Margret do, they share a playful natural chemistry. "Maybe tonight, I'll be the boss / And tomorrow night, *I'll* be the boss," Stefani coos near the end, leaving Setzer to mutter, "Whoa."

Best of all was "Sleepwalk," which earned Setzer a Grammy for Best Pop Instrumental Performance in 1999. Setzer had a history with the chart-topping 1959 instrumental by Santo & Johnny, Brooklyn brothers whose use of steel guitar gave their music an otherworldly quality. Stray Cats covered "Sleepwalk" on *Choo Choo Hot Fish*, and five years before that, the Santo & Johnny original soundtracked a key scene in the Richie Valens biopic *La Bamba*, which features Setzer very briefly as '50s rocker Eddie Cochran. In the 32 highly capable hands of the Brian Setzer Orchestra, "Sleepwalk" becomes a lush, tranquil swoon-fest.

Setzer picked up two Grammys in 1999; the other was for "Jump, Jive an' Wail," the most fortuitous cover choice on the album. *The Dirty Boogie* came out two months after the Gap premiered its "Khakis Swing" commercial, which had millions of Americans humming Louis Prima's 1956 original. Setzer hadn't planned on remaking the song, and in fact, a "Jive"-free version of *The Dirty Boogie* was finished and ready to ship before the Gap ad debuted. The label even sent out advance copies of the CD. Whalley then convinced Setzer to go back into the studio and record the song. This was almost certainly after the commercial came out, though Setzer's manager, Dave Kaplan, says he can't recall exactly when Whalley had the idea. Either way, Setzer was reluctant, until he realized he could give Prima his high-octane big band treatment. "I wrote all the charts, put a modulation in there, put a great guitar solo, slap bass," Setzer says in his episode of *VH1 Legends*. "All of a sudden, I went, 'Oh, it's got some magic to it.'"

In the second half of 1998, "Jump, Jive an' Wail" was everywhere: radio, TV, weddings, and swing dance classrooms across America. The single reached #2 on Billboard's Adult Modern Rock Tracks chart, #23 on the Mainstream Top 40, #14 on the Adult Top 40, #23 on Hot 100 Airplay, and #15 on Modern Rock Tracks. Setzer and the band shot a flashy music video starring sexy knicker-flashing swing dancers that went into heavy rotation on VH1. In October, *The Dirty Boogie* peaked at #9 on the Billboard 200, giving Setzer his first Top 10 album since Stray Cats' *Built for Speed* in 1982. "You know it's a hit when you get sick of hearing it," Setzer said.

Out on the road, Setzer's audience had grown to include more than just swing heads and Stray Cats fans. "What's incredible is that there are high school kids who are into it," Whalley told the *Los Angeles Times* in August 1998, right after the Brian Setzer Orchestra packed the 3,000-capacity Hammerstein Ballroom in New York City. "The music is fun, there's dancing that goes along with it, and it's something you can do with a date. . . . You never know how long a trend is gonna last. But people thought rap wasn't gonna last, and that's been around for a pretty long time."

Due in part to the overexposure of the Gap ad and Setzer's "Jump, Jive an' Wail," the trend didn't last a whole lot longer. Setzer got a little taste of the backlash when he showed up for the Grammys in February 1999 and crossed paths with punk legend John Lydon, aka Johnny Rotten, on the red carpet. Lydon was covering the event for VH1, and rather than congratulate Setzer—who happens to be an avowed Sex Pistols fan—he gave Brian a calendar, implying that anyone playing swing music in the '90s had no clue what year it was. That diss notwithstanding, it was a triumphant evening for Setzer, who went inside the Shrine Auditorium and won his first-ever Grammys. "That means the most, that you're getting that recognition from your peers, from other musicians," Setzer says on *Legends*. "That's the plum. That's the biggest deal of my life."

Speaking with the *Orange County Register* in 2017, Setzer looked back on the '90s swing revival as something that happened almost tangentially to his big band but helped push it over the top. He admitted the fad was "a bit of a double-edged sword," given the media backlash, but he also remembered all the opportunities it created. "Then there was the other side of it, where people were going crazy for the music," Setzer said. "I wasn't riding my first wave so I kind of knew how to dodge certain things or to take things with a grain of salt, but man, we were flying and selling out shows all over the country." The Brian Setzer Orchestra even played Woodstock '99, where they were the only representatives of the late-'90s ska-swing hooray-for-horns era. Youth culture was shifting back toward heavier music, and the fest is best remembered for violence-inciting performances by nu-metal monsters Korn and Limp Bizkit. On the final night, fans overturned ATMs and set fire to fences and vendor booths. Across the weekend, there were numerous reports of sexual assaults. MTV's Kurt Loder later described "waves of hatred bouncing around the place."

Retro-swing was a distant memory by the time the Brian Setzer Orchestra returned in August 2000 with their fourth album, *Vavoom!* Alongside eight solid originals that feel like *Dirty Boogie* outtakes, Setzer delivers choice covers of Bobby Darin's 1959 rendition of "Mack the Knife," the Cadillacs' 1954 doo-wop classic "Gloria," and Duke Ellington's 1936 exotic jazz standard "Caravan," which earned Setzer another Grammy for Best Pop Instrumental Performance. For "Pennsylvania 6-5000," a swing standard associated with Glenn Miller, Setzer let upstart producer David Darling fire up the computers and employ some hip-hop–style drum loops and other effects. "We went into that Pro Tools land, which is like, 'Danger, Will Robinson!' I've never gone there!" Setzer told *Mix*. "[Darling] said, 'Trust me. We're going to scuff this up, and it's going to sound unique. . . . All of that just added to taking it away from the 1940s sound and making it seem somehow year 2000. And I think it worked."

An inspired pick for lead single might've been "Americano," Setzer's take on the '50s Italian jazz tune that had recently been popularized in the 1999 film *The Talented Mr. Ripley*. Setzer leads the orchestra through a romping version and clearly gets a kick out of the revised lyrics, which paint Americans as whiskey-swilling, rock 'n' roll–loving, showgirl-chasing, Cadillac-driving strivers. Setzer's grinning performance suggests he can live with those generalizations.

Unfortunately, the album's lead single was "Gettin' in the Mood," a corny twenty-first-century update of "In the Mood," another swing standard linked to Glenn Miller. It's a painfully obvious cover choice that's done no favors by Setzer's new lyrics or trumpeter Kevin Norton's regrettable rap. Not even a video filled with hot rods and poolside babes could save "Gettin' in the Mood." It missed the charts, and *Vavoom!* stalled at #62 on the Billboard 200.

It would be nine years before the Brian Setzer Orchestra released another album of original material, the film noir–inspired 2009 collection *Songs from Lonely Avenue*. In the intervening years, the big band made two Christmas albums, plus 2007's *Wolfgang's Big Night Out*, a largely instrumental LP based on works by Beethoven, Mozart, Tchaikovsky, and others. On the solo front, Setzer honored his greasy deities on 2005's *Rockabilly Riot Vol. 1: A Tribute to Sun Records* and released a trio small-band albums rooted in rockabilly but not stuck there.

In 2019, Setzer regrouped Stray Cats for the third time in the twenty-first century and recorded the album *40*, a celebration of four decades in the business. The Cats toured Europe and North America that summer, and later in the year, Setzer planned to front the orchestra for his annual Christmas Rocks! Tour, a tradition dating back to 2003. Unfortunately, Setzer was forced to cancel the trek in November 2019 due to a bout with tinnitus.

Setzer's yuletide infatuation is on-brand with his retro aesthetic. He's Bing Crosby in creepers, Andy Williams with full-sleeve tattoos. Whether jamming on "Here Comes Santa Claus" or "Stray Cat Strut," the Brian Setzer Orchestra is never a novelty in the eyes of its creator. It's a tool for shaking up and straining the various flavors of American music he's savored since childhood.

"I don't know what to say about having kept this band together for 25 years," Setzer told *Orange County Register* in 2017. "There's no real way, with the cost that goes into it and with people's shifting musical taste that this should have even lasted a month. It started off with a very slow ascent and it just keeps going. I don't know what to say about it, but I'm certainly happy it got there, and I love the musical aspect of being in a big band. It's just great to play with that big, beautiful band."

CHAPTER 11

Swinging at the Margins

Ask any '90s child about the swing revival, and if they were even remotely aware of the phenomenon, they'll mention Cherry Poppin' Daddies, Brian Setzer Orchestra, and Big Bad Voodoo Daddy. Savvier consumers of pop culture will throw in Squirrel Nut Zippers, and those who really know what's up will give props to Royal Crown Revue.

But neo-swing wasn't just about the Big Five. All across America—and especially in San Francisco—there were scores of also-swungs who packed clubs and moved bodies without the benefit of MTV. Some preferred it this way. Others had the will and skill to chase a mainstream audience but never got that kiss from Lady Luck.

■ ■ ■

In 1989, San Francisco was a powder keg of retro-cool waiting for the right Zippo to light the fuse. "L.A. didn't have a scene; they had a band. San Francisco had a scene, but we didn't have a band," says Michael Moss, the Frisco scenester who founded *Swing Time* magazine in 1995. The band down in L.A. was Royal Crown Revue, and in 1992 they made their first San Francisco appearance at Cafe Deluxe, a recently opened art deco–style nightclub on the corner of Haight and Ashbury, hippie central two decades earlier. Moss was there.

"It wasn't a place where you saw zoot suits and stuff like that—it was just a cool bar," says Moss. "One night, all of a sudden, these dudes in zoot suits showed up, like six of them, and they packed a bunch of gear and set it up and started to play. And then 20 more people, audience members, came in, all decked out. It was Royal Crown Revue. It blew my mind so hard. The next day, I was like, 'I'm buying a suit. That was dope.'"

Royal Crown Revue found a second home in San Francisco and synthesized a scene of artists and music lovers already rediscovering mid-century American culture. One of the bands established in the city before Royal Crown Revue touched down at Club Deluxe was Lavay Smith & Her Red Hot Skillet Lickers, a swinging blues-jazz combo with its very own pinup queen front woman.

Born in Southern California, Smith spent part of her childhood in the Philippines, where her father was sent on business. As a teenager, Smith would venture off the naval base where her family lived and sing rock and pop hits for drunken sailors in nearby Olongapo City. It was a wild place for a 14-year-old, but Smith had a fine mentor in Sampaguita, the "Queen of Filipino Rock 'n' Roll."

The good times ended when Smith was 16 and the family moved back to the States. They settled in sleepy suburban Orange County, where Smith rebelled against the blandness by listening to trailblazing Black female blues singers like Bessie Smith, Dinah Washington, and Billie Holiday. She discovered this music via the 1980 compilation album *Mean Mothers: Independent Women's Blues, Volume 1*. Featuring songs like Bessie Brown's "Ain't Much Good in the Best of Men Nowadays" and Blue Lu Barker's "I Don't Dig You Jack," *Mean Mothers* is a celebration of Black women who dared to sing their truth in the '20s and '30s. Smith, a white girl who'd been halfway around the world and experienced more than her peers, found the music irresistible.

"Songs about feminism and independence, that's what I was attracted to," says Smith. "It was absolutely punk-rock music. They were incredibly powerful from the women's position. Despite the fact they were kicked down, their humanity still shines."

Smith's desire to make music and get the hell out of Orange County eventually brought her to San Francisco, where she met a pair of fellow whippersnappers with a taste for the old stuff: guitarist Craig Ventresco, who could play just like blues king Big Bill Broonzy, and pianist Christ Siebert, who would become Lavay's musical and romantic soulmate. Through a jam session, Smith enlisted Oscar Meyer, a Black trumpeter who, at the age of 45, had two decades on everyone else in the band. "It was kind of cool that we were multigenerational and multiracial, but mostly young," Smith says. "It was unusual for anybody to be doing this music, especially the way we were doing it."

Named for Jelly Roll Morton's Red Hot Peppers and Georgia fiddler Gid Tanner's '20s-era band the Skillet Lickers, Smith's crew began playing around town. Everyone from rockabillies and punks to regular people who liked jazz and blues were coming to see Lavay vamp her way through decades-old songs that still felt fresh and powerful. She wore vintage cocktail dresses and tucked flowers in her hair like Billie Holiday. The band was hot in every sense of the word, but Smith agrees with Moss: what really catalyzed the San Francisco swing scene was the arrival of Royal Crown Revue. "They just excited people," says Smith. "I'm sure their crowd was more straight rockabilly and hipster because they're so cool."

The Skillet Lickers soon welcomed a pair of veteran instrumentalists with sterling résumés: saxophonist Bill Stewart, who'd played with jazz great Lionel Hampton, and trumpeter Allen Smith, who'd recorded with Duke Ellington and Benny Goodman and performed with Frank Sinatra and Ella Fitzgerald. "We were like from 21 to 80, and we were really proud of that," Smiths says. "These older guys were around when swing turned to bebop, so these were the magic people. You know how magic it is at twilight? That's what the sound between swing and bebop is."

For the first half of the '90s, Lavay Smith & Her Red Hot Skillet Lickers existed purely as a live act. They had no burning desire to make a record, but fans kept asking for one, so they hit the studio and made 1996's sublime

One Hour Mama, named for the playfully suggestive Ida Cox ditty that ends the album. While Big Bad Voodoo Daddy and Cherry Poppin' Daddies rode heavy rock-powered jazz beats into the mainstream spotlight, Smith and the boys kept things light, with plenty of winking humor and tasteful sexuality. Released on their own Fat Note Records, *One Hour Mama* consists solely of covers. The group's faithful approach to blues and jazz from the '30s, '40s, and '50s kept them somewhat on the fringes of retro-swing, a movement Smith nevertheless supported.

"I thought it was so wonderful that so many people were starting to check out jazz and blues and learn how to dance," she says. "It was the kind of revolution we needed. We needed to get back to music we can all listen to as a family, as a group. You don't want to go out and listen to indie rock with your grandma and your dad."

Such talk, plus retro-swing's throwback fashions—men in suits, women in dresses, everyone reinforcing traditional gender roles—might seem politically conservative. It did to Mark Gauvreau Judge, the author and journalist who would become a topic of national conversation in September 2018, when his beer-loving high school buddy Brett Kavanaugh, then a nominee for the U.S. Supreme Court, went before the Senate Judiciary Committee facing allegations he committed sexual assault as a teenager. (Kavanaugh's accuser, Christine Blasey Ford, claimed that Judge was in the room when the incident took place.) In the late '90s, after he'd quit drinking and published his 1997 memoir *Wasted: Tales of a GenX Drunk*, Judge immersed himself in the Washington, D.C., swing scene. He viewed the music and its attendant fashions and social customs as a return to civility after the scourges of '60s liberalism and feminism. Swing was making America great again, and he was all too happy to hit the dance floor.

Judge once wrote favorably of Lavay Smith & Her Red Hot Skillet Lickers in the *Washington Post*, but it was not a mutual admiration society. "He tried to put his own values into it and say, 'This is a conservative movement,'" says Smith. "Of course he met us, and we're like, 'What the fuck

FIG.15 Lavay Smith (*center*) is all smiles with Carmen Getit of Steve Lucky & the Rhumba Bums (*left*) and jazz-blues singer Kim Nalley (*right*). Photo: Mark Jordan.

are you talking about, man? That's not what we are after.' My whole message is about feminism and empowerment, not about being *in your place*."

On their second album, 2000's *Everybody's Talkin' 'Bout Miss Thang*, the Skillet Lickers threw some original songs into the mix. "You know I got to be the boss / But daddy, you can wear the pants," Lavay sings on the va-va-va-vooming opener "The Busy Woman's Blues," a fine summation of her brand of feminism. With arrangements from David Berger, the founding conductor of Lincoln Center Jazz Orchestra, *Miss Thang* is sweet and airy like lemon meringue. The album reached #24 on Billboard's Jazz Albums chart and earned a rave from *JazzTimes*.

After releasing their third record, 2009's *Miss Smith to You!*, the group eased back on touring and focused on local gigs. As of 2019, they were prepping a new album, *Crazy in Love with Patsy Cline*, inspired not just by the titular country heroine but also by Ray Charles. The band's versatility and ability to forge connections between various strains of American music are among the reasons they've remained a San Francisco institution long after the collapse of the swing scene.

"We really were always based more on jazz and the feeling of the music," Smith says. "A lot of the other bands, which I love, have a great sound and a niche. It's just different from ours. A lot of them might use more backbeat, a little more rock 'n' roll. That could be to their advantage. You may go out and play a suburb, and people can dance better with that damn backbeat. That helped some groups. In America, it's all about marketing."

■ ■ ■

Michael Moss of *Swing Time* remembers having long debates with Chris Siebert of the Skillet Lickers about traditionalism versus experimentation in neo-swing. "I knew in my heart that the punk-rock element was really important to making it a contemporary thing and not just some nostalgia thing," Moss says. That's why he championed bands like Cherry Poppin' Daddies and hometown heroes the New Morty Show, the rare swing band that could cover X, Billy Idol, and Metallica—all in the context of a glitzy Vegas lounge-swing spectacular.

The New Morty Show was the brainchild of trumpeter Neal "Morty" Okin, a Michigan native who moved to the Bay Area in 1991. Okin was then a member of the Psychedelic Lounge Cats, a group he joined while studying at Eastern Michigan University. The Cats had gone as far as they could in the Midwest and decided to move to either New York City or San Francisco. The latter seemed more manageable, so westward they went.

Okin had been in San Francisco less than a month when he befriended Club Deluxe bartender and man-about-town Larry Castles, aka Vise Grip. The son of a local vaudeville entertainer, Grip was a onetime hardware store owner (hence his nickname) whose first foray into music was fronting the hardcore punk band Hard Attack in the late '70s. He'd always loved swing, though, and when the scene took shape in the early '90s, he formed a band called St. Vitus Dance. They debuted in 1992 with Okin in the lineup.

With his towering pompadour and taste for vintage fashions, Okin felt right at home in America's retro mecca. "I'd be riding around on my scooter in a fucking suit," he says. "I was playing seven nights a week in tons of different bands. All different styles of music. There was so much music going on here at that time. Ska, punk, rockabilly, swing: it was all one giant scene."

Okin's ska adventures included gigging and recording with Bay Area favorites Undercover S.K.A. and even playing on Skankin' Pickle's 1994 masterwork, *Sing Along with Skankin' Pickle*. He stepped up his freelance game after being fired from St. Vitus (supposedly because he never had an extension cord for his music stand light) and quitting the Psychedelic Lounge Cats. The freedom was nice, but it sucked being at the mercy of other people. So Morty started his own band.

He'd always been a fan of Louis Prima and Keely Smith, the husband-and-wife team who helped put Vegas on the map in the '50s with their music-and-comedy show. Smith played the cool cucumber to Prima's spicy meatball while saxophonist Sam Butera and his band the Witnesses kept the music thumping. The New Morty Show was a '90s update of the Prima-Smith thing, though the real inspiration was the more obscure act Ray Anthony and His Bookend Revue. Like Prima, Anthony was an Italian American trumpeter and bandleader who put together a hard-swinging '50s variety show. The 1969 album *The New Ray Anthony Show*, recorded at the Sahara in Vegas, blew Okin's mind. "It was just the cheesiest thing in the world," says Okin. "It was so awesome."

Okin found his Keely Smith in Connie Champagne, a punk-turned-lounge-singer who was singing backup for the popular soul and blues band Veronica Klaus's Heart and Soul Revue. Champagne was a Keely superfan, and for a little while the band was called the New Morty and Connie Show. When St. Vitus Dance broke up, Okin tapped Vise Grip to play the Prima role, and the chemistry was undeniable. The New Morty Show packed houses in San Francisco and began touring the country—not easy for a 10-piece band. "It was very, very difficult," says Okin. "For tons of different reasons. A lot of egos. A lot of drugs. A lot of alcohol. I was basically running a business, and I was 24 years old."

In addition to the comedic interplay between Grip and Champagne, the New Morty Show's unorthodox cover choices helped to differentiate the group from its retro-swing peers. The Psychedelic Lounge Cats had "lounged up" Ozzy Osbourne and the like, so Okin was well equipped to create swing arrangements of Billy Idol's "White Wedding" and Metallica's "Enter Sandman." Metallica guitarist Kirk Hammett was so impressed by Morty's crew that he hired them for a couple of his Christmas parties. Another celebrity fan was Robin Williams, who'd come see the band at the San Francisco club Bimbo's. In 1996, the New Morty Show made a quickie appearance in the Francis Ford Coppola film *Jack*, starring Williams as a boy who ages at four times the normal speed. Unfortunately, Okin says, the band was given a "goofy" song to perform and didn't get featured anywhere near as prominently as Royal Crown Revue in *The Mask* or Big Bad Voodoo Daddy in *Swingers*.

FIG.16 The New Morty Show prepare to swing some
Metallica tunes. Photo: Mark Jordan.

By early 1997, the New Morty Show had signed a deal with Atlantic
Records, but the whole thing fell apart before they could make a record.
"All I heard was they sensed inner turmoil in the band, and they didn't
want to put all this money into us and think that we're going to break
up a year later," Okin says. "They weren't wrong about inner turmoil. I
mean, fuck, it's a 10-piece band. Not everybody gets along. Where they
got that from is the question. I think I know, but I'm not going to say
anything."

The backup plan was Slimstyle Records, a fledgling Arizona label founded by recent college graduate Jack Vaughn. Vaughn's parents worked in the Foreign Service, and he spent part of his teen years in Guatemala, where he claims to have started that nation's first-ever punk band. "We were probably the last," Vaughn says. While in Guatemala, he started Third World Underground, which released a bunch of "awful punk rock" before he moved back to the States for college. While at school, he incorporated Third World Underground and began issuing proper albums, including a Washington, D.C., indie rock compilation and the debut album by Jonathan Fire*Eater, members of which would go on to form celebrated '00s indie rockers the Walkmen.

After graduating from the University of Arizona in 1996, Vaughn decided he was done with noisy guitar music. "I felt like ska was a good counterbalance to the aggravated guitar rock that came to dominate everything," he says. "It was guys in suits playing melodic music, and women were coming to the shows again. Everyone was dancing. It was a complete antithesis of what had come before and had gotten so boring."

Vaughn started Slimstyle primarily as a ska label in 1997 but soon fell in love with the neo-swing scene. Like Michael Moss, who would become a collaborator and co-executive producer on Slimstyle's most successful CD, Vaughn was all for bands giving swing the modern treatment. "There was a real point among purists going, 'Well that's not real swing,'" says Vaughn. "And I felt like saying, 'Of course it's not. It's an updated take on it.' We're not trying to be Benny Goodman. We're trying to bring the energy of what had come before rock 'n' roll and put it into this music to create something new. . . . In retrospect, it wasn't nearly as cool as we thought at the time. But during that era, it was really pretty great."

Because Vaughn spent much of his initial Slimstyle investment signing ska bands, he didn't have a ton of money left for building his swing roster. After failing to land Big Bad Voodoo Daddy, Vaughn went looking for second-tier groups still up for grabs. He signed the New Morty Show,

San Francisco's Blue Plate Special, and the hard-charging Tucson swing-abilly outfit Hipster Daddy-O and the Handgrenades. Before any of them released their Slimstyle debuts, the label issued *Swing This, Baby*, the defining compilation CD of the '90s swing movement.

Featuring tracks by Big Bad Voodoo Daddy, Royal Crown Revue, Cherry Poppin' Daddies, and the Brian Setzer Orchestra, among others, *Swing This, Baby* was perfect for newbies who wanted to learn what neo-swing was all about. Vaughn cut a production and distribution deal with Beyond, a new label affiliated with BMG, and the CD hit shelves in August 1998, mere months after the Gap's "Khakis Swing" spot. It shipped more than 250,000 copies and reached #146 on the Billboard 200. At least some of those sales were thanks to Fritz Striker's cover painting of a woman in a fedora, blazer, and black stockings sitting on the hood of a car, holding a martini. She was originally clutching a tommy gun, but Walmart—which sold *actual* guns—made them change it.

While Vaughn handled the business end, Moss used his connections to secure the talent. "Bands that hated each other, I was able to get on this record. I will not say who they are, but there was a lot of competition at this point, and some bands didn't want to be on the same record." Moss begrudgingly included "(Everytime I Hear) That Mellow Saxophone" by Brian Setzer Orchestra after the band asked to be included.

"I really felt—and I still feel this way, honestly—that Setzer took a lot of the attention away from more deserving bands," Moss says. "He was kind of a Johnny-come-lately on that scene." Moss tried to get Squirrel Nut Zippers and the Mighty Blue Kings, a popular jump blues band out of Chicago, but neither wanted to be associated with the retro-swing movement.

Swing This, Baby includes the New Morty Show's "Knockin' at Your Door," a showcase for Okin's trumpeting and the cheeky interplay between Vise Grip and Connie Champagne. The song was featured on the New Morty Show's 1998 debut album, *Mortyfied!* Slimstyle pushed "Out of Control," a spry tune with fairly dark lyrics about drug use, as the first single.

Okin would've preferred their cover of "Enter Sandman," which might've been novel and rocking enough to break big.

"Look at Save Ferris—they had 'Come On Eileen,'" says Okin. "Obviously, it wasn't their song, but it became a great hit for them. To me, it doesn't matter what song would have done it. Just that it gets done." As it happened, *Mortyfied!* sold about 10,000 copies, more than double what Blue Plate Special did with their debut, *A Night Out With.* "For a small independent, great, I can make money off of that," says Vaughn. "But it wasn't enough to sustain itself, especially when you had to put them on the road."

Even if the New Morty Show had crossed over with a big radio hit, their time in the spotlight would've been brief. Slimstyle's phone simply stopped ringing in July 1999, as swing became overexposed. "I would never say this at the time, but in hindsight, there was definitely a novelty aspect to it," Vaughn says. "It just got too big too quickly and really burned bright. When genres previously had come to the forefront, they built slowly, built more of an audience, built more of a bedrock, and then slowly faded away. The graph on this one was straight up and down."

Even in San Francisco, things got bleak. "It died pretty quick here," says Okin. "It was within a year of everything. Dance lessons everywhere. More of the hardcore people that just wanted to watch good music and party and dance for fun and drink like fish stopped going to a lot the clubs that bands were playing." The boozers were replaced by the hardcore swing dancers who never drank alcohol, the lifeblood of club owners. They showed up with their own bottled water.

"I don't want to *blame* blame the dancers, but it was a bummer," says Okin. That's why the Morty Show didn't do a whole ton of hardcore swing shows just for dancers. We did a ton of ska shows. A ton of rock shows." At the same time the audiences were changing, personnel shake-ups were taking their toll. On the tour supporting *Mortyfied!* Kat Starr from the San Francisco cabaret band Beach Blanket Bingo replaced Connie Champagne, and soon after, Vise Grip started a family and retired from the road. Okin grabbed two new singers for 2000's *Rigormorty*, but the magic was gone. By 2003, Okin had decided to put the band on hold. He reunited with Champagne and Grip in 2006 but realized after a few years that the New Morty Show had reached their logical conclusion.

After swing's demise, Vaughn tried to make Slimstyle work for another couple of years. He signed surf and Latin dance artists who were musically similar to swing and ska but—crucially—not swing or ska. By 2002 he'd put the label on hold and moved to New York City to launch a record label for the cable network Comedy Central. Vaughn reactivated Slimstyle in 2011 to release an album by Movits, a Swedish hip-hop–swing band he learned about from comedian Stephen Colbert. Slimstyle has gone on to release albums by legacy acts like Local H, Ian Hunter, and Dexys, formerly known as Dexys Midnight Runners.

Since swing's death, Okin has blown his horn for all kinds of different bands. In 2009 he debuted a 14-piece Michael Jackson tribute band called Neverland, which later changed its name to Foreverland after legal threats from the King of Pop's estate. In 2012 Okin left Foreverland and launched the Purple Ones, a 12-piece tribute to Prince.

Even though "Enter Sandman" never became the smash he thought it could've been, Okin looks back on the New Morty Show's run as some of the best years of his life. While Moss and others describe the retro-swing movement as fundamentally countercultural and subversive, Okin takes a lighter view. "You could wear killer clothes for dirt cheap," he says. "You looked good and felt good, and you could definitely stand out. I don't think it was anything political. It was a way to show that young kids could go out for an elegant evening. See a killer show. And it would be hip. It's not like your grandparents' swing music."

■ ■ ■

Timing was crucial in the ska and swing revivals. Just ask John Bunkley, the Detroit singer, songwriter, and musician who could've been a contender in both movements. Bunkley's best chance for big-time success came with the Hemi-powered jump blues combo the Atomic Fireballs, who signed with the Atlantic Records affiliate Lava and released the incendiary *Torch This Place* in 1999.

When the band went into the studio with Bruce Fairbairn, the producer behind Bon Jovi's 1986 breakthrough *Slippery When Wet* and Aerosmith's 1993 mega-seller *Get a Grip*, swing was still red hot. When the record came out, it was dead in the water. The album tanked, and the Fireballs were dropped—but not before landing a song on the *American Pie* soundtrack and appearing in another 1999 film, *Three to Tango*, starring Matthew Perry and Neve Campbell.

Compared to swing, ska was much more established by the time the majors came calling in the mid-'90s. There had been quality bands all over the country since the '80s, and Bunkley fronted one of them, Gangster Fun. He started the group at Oakland University in Rochester, Michigan, located about 30 miles from his hometown of Detroit. Heavily influenced by 2 Tone, Gangster Fun were the only game in town as far as Michigan ska in the late '80s was concerned. "When we would play, it wasn't like three or four ska bands on the bill," Bunkley says. "It would be us, then a New York Dolls–type band or a punk band." Gangster Fun played with ska legends Desmond Dekker and the Skatalites, but they also shared bills with Bad Brains and Fugazi.

Bunkley quit Gangster Fun in the early '90s after singing on their 1989 debut, *Come See, Come Ska*, released on the Welsh label Ska' Records. He left because he was working on a graduate degree in sociology, and because his bandmates weren't interested in touring beyond Michigan. Gangster Fun carried on playing locally with another singer while the Detroit bands they inspired rose to national attention. "Sometimes when you're the first in an area, you pave the way for other people bigger than you," Bunkley says. "It happens in every musical genre. We paved the way for the Suicide Machines and Mustard Plug. We're great friends with those guys, and we were nothing but happy for their success."

After finishing his graduate program, Bunkley learned the art of glass blowing and went to work at Greenfield Village, a Michigan museum that lets you experience life in the nineteenth century. He shifted his focus to the mid-twentieth century with the Atomic Fireballs, which he started with trumpeter James Bostek in 1995. Bunkley's plan was to play the jump blues he'd grown up loving thanks to his grandmother. He knew of Squirrel Nut Zippers and Royal Crown Revue—bands he rates very highly—but was unaware of the West Coast scene. Together with Bostek, he put together a Fireballs lineup that included jazz-schooled horn players and pianist Randy Sly, who'd done time in the ska-leaning worldbeat band Bop (Harvey) and the Verve Pipe, soon to become one-hit wonders with 1997's "The Freshman." The Fireballs played their first show on Valentine's Day 1996 at Detroit's Majestic Theatre and nearly sold the place out.

The Fireballs arrived fully formed, offering something very different from the other neo-swing bands. Piano tap-danced over pounding drums while Bunkley growled like a punk-rock Louis Armstrong and the horns wailed away. "The jazz guys, they always wanted to base the horns around the Basie big band, Kansas City jump," Bunkley says. "Never once was Glenn Miller mentioned. Never once was Sinatra mentioned. No crooners were ever mentioned. It was all shouting and all Basie."

It was a bit too heavy for some audiences. The Fireballs played their first East Coast show at the New York Supper Club. "We go into the club, and the guy who runs it, or the promoter, hands me a set list, and it's all cover songs," says Bunkley. "'Yeah, we want you to do this Cab Calloway song. You need to do this Glenn Miller song.' I'm like, 'Fuck this. We don't do this. Did you read what we're about? We do originals. East Coast bands would do stuff like that. They were wedding bands. They sounded like wedding bands. And it was lame." To top it all off, some of the swing dancers in attendance complained that the Fireballs were blazing too darn fast. "My mom danced," Bunkley says. "She's seen us a zillion times. She's got 30 years on me."

The Atomic Fireballs found a more receptive audience on the 1998 Warped Tour. Bunkley got to catch up with Tim Armstrong of Rancid, whom he knew back in his Gangster Fun days, and play basketball with blink-182 and the Aquabats during downtime. Warped gave the Fireballs a chance to play for kids who couldn't get into 21-and-over clubs and might've never seen the band otherwise. They gave it everything they had for 30 minutes, then got back in the van and drove to the next city.

In the wake of 1998's *Birth of the Swerve*, an eight-song indie release featuring five tracks that would end up on *Torch This Place*, Bunkley fielded phone calls from 12 labels. Among the execs blowing up Bunkley's line was Ahmet Ertegun, the legendary Atlantic Records founder and R&B lover who'd shaped the careers of Ray Charles and Aretha Franklin. Bunkley loved all that music and even knew Aretha personally—the choice seemed obvious. "A lot of labels, like Roadrunner and Universal, we thought they were just jumping onto the swing thing," says Bunkley. "But so was Lava/Atlantic. We thought, 'Hey, they see us as a rhythm and blues band, a jump blues band.' They really didn't."

The next decision after picking a label was selecting a producer. Steve Lillywhite (U2, Dave Matthews Band, the Rolling Stones) wanted $2 million and 10 points, or 10 percent royalties. The Fireballs didn't have that kind of budget, so they recorded with Bruce Fairbairn from October through December 1998—the waning days of the swing revival, it turned out. They emerged with an album that played on exotic themes—voodoo hexes, love potions, et cetera—and moved at such a brisk clip that stodgy swing dancers were sure to complain.

The lead single, "Man with the Hex," opens with lines cribbed from Cary Grant in the 1947 comedy *The Bachelor and the Bobby-Soxer*, via David Bowie's *Labyrinth* hit "Magic Dance": "You remind me of a man / (What man?) / The man with the power? / (What power?) / The power of voodoo (Who do?)." Bunkely wrote the whole thing on his guitar in 10 minutes. Despite its raging beat and strong hook, the single never caught on, though it does share space with Sugar Ray, Third Eye Blind, Goldfinger, and blink-182 on the *American Pie* soundtrack. Bunkley suspects there was some behind-the-scenes finagling from Atlantic: "You have to take this band if you want Sugar Ray on the soundtrack."

A combination of things extinguished the Atomic Fireballs. As the label lost faith in the group, some of Bunkley's bandmates became jealous that he was getting all the attention. Then it became harder and harder to book shows. Some clubs mandated that swing acts participate in pre-show dance lessons, while others refused to book swing nights altogether because the hardcore dancers drank water, not alcohol. Finally, the label made Bunkley an offer he couldn't possibly accept. "They said, 'Hey, the band's not gonna go far. When we put out the record, we knew you weren't going to make it. So what do you want to be? You're the only Black guy on our label. Do you want to be Lenny Kravitz, or do you want to be Seal?'" Bunkley says. "I'm like, 'I'm from fucking Detroit. Lenny Kravitz or Seal? I don't really want to play anymore.'"

Thankfully, Bunkley has continued making music. His Bandcamp page is full of cool tunes ranging from the mellow jazz of 2015's *Thoughts* album to the instrumental ska of his 2019 single "Tura." If nothing else, Bunkley says, the Atomic Fireballs were right behind the Big Five swing bands in terms of popularity—the lower tier of the upper tier. The problem with the movement, he says, is that everyone focused on the costume instead of the music.

"Everything's like, 'We're smoking cigars. We're wearing zoot suits. We're wearing big fedoras,'" Bunkley says. "It looked like a cartoon. A lot of people that I know would say, 'I don't want to go to a swing show because I don't know how to dance.' That's what hurt it, but that's also what made it take off real big, too."

The Beats Go On

On a sunny Saturday in August 2019, the Mighty Mighty Bosstones staged their second annual Cranking & Skanking Fest at the Met Courtyard in Pawtucket, Rhode Island. The Bosstones faithful arrived early, ostensibly to catch the trio of terrific undercard bands: Buck-O-Nine, Voodoo Glow Skulls, and newly reunited local heroes the Amazing Crowns, whose punky rockabilly sound was a hit with ska fans back in the late '90s.

The crowd skewed a little older, but near the front of the entrance line, there were a couple of young skater dudes who must've been about 16. They knew the Bosstones, obviously, but talking before the show, they realized they'd never heard Voodoo Glow Skulls. Fortunately, these teens were living in an age of miracles and wonder; one grabbed his iPhone, tapped Spotify, and held the tiny speaker between his and his buddy's ear. Satellites that weren't in the sky when the Glow Skulls released 1995's *Firme* beamed the berserk "El Coo Cooi" down from outer space and onto Main Street, Pawtucket. The boys smiled wide, and one said what the other surely was thinking: "This is awesome!"

Two decades into the twenty-first century, ska is still reaching pockets of young Americans. These amateur skankers are too young to remember just how uncool ska became around the turn of the millennium, when casual fans abandoned the genre and industry tastemakers began pushing other sounds, like nu-metal, garage rock, and emo. In 2004, as the ska faithful began peeking their heads above ground, Dave Kirchgessner of Mustard Plug launched the aptly named Ska Is Dead Tour. Alongside Mustard Plug, the trek featured Big D and the Kids Table and Catch 22, popular East Coast ska-punk bands whose debut albums arrived after ska's 1997 boom time. Ska Is Dead attracted more than 1,000 fans in some markets, and the tour returned several times before the decade was out. One of the headlining bands, the Catch 22 offshoot Streetlight Manifesto, even kept ska on the charts, placing three albums on the Billboard 200 from 2007 to 2013.

Still, ska remained an object of ridicule. In a 2016 episode of the Fox sitcom *Brooklyn Nine-Nine*, comedian Andy Samberg's character flashes back to 1998, when he appeared on the local TV news in full rudie regalia, telling a reporter, "Ska defines who I am as a person, and I will never turn my back on ska." He's meant to look like a jackass, and flashing forward again, Samberg admits he ought to regret that phase of his life.

Jokes aside, ska's not dead. As of 2020, most of the bands interviewed for this book are still active in some capacity. There are also new groups making noise, most notably Rancid-approved ska-punk revivalists the Interrupters, who took their thoroughly Rancid-like "She's Kerosene" to #4 on Billboard's Alternative Songs chart in 2018. According to *Billboard*, it was the first ska hit on alternative radio for a female-fronted band since No Doubt.

On a more underground tip, staunchly DIY singer-songwriter Jeff Rosenstock, formerly of the ska-punk band the Arrogant Sons of Bitches and the punk collective Bomb the Music Industry!, garnered glowing reviews with his ska-dusted 2016 pop-punk album WORRY. (Check out the song "Rainbow.") Further below the radar, new ska bands like the Scotch Bonnets from Baltimore, the Prizefighters from Minneapolis, and Catbite from Philadelphia are holding it down for folks who read ska blogs and actively participate in the scene. Florida musician Jeremy Hunter, aka Ska-tune Network, has become a social media star and genre ambassador by posting ska covers of popular songs, as well as original material. Hunter was among those interviewed for a September 2020 BrooklynVegan story whose headline, "Ska Is Thriving," speaks to the wealth of bands bringing the genre into the new decade.

In 2020, the newly formed and potentially game-changing New Orleans band Bad Operation began using the term "New Tone" to describe their socially conscious brand of 2 Tone–indebted ska. Hunter and others soon adopted the New Tone tag, rejecting the notion of a "fourth wave" and the antiquated metrics of success—chart hits, radio airplay—it implies. Regardless of what the traditional gatekeepers say, the state of the ska is strong.

There have also been freak ska sightings on the pop charts. Scottish EDM DJ Calvin Harris teamed up with superstars Pharrell Williams, Big Sean, and Katy Perry for 2017's "Feels," a slick pop-funk bop with a pronounced ska influence that reached #20 on the Hot 100. The Jonas Brothers went a similar route with 2019's "Only Human," a reggae-pop jam with enough skankability to get ska Reddit talking. One might chalk these oddities up to the same '90s nostalgia that had '10s pop stars like Charli XCX and Dua Lipa shouting out Gwen Stefani as a major influence.

Swing didn't survive into the 2000s as stubbornly as ska did. Nevertheless, many of the swing groups profiled in this book are still doing their thing in 2020. Across the country—and indeed, around the world—oodles of new swing groups are playing to loyal Lindy Hoppers and jazz enthusiasts. Some are taking the retro thing even further. In the 2010s, young people in NYC and elsewhere went full Gatsby and sparked a hot jazz revival. *Vanity Fair* ran a piece in 2013 titled "How a Swath of 20-Somethings Have Tuned In to 1920s Pop."

Some semblance of swing has also flourished on the Internet, compliments of bandleader Scott Bradlee and his Postmodern Jukebox, an ensemble whose schtick is remaking modern pop hits in retro styles, including swing and ragtime. Bradlee's viral covers of songs like Radiohead's

"Creep" and Meghan Trainor's "All About That Bass" have earned the group more than 4.5 million YouTube subscribers. There's also something called "electro swing," a European dance genre that sounds exactly how you'd imagine. The less said about that, the better.

Regardless of how close ska or swing comes to reclaiming the spotlight, it's unlikely either genre will infiltrate pop culture in quite the same way it did in the mid-to-late '90s, when the conditions were just right. Grunge died, the economy boomed, and if you could keep your mom from picking up the phone while you dialed into AOL, the Internet pointed toward a bright future for humanity. Youth culture turned upbeat, and for a couple of years, suits and trombones made a lot of sense.

Which isn't to say all '90s ska and swing bands were writing in response to this era of good feelings. Both scenes predated Clinton's first inauguration, and many of the bands profiled in this book did take on serious political and social issues. But it's no accident these sounds bubbled up into the mainstream when they did. The popularity of ska and swing reflected what was happening in the wider culture.

Try to imagine ska or swing exploding five years earlier, during Nirvana's reign, or five years later, in the aftermath of 9/11, with America at war. From dance-punk and emo to trap, the hip-hop subgenre that came to dominate all areas of popular music in the late '10s, the major musical trends of the twenty-first century have tended to be moodier and more introspective than anything in the years immediately preceding Y2K. (A brief reprieve came during the Obama years, when EDM had America's youth waving glow sticks.) In the late '10s, one of the most popular bands in the much-diminished alternative rock field, twenty one pilots, wrote a lot about depression and anxiety, just like major pop stars Ariana Grande and Billie Eilish. Young people raised in the age of social media, opioids, COVID-19, and crippling student-loan debt could probably use a good old-fashioned ska dance party, but they're finding catharsis in other ways.

So for now, ska and swing belong to scenesters and subcultures and those in the know. They also live on in the hearts of those '90s kids who once found comfort, joy, community, and maybe even political awakening in these danceable sounds.

In November 2019, Spring Heeled Jack, leaders of the once-hardy Connecticut ska scene, played a show to celebrate the twenty-first anniversary of *Songs from Suburbia*, a locally beloved mix of pop-rock and ska released on Ignition Records, a subsidiary of Tommy Boy, in 1998. It was a cold night in Connecticut two days after Thanksgiving, and the crowd at Toad's Place in New Haven was sparse yet spirited. Spring Heeled Jack's lineup included a couple of noteworthy former members: trombonist Chris Rhodes, now a Mighty Mighty Bosstone, and saxophonist Peter "JR" Wasilewski, who's played with Less Than Jake since Spring Heeled Jack broke up in 2000. (SHJ reformed with new horn players in 2013.) Toward the end of the set, Wasilewski said something that resonated with at least one 30-something in the audience hoping to recapture a little piece of his youth. "I didn't go to my high school reunion," Wasilewski said. "This is my high school reunion."

Source Essays and Further Reading

INTRODUCTION: BRING ON THE HORNS

The intro includes quotes from my interviews with Michael Moss, Jon Pebsworth, Dave Kirchgessner, and Steve Perry. All four of these guys pop up later in the book.

CHAPTER 1: NOISE BRIGADE

The bulk of this chapter derives from my interviews with Dicky Barrett and Joe Gittleman, whose kindness will not be soon forgotten. Barrett's quote about becoming "Boston's first 'rude boy'" comes from Greg Kot's "Ska, Ska, Ska," *Chicago Tribune*, July 17, 1997. Mercury Records A&R Bob Skoro predicts platinum sales for the Bosstones in "Hunt for 'Next Big Thing' Unearths Ska Underground," *Billboard*, January 15, 1994. Barrett spoke to MTV in August 1997 about James Michael Curley, the inspiration behind "Rascal King." For a description of Bosstones saxophonist Kevin Lenear kicking over an amplifier in Cologne, Germany, see "Mighty Mighty Nate," *Brown Alumni Magazine*, March/April 1999.

CHAPTER 2: TRAPPED IN A BOX

This chapter draws from my interviews with Adrian Young and Eric Wilson, both of whom I was thrilled to interview. The quotes from Sublime associate Miguel Happoldt that open the chapter come from Lilledeshan Bose's "Miguel Happoldt Says 'No Doubt Was Like Richie Cunningham and Sublime Was Like Fonzie,'" *OC Weekly*, September 14, 2012. Jeff Apter's thoroughly researched 2007 book *Gwen Stefani & No Doubt: A Simple Kind of Life* was an invaluable source for the No Doubt sections of this book—particularly the passages about the band's early years. Gwen Stefani's self-deprecating quotes about her early life come from Rob McGibbon's "Golden Girl 'Gwen Stefani' Leaps from Frog to Princess," *Daily Mail*, March 2, 2007, and Jill Kopelman's "New Again: No Doubt," *Interview*, August 21, 2012. For more on Gwen's reaction to John Spence's suicide, see Kennedy's "Ms. Doubtfire," *Spin*, June 1996. To learn more about Sublime's formation, watch the 1998 documentary *Sublime: Stories, Tales, Lies & Exaggerations*. Evan Rytlewski's review of *40oz. to Freedom* ran on Pitchfork on February 25, 2018. Eric Wilson discusses his pre-Sublime life in Stephen Laddin's "Eric Wilson Does It for the Love of Music," *High Times*, May 29, 2019. Brad Nowell discusses his efforts to avoid singing like a Jamaican in Jamie Tierney's "In Name Only," *Slam Magazine*, November 1, 1995. Tom Dumont compares the L.A. metal and ska scenes in *BAM Magazine*, November 17, 1995. Gwen Stefani recalls her initial run-in with Jimmy Iovine in Jonathan Van Meter's "Gwen Stefani: The First Lady of Rock," *Vogue*, April 1, 2008. Brad Nowell's widow, Troy Dendekker, discusses her late husband's heroin troubles around the time of *Robbin' the Hood* in Mark Kemp's "Bradley Nowell: Life After Death," *Rolling Stone*, December 25, 1997. For more on Tazy Phyllipz breaking "Date Rape" on KROQ, check out Tazy's December 8, 2001, interview with the *Full Value Review*. Eric Stefani discusses his decision to leave No Doubt in Mike Boehm's "Without No Doubt," *Los Angeles Times*, October 30, 1996. For more on Brad Nowell's final days, check out David Grad's "Sublime's Late Brad Nowell Could Have Had It All . . . ," *Guitar World*, October 1997.

CHAPTER 3: THE CONTENDER AND THE KINGS OF SWING

The story of Royal Crown Revue is based largely on my interviews with Mando Dorame and Daniel Glass. The Big Bad Voodoo Daddy sections derive from my interview with bandleader Scotty Morris. These were the first three people I interviewed for the book, and I owe them a huge debt of gratitude. I relied heavily on V. Vale's 1998 book *Swing! The New Retro Renaissance* for information on RCR's formation and Eddie Nichols's early years. Nichols describes his initial songwriting efforts in Tim Parson's "Royal Crown Revue

Swings into Harrah's Tahoe," *Lake Tahoe Action*, September 25, 2008. Morris tells the story of BBVD's rise and fall and shares his thoughts on Brian Setzer covering "Jump, Jive an' Wail" on the "Swing in the '90s" episode of the *Dig Me Out* podcast, September 20, 2016. For more on Nichols's run-ins with the law in Toledo, Ohio, check out "Royal Crown Revue's Singer Pleads to Lesser Charge," published on MTV.com on November 24, 1998.

CHAPTER 4: SKANKING BEHIND THE ORANGE CURTAIN

Much of this chapter is based on my interviews with Aaron Barrett of Reel Big Fish and Monique Powell of Save Ferris. Both were extremely generous with their time and thoughtful with their answers. For more on Epic Records A&R exec David Massey signing Save Ferris, read Sara Scribner's "Save Ferris Steps Out of O.C. Ska Pack," *Los Angeles Times*, October 4, 1997. Brian Mashburn talks about the surprisingly lascivious meaning behind "Come On Eileen" in an interview with Bradley Bambarger for the issue of *Billboard* dated November 29, 1997. Powell explains why it's OK to compare her to Gwen Stefani in Craig D. Lindsey's "Trading Spaces," *Houston Press*, May 15, 2003. Powell discusses the difficulty faced by female artists in the alt-rock field in Derek Palva's "Band Preserves Some Favorites for the Stage," *Honolulu Advertiser*, March 1, 2002.

CHAPTER 5: CALIFORNIA SKAQUAKE

This chapter hinges on interviews I did with Mike Park of Skankin' Pickle and Asian Man Records fame, Jorge Casillas from Voodoo Glow Skulls, and Jon Pebsworth from Buck-O-Nine. Huge thanks to all three. Thanks also to Tazy Phyllipz, who chatted with me about the history of California ska. I briefly summed up the career of Dance Hall Crashers using information from Mike Boehm's "Dance Hall's Path Furthers Young America's Education in a Hybrid of Ska-Pop-Punk," *Los Angeles Times*, January 13, 1996. For more of Mike Park discussing the racism he faced growing up, see John Roos's "Ska-lapalooza: United They Jam," *Los Angeles Times*, April 3, 1998. To learn more about the criticism surrounding Park's Ska Against Racism Tour, check out J. R. Jones's "Ska's Lost Cause," *Chicago Reader*, July 23, 1998. Jennifer Vineyard voices similar concerns in "Politics Aside, It Was a Party," *Los Angeles Times*, April 7, 1998. For the story of young Eddie and Jorge Casillas lip-syncing to metal records with drummer Jerry O'Neill, check out the summer 2002 issue of the zine *Sink Hole*. Frank Casillas discusses the Glow Skulls' stint on Victory Records in Brian Blueskye's "From the Backyards of Riverside: Ska-Punk Legends the Voodoo Glow Skulls Head for the Hood," *Coachella Valley Independent*, July 12, 2013. Frank Casillas explains how Black and Mexican music informed the VG sound in "Voodoo Glow Skulls on Touring with the Toasters, Mixing Hardcore with Ska and Staying in the Game

Since the '80s," an interview I conducted for Diffuser.fm, published on September 16, 2013. John Feldmann of Goldfinger discusses seeing the English Beat in 1983 in a January 2019 interview with KROQ's *The Kevin & Bean Show*. Feldmann talks about wanting Goldfinger to have a "mod element" in an interview with the reggae-rock website The Pier, published on October 24, 2017. For more on Feldmann selling shoes, forming Goldfinger, and ditching ska after *Hang-Ups*, check out issue #7 of *Sink Hole*, published in 2001. For more on Electric Love Hogs, check out "John Feldmann: The Man with the Midas Touch," published on January 21, 2016, on the website Louder. There's more about the making of Goldfinger's first album in "Goldfinger's Debut Album Turns 20: John Feldmann Reflects," published on the Fuse website on February 26, 2016. Feldmann discusses his aversion to political songwriting in Sandy Masuo's "Goldfinger Explores True Meaning of Punk," *Los Angeles Times*, August 16, 1996. Feldmann discusses why people need festivals like Back to the Beach in Brittany Woolsey's "Coachella of Ska," *OC Weekly*, April 24, 2018.

CHAPTER 6: ONE NATION UNDER SKA-PUNK

This chapter is based largely on my interviews with Chris DeMakes, Jay Navarro, Billy Spunke, and Dave Kirchgessner. All four spoke to me at length and told terrific stories about their '90s adventures. For more on Less Than Jake's early years and tenure with Capitol Records, check out the July 2015 episode of Damian Abraham's *Turned Out a Punk* podcast, featuring an interview with Vinnie Fiorello. Fiorello talks about the concept behind *Hello Rockview* in Gen Handley's "Rank Your Records: Less Than Jake's Vinnie Fiorello Rates the Ska-Punk Band's Eight Albums," *Noisey*, June 25, 2015. Chris DeMakes's podcast, *Chris DeMakes a Podcast*, was also a valuable source, especially regarding the band's use of Pro Tools.

CHAPTER 7: OLD'S COOL

The chapter on traditional ska is based on my interviews with Greg Lee, Vic Ruggiero, and Jeff "King Django" Baker. Dave Hillyard's quote about Hepcat's influences comes from the "Story of U.S. Ska" series he originally wrote for his MySpace blog, which was republished on the website Lawless Street in 2014. For more on the Slackers' early years, check out 2007's *The Slackers: A Documentary*, an excellent overview of the band's career up to that point. King Django discusses the making of *Roots & Culture* in Chris Nelson's "King Django Mixes Reggae and Yiddish *Roots & Culture*," published on MTV.com on November 26, 1998.

CHAPTER 8: EAST SIDE BEAT

Most of this chapter is based on my interviews with Steve Shafer, Stephen Jackson, Mikal Reich, Brendan "Brendog" Tween, and Greg Robinson. Rob "Bucket" Hingley—who

declined to speak with me for this book—discusses the rise and fall of Moon and the future of the music business in a summer 2004 interview with the online music magazine *In Music We Trust*. For more of Bucket's thoughts on the difficulties facing working musicians in the digital era, check out the episode of Northern Ireland's *Ska Craze* radio show from April 15, 2016. For more on Bucket's pre-Toasters musical endeavors and Moon's early days, check out the excellent interview posted on the website Marco on the Bass on March 12, 2010. Bucket talks about buying his first ska record—Millie Small's "My Boy Lollipop"—in a September 12, 2012, interview with the blog *Tone Deaf*. For more on Bucket vowing to create an American ska scene after seeing a poorly attended English Beat show, see George Lang's "Ska Lured Musician to Stage," *The Oklahoman*, February 11, 2005. To get the full story on the Unity 2 leaving the Toasters, Coolie Ranx joining, and the band signing to Folk & Morrow booking, check out Steve Shafer's "Shots in the Dark: The Toasters' 'Frankenska,'" Duff Guide to Ska, May 20, 2018. For more on ex-Pietaster Tal Bayer, who built an impressive rugby program at Perry Street Prep Public Charter in Washington, D.C., check out Rick Maese's terrific "A Coach's Painful Farewell to a Rugby Program He Built and the Players He Loves," *Washington Post*, June 22, 2013. For more on how the Bosstones saved the Pietasters from breaking up in the mid-'90s, see Chris Nelson's "Bosstones Singer Sweetens Pietasters Future," published on MTV.com on

September 5, 1997. Jackson discusses playing with James Brown, Joe Strummer, and others in Josh Eiserike's "Party Hard," *Daily Progress*, January 11, 2008.

CHAPTER 9: MISFITS OF SWING

This chapter is based on original interviews with Steve Perry and Jimbo Mathus—terrific conversationalists, both. For more on CPD's interactions with late-night talk show hosts, check out Dominick A. Miserandino's 2000 interview with Perry for the Celebrity Cafe. Perry discusses his work at the Cresko Lab in a story titled "Science & Swing," available on the University of Oregon website. Tom Maxwell's fantastic 2014 memoir *Hell: My Life in the Squirrel Nut Zippers* provided crucial insights for this chapter, particularly the section about Maxwell's writing of "Hell." For more on Squirrel Nut Zippers' entire '90s run, including the circumstances that led to "Hell" becoming a radio hit, see Allison Hussey's "Hell Is Hot: How Squirrel Nut Zippers Accidentally Sold a Million Records," *Indy Week*, August 16, 2016. Maxwell voices his distaste for the '90s swing revival in Gerry Galipault's "Tom Maxwell: An Ex–Squirrel Nut Zipper Does Good," Pause & Play, June 18, 2000. For more on the legal dispute that pitted Tom Maxwell and Ken Mosher against Jimbo Mathus and the other remaining Zippers, read David Menconi's "Squirrel Nut Zippers: What Happened, a Zippers Opera," *News & Observer*, May 14, 2006.

CHAPTER 10: STRAY CAT SWINGS

Brian Setzer politely declined my interview request for this book, so this chapter is based entirely on secondary sources. Setzer discusses swing's place in the American psyche in Matt Ashare's "Out of the Mosh Pit and into the Swing," *Boston Phoenix*, July 20, 1998. For more on Setzer's early interest in New York City jazz bands, see George Varga's "Brian Setzer Talks Big Band Swing, Rockabilly Romps, 2017 Solo Plans, Surfdog and More," *San Diego Union-Tribune*, December 14, 2016. For more on Setzer's first time jamming with a horn section, see the 2002 book *Playing from the Heart: Great Musicians Talk About Their Craft*, which compiles interviews Setzer conducted with *Guitar Player* in 1994, 1998, and 2001. Setzer's quote about his horn players making good money as in-demand session players comes from a 1996 MusicPlex / Lazar Productions interview reprinted on the Rockabilly.net website. Another great resource in writing this chapter was the Brian Setzer episode of *VH1 Legends*, which touches on the formation of the big band, the switch to Interscope, and Setzer's trepidation about recording "Jump, Jive an' Wail." Setzer talks about hitting his stride on the second BSO album in Buddy Seigal's "Guitar Slinger Strays Again," *Los Angeles Times*, July 22, 1998. For more on Setzer working with producer Phil Ramone on *Guitar Slinger*, check out the iMusic interview reposted on Rockabilly.net. For Setzer discussing his bass player Tony Garnier, see G. Brown's "Brian Setzer Orchestra Drowns Out the Skeptics," *Denver Post*, August 1, 1998. Setzer discusses recording the rhythm section live on *The Dirty Boogie* in a November 1998 *Guitar Player* interview with Andy Ellis. Whalley from Interscope discusses Setzer's broad appeal in Elysa Gardner's "Back in the Swing of Things," *Los Angeles Times*, August 2, 1998. Setzer takes stock of the BSO's quarter-century run in Kelli Skye Fadroski's "Brian Setzer Reflects on 25 Years of the Brian Setzer Orchestra as It Prepares to Celebrate Its Anniversary at the Hollywood Bowl," *Orange County Register*, July 26, 2017. For more on Setzer's embrace of Pro Tools on *Vavoom!* see *Mix*, January 1, 2001.

CHAPTER 11: SWINGING AT THE MARGINS

This chapter is based almost entirely on my interviews with Michael Moss, Lavay Smith, Morty Okin, Jack Vaughn, and John Bunkley. All five have interesting stories to tell, and it was an honor to speak with them for this project.

CONCLUSION: THE BEATS GO ON

I end this chapter with an onstage quote from Peter "JR" Wasilewski of Spring Heeled Jack, the first ska band I ever saw in concert. As a Connecticut native, I deeply regret being unable to feature SHJ more prominently in this book. Alas, I had a limited word count, and they didn't fit neatly into any of the chapters. I close with the JR quote as a tribute to

the band that set me down the path toward writing this book in the first place.

FURTHER READING

Apter, Jeff. *Gwen Stefani & No Doubt: A Simple Kind of Life*. Omnibus Press, 2009.

Augustyn, Heather. *Ska: An Oral History*. McFarland, 2010.

——. *Ska: The Rhythm of Liberation*. Scarecrow Press, 2013.

Jones, J. R. "Ska's Lost Cause." *Chicago Reader*, July 23, 1998.

Kemp, Mark. "Bradley Nowell: Life After Death." *Rolling Stone*, December 25, 1997.

Kot, Greg. "Ska, Ska, Ska." *Chicago Tribune*, July 17, 1997.

Marshall, George. *The Two Tone Story*. S.T. Publishing, 1997.

Maxwell, Tom. *Hell: My Life in the Squirrel Nut Zippers*. Oyster Point Press, 2014.

Playing from the Heart: Great Musicians Talk About Their Craft. Edited by Robert L. Doerschuk. Backbeat Books, 2002.

Vale, V. *Swing! The New Retro Renaissance*. V Search Publications, 1998.

Index